The **First Strike**

The

DOOLITTLE RAIDER DON SMITH

First Strike

Paul Higbee

South Dakota Historical Society Press

Pierre

Library of Congress Cataloging-in-Publication data
Higbee, Paul, author.
The first strike : Doolittle raider Don Smith / Paul Higbee.
Pierre : South Dakota Historical Society Press, [2019] |
Includes bibliographical references and index.
LCCN 2019026156 | ISBN 9781941813126 (cloth)
LCSH: Smith, Donald G., 1918– | Tokyo (Japan)—History—Bombardment, 1942. |
Bomber pilots—United States—Biography. | United States. Army Air Forces.
Bombardment Group (Medium), 17th—Biography. | United States. Army Air Forces—
History—World War, 1939–1945. | World War, 1939–1945—Aerial operations, American. |
Doolittle, James Harold, 1896–1993. | Belle Fourche (S.D.)—Biography.
LCC D767.25.T6 | DDC 940.54/4973092 [B]—dc23
LC record available at https://lccn.loc.gov/2019026156

Printed in the United States of America

The paper in this book meets the guidelines for permanence and durability
of the Committee on Production Guidelines for Book Longevity of the Council
on Library Resources.

Please visit our website at sdhspress.com

23 22 21 20 19   1 2 3 4 5

Cover and frontispiece: Donald G. Smith (second from right) and three members
of his crew are given a farewell from a Chinese village in late April 1942 (bottom).
ww2db.com; One of the B-25s from the Doolittle Raid takes off from the deck of the
USS *Hornet* (top). *National Archives*; A restored B-25 retains the look of those used
in the Doolittle Raid. *NNehring/iStock*

Designed and set in Utopia type by Rich Hendel

In memory of my father,

Walter Higbee,

who survived fighting in World War II

and, by example,

instilled in me a love of writing and

twentieth century history.

Contents

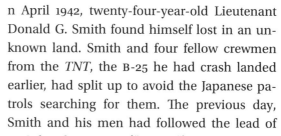

n April 1942, twenty-four-year-old Lieutenant Donald G. Smith found himself lost in an unknown land. Smith and four fellow crewmen from the *TNT*, the B-25 he had crash landed earlier, had split up to avoid the Japanese patrols searching for them. The previous day, Smith and his men had followed the lead of Lieutenant Colonel James H. ("Jimmy") Doolittle as he guided a total of sixteen bombers toward Japan for the first American attack against that empire since the entry of the United States into World War II. Now, on the Chinese island of Nantien, Smith followed a guerilla soldier, hoping that his guide would lead him to a rendezvous point with the rest of his squad. Beyond that objective, he and his men had only one goal: reach the safety of Chungking, China.

Although Don Smith was a significant figure in what came to be known as the Doolitte Raid, his story has long been overlooked. Smith died at a young age, leaving no memoir, diary, or personal interviews about his experiences. He did, however, write home regularly to his parents in Belle Fourche, South Dakota, and his correspondence gives insight into one of the most famous attacks in American military history, one that lifted the spirits of Americans still reeling from the destruction at Pearl Harbor. Beyond that, Smith's words reveal the life of one young man, representative of thousands of others, as he navigated through Army Air Corps training and the early months of World War II.

Of all people, J. R. R. Tolkien might seem among the least likely to inspire a project on the Doolittle Raid, but it was the British fantasy writer who first led me to examine the attack in depth. In 1992, while writing a magazine-length biography of Tolkien for the University of Notre Dame's alumni and continuing education publication, I studied the daring strategies of Jimmy Doolittle, General Henry H. ("Hap") Arnold, and Vice Admiral William F. ("Bull") Halsey that made the operation a success. I got pulled down that rabbit hole after learning Tolkien knew a good deal about World War II aviation and that some of his literary inspirations were American—barefoot Kentucky lads who morphed into hobbits, for example. I wondered whether the author had found inspiration for the central plot of his trilogy, *The Lord of the Rings*—the story of a secret fellowship that ventured into the heart of enemy territory to destroy their enemy against long odds—from Doolittle's top-secret, nearly suicidal mission.

While I dropped my hypothesis after determining that Tolkien had done his first drafts prior to World War II, my research detour left me well prepared a decade later when Teresa Schanzenbach, then director of the chamber of commerce in Belle Fourche, South Dakota, called to discuss the Doolittle Raid. Her community was preparing to honor Don Smith on the anniversary of the raid and asked if I would write about him and the 18 April 2001 ceremony for *South Dakota Magazine.* Of course, I answered, a little chagrined that in my earlier study I failed to notice the Raider who had grown up just fifteen miles from where I did and with whom I shared similar experiences as a young person. I learned quickly that South Dakota's fingerprints were all over the Doolittle Raid.

In her telephone call, Schanzenback said Smith was well-known to South Dakotans before the raid because of his football career at South Dakota State College, leading me to imagine a big-man-on-campus type who evolved into a gung-ho warrior. Nothing, I learned in Belle Fourche the day of the ceremony, could have been further from the truth. Smith's cousin, Ruth Streeter Woodall, generously took the time to illuminate his character, painting a portrait of a reserved, modest, and always considerate young man.

Speaking to surviving raiders was the most rewarding part of writing this book. I had the opportunity to talk with David Thatcher, who drove from Montana for the ceremony. He confirmed his friend possessed the qualities Woodall described during their military service. The same week, I spoke on the telephone with Smith's flight engineer over Japan, Edward Saylor, and he expressed deep admiration for a man he called "a straight arrow." Further down the line, I met Smith's friend and fellow raider Thomas Griffin. He greatly enjoyed chatting with anyone interested about the raid. It is an understatement to say they were all happy to help tell Smith's story. Later in the process, after learning Thatcher and Saylor's own stories, I could scarcely believe I had had personal contact with these historic figures.

Letters Smith sent to his parents during Army Air Corps training and the war were a central source. Smith's commitment to writing home reminded me of my late father, Walter Higbee, and my uncle, Max Higbee, army and navy servicemen respectively. Like Smith, they were sons of a heartland livestock veterinarian and part of the operations in the Pacific. Both men would have cringed at being called heroes, just as I believe Smith would have done.

As Teresa Schanzenbach hoped, I published a magazine article about Smith in *South Dakota Magazine* in 2002, which inspired further study. In 2007, after helping my frequent collaborator, Julia Monczunski, produce a broadcast feature for South Dakota Public Radio with Ruth Woodall's guidance, I approached the South Dakota Historical Society Press about a book-length biography. With this book in the works, family friend Maggie Speirs tracked down records of Smith's years as a student at South Dakota State College, now South Dakota State University. Smith's remarkably low profile, despite playing varsity and intramural sports and belonging to a wide range of academic and social organizations, complicated her already difficult task. Still, the librarians at the Hilton M. Briggs Library provided valuable help in tracking down materials.

The same was certainly true at other archives and libraries across the state, especially when librarians learned the identity of my subject. Matthew Reitzel, archivist for the South Dakota State Historical Society, pulled materials from the State Archives at the Cultural Heritage Center in Pierre that I had only hoped existed: the printed program from the Doolittle Raider Annual Reunion in Rapid City in 1978, a file on Japanese balloon bombs, and Steve Nelson's audio tape recordings of the raiders reminiscing at the 1978 reunion. Kay Heck at the Belle Fourche High School Library discovered school newspapers from the 1930s in a wooden cabinet the day after having informed me that Smith's years predated the beginning of the school's yearbook. Staff at the Belle Fourche Public Library, Brookings Public Library, E. Y. Berry Library-Learning Center at Black Hills State University, Grace Balloch Memorial Library in Spearfish, and Rapid City Public Library also did the hard work of tracking down additional sources.

Staff at the Tri-State Museum, the repository for Smith's letters, took great interest in the project. They invited me to present a program about Smith in 2011, during which I learned as much from my audience as they did from me. Several people in attendance had stories to share nearly seventy years after Smith's death. Museum staff members Kristi Thielen and Rebecca Dagel helped in multiple ways, including making photographs available for this book. During that same trip, Jack Wells invited me to his home in Belle Fourche, along with Harold Brost, to discuss memories of the community Smith knew in his youth and, in Brost's case, memories of Smith himself.

On the other side of the state, in Mitchell, former Army Air Corps combat pilot and United States Senator George S. McGovern was generous in sharing his recollections of Air Corps culture. He also described growing up on the prairies in the 1920s and 1930s when flight fascinated a young generation of adventurers because, he explained, South Dakota "was the land of open skies." I am also grateful to another former United States Senator from South Dakota, Larry Pressler, for documenting Senator William J. Bulow's thinking in his book, *U.S. Senators from the Prairie*.

I enjoyed reading the reporting of two late South Dakota journalists, my friend Ron Bender and the imitable Robert Casey. Both men provided important coverage of the raiders at different points in time that contributed to this project. It was a pleasure to make the acquaintance of Janice Evans, Ruth Woodall's daughter, who shared family insight as well as notes and clippings they had saved. Nancy Tystad Koupal, the staff of the South Dakota Historical Society Press, and an anonymous reader provided encouragement throughout the process and offered suggestions on how to expand Smith's story, including research into South Dakotans' opposition to military action in the years just prior to World War II.

Karen Laumer helped me tremendously in technical aspects of preparing the manuscript, including organizing footnotes. My bookseller daughter, Julie Higbee, located long-out-of-print publications for my research. Finally, my wife Janet offered constant support, even on the day we left for vacation in 2018 with an extra suitcase packed with heavy research materials so I could revise and extend the book after days spent sightseeing.

The **First Strike**

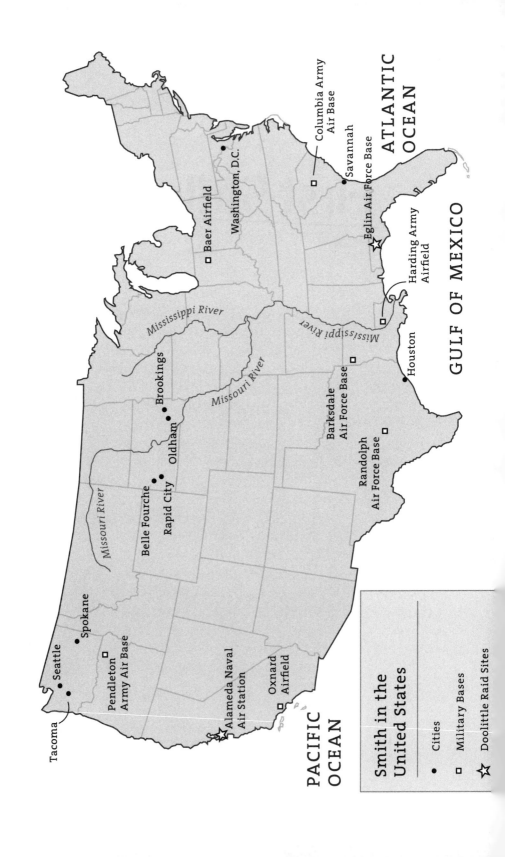

ATLANTIC OCEAN

GULF OF MEXICO

PACIFIC OCEAN

Columbia Army Air Base

Savannah

Eglin Air Force Base

Harding Army Airfield

Houston

Baer Airfield

Washington, D.C.

Mississippi River

Mississippi River

Brookings

Missouri River

Oldham

Belle Fourche

Rapid City

Barksdale Air Force Base

Randolph Air Force Base

Missouri River

Spokane

Seattle

Pendleton Army Air Base

Alameda Naval Air Station

Oxnard Airfield

Tacoma

Smith in the United States

• Cities

▫ Military Bases

★ Doolittle Raid Sites

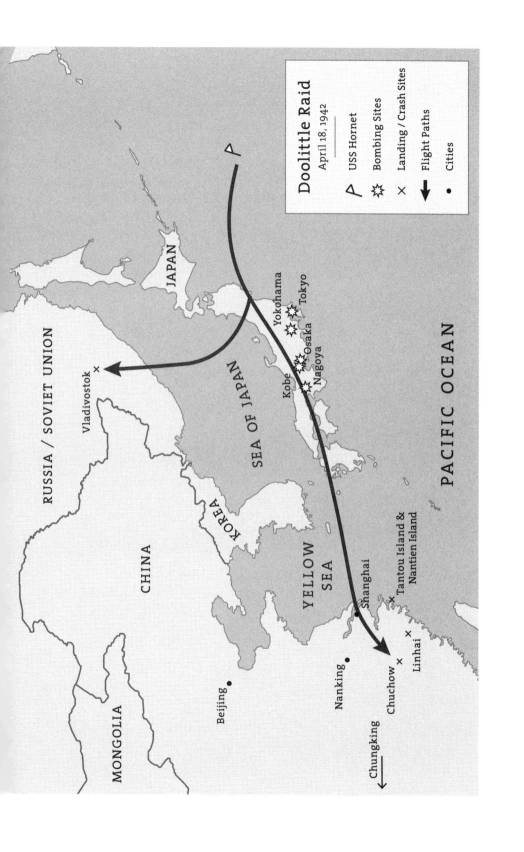

Doolittle Raid
April 18, 1942

- Ρ USS Hornet
- ✿ Bombing Sites
- ✕ Landing / Crash Sites
- ⬇ Flight Paths
- • Cities

MONGOLIA

RUSSIA / SOVIET UNION

Vladivostok ✕

CHINA

Beijing •

JAPAN

KOREA

SEA OF JAPAN

Yokohama
Tokyo
Osaka
Kobe
Nagoya

Nanking •

YELLOW
SEA

Shanghai •

Chungking ⬇

Chuchow ✕
Linhai ✕

Tantou Island &
Nantien Island ✕

PACIFIC OCEAN

n Saturday morning, 18 April 1942, sixteen United States Army Air Corps planes prepared to take off from the aircraft carrier USS *Hornet*. One hundred thirty-four days had passed since Japanese planes bombed the United States Naval Station Pearl Harbor in Hawaii, drawing the nation into World War II. Once the sixteen American planes became airborne, the pilots were to fly them low for six hundred miles over the Pacific Ocean and bomb targets in Japan. The takeoffs alone would be anything but routine.[1]

In fact, some of those present worried that none of the aircraft would make it aloft. The United States Navy had designed the *Hornet*'s flight deck for small, single-engine fighter planes. On this day, land-based, twin-engine B-25 Mitchell bombers, each loaded with four bombs weighing five hundred pounds apiece, a crew of five, and fuel for a long trip, occupied the runway. Typically, B-25 pilots required a thousand feet of tarmac to get airborne, but for this mission each had less than five hundred. While they had practiced on short runways on land, the roll and pitch of the *Hornet* as it cruised the Pacific changed conditions considerably. This day's sea was rough. Each pilot and crew member knew that if his plane malfunctioned and sat disabled on the deck, it would end up in the ocean so the next plane could attempt a takeoff within three or four minutes. Should a plane fail after takeoff, landing it back on the ship's deck would be impossible.[2]

As it turned out, plane after plane soared into the sky. By the time the fifteenth B-25 sat revving its engines, waiting for the takeoff signal, even the most casual observer would have understood the procedure: wait to taxi until the *Hornet*'s bow was moving upward so that it would be dropping down at takeoff. Lieutenant Donald G. ("Don") Smith, a twenty-four-year-old South Dakotan, piloted Plane Fifteen, which its crew named the *TNT*. Smith made his takeoff look simple, climbing into the sky well ahead of the ship's stern. Plane Sixteen followed successfully, making the mission's takeoff phase a complete success.[3]

The squad's leader, Lieutenant Colonel James H. ("Jimmy") Doolittle, piloted the first plane. A well-known former test pilot turned military aviation pioneer, Doolittle helped the United States Army fully understand the offensive potential of modern warplanes. This attack would demonstrate the aggressive possibilities of airpower during the war. Doolittle, having come up with the plan, also had the responsibility of training his pilots. In coming years, Americans would fittingly remember the mission as the Doolittle Raid.[4]

Few other times in American history have called for aggressive military action more urgently than the situation in the Pacific in spring 1942. The United States and its allies had suffered a demoralizing series of defeats that winter across Asia, including the Pacific islands, and many worried for the security of the American West Coast.[5] "America had never seen darker days," Doolittle later wrote.[6] Indeed, losing the war seemed possible.[7]

As soon as the B-25s got aloft, most made a circle and briefly aligned themselves with the *Hornet* so that navigators could check their compasses against the ship's direction. The Doolittle plane was bound for Tokyo. Smith's plane would reach the Japanese coast south of Tokyo and fly west to Kobe, an industrial port wedged between mountains and sea.[8]

As Smith flew a few hundred feet above the water, he and his crew had about five hours to contemplate a sudden change of plans. "The plan was to take off at dusk, bomb at night, and land in China the next morning," remembered Edward J. Saylor, Smith's flight engineer that day. "But the navy spotted a Japanese fishing trawler and thought maybe the boat spotted us [the *Hornet*]. So the navy got nervous the boat had reported us and we took off early."[9] What had been planned as a nighttime raid became a daylight attack with more than two hundred miles of distance added to the flights. The adjustment cast doubt on whether the B-25s had enough fuel to strike, escape Japanese airspace, and land at a Chinese airfield as intended.[10] "When we took off we didn't know where we'd land," said Saylor. "Of course, there was a good chance we'd get shot down, anyway. They told us to get out however we could."[11]

Still, it was not a suicide mission. Saylor would later say he never met a better pilot than Don Smith. On 18 April, Smith confirmed that reputation. The new, state-of-the-art B-25 also inspired confidence. Noisy twin-propeller engines powered the bomber, which measured nearly fifty-three feet long and had a sixty-seven-and-a-half-foot wingspan. The North American Aviation Company began rolling the airplanes out of their factories in 1941. Occasionally, Army Air Corps training involved flying the B-25s on long sorties across the United States.[12] Smith told his parents he hoped one day to buzz his hometown of Belle Fourche, South Dakota. "If you see a brown colored plane with twin tail surfaces flying real low it will probably be me," he wrote in a letter eight months before the Doolittle Raid.[13]

Before Smith's plane reached the coast of Japan, someone onboard switched on a radio and, through headphones, picked up music from a Japanese radio station. The music continued for an hour as the plane flew toward Kobe, but then it stopped abruptly. An alarm sounded, and someone in the studio shouted. Doolittle and nine other pilots had reached Tokyo and released their bombs.[14] "In from the sea swept a fleet of U.S. bombers," *Time* reported the following week, "and for the first time in 2,602 years the island cities of Japan were subjected to enemy assault. Smashed in an instant of terror was the myth of immunity the people of Japan have accepted for generations as gospel."[15]

The "myth of immunity" held that, as an island in the world's widest sea, no invader could reach Japan as long as the nation maintained a strong navy. Indeed, in the early stages of World War II, many believed that merely planning for a possible homeland attack amounted to an insult against the Imperial Japanese Navy. As for airstrikes, Prime Minister Hideki Tojo, previously a general in the Imperial Japanese Army, insisted that Japan had nothing to fear, unlike its counterparts in Europe where enemy bases sat just across borders. He further stated that Japan's one- and two-story buildings made them somehow less vulnerable to air strikes than the taller European cityscapes.[16]

The Tokyo residents who witnessed the 18 April attack described the B-25s in much the way Smith hoped his Belle Fourche friends might one day observe his airplane: close enough to make out details. To avoid detection, the raiders came in low, just above the treetops, then climbed to twelve hundred feet before dropping the bombs so they might escape shock waves. They found Japan's military almost completely unprepared. The trawler Saylor described had indeed spotted the *Hornet* and radioed a report before being sunk by the Americans. Other Japanese civilian vessels that formed a "picket" of observers more than six hundred miles off the coast reported the carrier as well. Leaders in Japan either did not view the reports as indicative of imminent attack or had not received them in time. As the planes roared over land, inexperienced anti-aircraft gunners fired but brought down no aircraft. Japanese fighter planes had patrolled Tokyo's airspace that morning but were mostly on the ground refueling when the B-25s arrived at 12:20 that afternoon. After the attack began, about forty Japanese fighters scrambled but apparently searched at altitudes much higher than the raiders' positions. The American airplanes, to use the raiders' jargon, "hugged the deck."[17]

Even before Smith took part in the raid on Japan, his service in the Army Air Corps had taken him well away from the American heartland. In a letter to his parents the previous year, he marveled at how much geography he had seen. "I have gone swimming in the Pacific, Gulf of Mexico, and the Atlantic, oh yes, also the Great Lakes," he noted.[18] Soon he could add the China Sea to his list. More significantly, he found himself thoroughly immersed in a war he had hoped would never involve Americans. Eight months earlier, in another letter, he had written, "I'm still a little afraid we will get ourselves in the mess, but what are we supposed to do about it, ruin our lives just because the rest of the world can't get along with itself?"[19]

In that letter, Smith expressed an isolationist's view of world affairs that was not surprising, given his South Dakota background. The Great Plains and Midwest had more citizens and politicians who spoke in favor of steering the United States clear of foreign disputes than anywhere else in the country. United States Senators William J. Bulow of South Dakota, Gerald Nye and Lynn Frazier of North Dakota, George Norris of Nebraska, and Robert M. La Follette, Jr., of Wisconsin regularly questioned why President Franklin D. Roosevelt insisted on increased military spending beginning in the late 1930s. Of this band of heartland critics, Nye had the most biting remarks, at one point seeming to revel in Adolf Hitler's ridicule of the president. Other American politicians and observers noted that residents of landlocked states were less likely to encounter recently arrived refugees who described the horrors playing out overseas. The heartland also sometimes expressed disdain for Americans on the East Coast who seemed more attuned to European culture and issues, especially viewed through a British lens, than to American life west of the Hudson River. People from the Great Plains and Midwest could easily put President Roosevelt in that category.[20]

Isolationists existed in all other sections of the country, however, and in 1935 they had become especially active on college campuses. Some isolationist groups organized "Peace strikes," while some student organizations demanded ending Reserve Officer Training Corps (ROTC) programs at their schools. That spring, Hitler boldly announced his intent to rebuild the German military in violation of the Treaty of Versailles that had ended World War I seventeen years earlier. The Nazi dictator seemed especially proud of an emerging German air force.[21] His declarations, along with Italian dictator Benito Mussolini's military campaigns in North Africa, alarmed world leaders, including President Roosevelt, who described 1935 as "hair-trigger times."[22] Many isolationists agreed but saw no need to overreact. They had strong voices on their side, including those who quoted George Washington's warning about "the insidious wiles of foreign influence."[23] The country's most celebrated aviator, Charles Lindbergh, would eventually announce himself as an isolationist, saying, "The destiny of this country does not call for our involvement in European wars. One need only to glance at a map to see where our true frontiers lie." He described the Atlantic and Pacific Oceans as formidable barriers, "even for modern aircraft."[24]

President Roosevelt, however, began thinking of airplanes in potentially life-saving roles should international matters turn grave. First, though, he heeded the isolationists and signed the Neutrality Act of 1935, a popular series of laws that forbade arms sales and, later, financial loans to overseas nations engaged in war. Gerald Nye led a Senate investigation that found certain American corporations had profited greatly during World War I. He worried that these same capitalists could influence war-making decisions in the 1930s as well.[25] Although Roosevelt always hoped to follow isolationist policies, he warned Americans there could come a time when human-rights abuses would cause the United States to act out of moral obligation. Still, in those instances, he hoped to respond in any way "short of war."[26] International developments increasingly challenged ideas of neutrality. The events of Kristallnacht on 9 and 10 November 1938 especially disturbed the president. On those two days, Nazis across Germany killed Jews and destroyed Jewish homes, synagogues, and shops. The Nazi government then forced Jewish citizens to pay for the damages.[27] "There comes a time in the affairs of men," Roosevelt said in the aftermath of those events, "when they must prepare to defend not only their homes alone but the tenets of faith and humanity on which their churches, their governments and their very civilization are founded. The defense of religion, of democracy, and of good faith among nations is all the same fight."[28]

As more stories of Jewish persecution emerged out of Europe, some United States officials pushed to relax immigration quotas as a short-of-war means to address the plight of European Jews, but polls found Americans firmly opposed to the idea. Even a bill to admit more refugee children failed to pass in Congress. The president also tried an American-led negotiated peace agreement to end the specter of United States involvement in a foreign conflict. On 15 April 1939, Roosevelt wrote to both Hitler and Mussolini listing thirty-one nations and asking these leaders to sign binding pledges not to invade them. The fascist Mussolini found the idea of a "distant spectator" stepping into European affairs so outrageous that he concluded Roosevelt's "infantile paralysis" made him delusional. Mussolini never responded to Roosevelt's message.[29]

Hitler, on the other hand, made a spectacle out of his reply. A few weeks after receiving the message, he stepped before the German Reichstag and ridiculed Roosevelt for two hours, during which he demonstrated a startling awareness of American history, including the dark past of Don Smith's South Dakota. Anyone who believed the United States came to dominate the North American continent through peaceful negotiations alone, Hitler asserted, should learn the history of the Lakota people. He also wondered how the United States could think about brokering international peace when it had brought down the League of Nations, the organization created specifically to resolve international conflicts peacefully, by deciding against membership. For some isolationists, Roosevelt's letters to the two heads of state violated the spirit of neutrality. Of Hitler's rebuke, Senator Nye said, Roosevelt "asked for it."[30]

By that time, Americans had become increasingly aware of matters on the other side of the world, where Japan, under Emperor Hirohito, had built an imperial empire in the western Pacific. The stiffest resistance the Japanese faced to that point came in China. When Japanese and Chinese troops fired on one another across the Marco Polo Bridge near Peking (Beijing) in the summer of 1937, the conflict turned brutal. Japanese officers used the exchange at the bridge as a justification to invade China and landed troops at Shanghai. They soon fought their way to the national capital of Nanking (Nanjing).[31]

The capital fell in December, but the Japanese punished Chinese citizens for the next six weeks—shooting, bayonetting, raping—resulting in at least two hundred thousand deaths. This violent campaign acquired the name "Rape of Nanking." The atrocities prompted some Americans to wonder how far and how swiftly a military capable of such brutality might advance. Even before the Rape of Nanking, most Americans sympathized with China, thanks to American missionaries who regularly reported home and to exotic coverage in *National Geographic* as well as Pearl S. Buck's popular 1931 novel, *The Good Earth*, which painted a sympathetic portrait of a Chinese peasant couple. Many Americans came to believe they understood something of China's people, culture, and day-to-day life, but their sympathy did not translate into believing that the United States should help resolve the conflict with Japan.[32]

Having read briefings describing aggression—much of it extreme—in both Asia and Europe, especially after the Japanese navy attacked the United States transport ship USS *Panay* on 12 December 1939, Roosevelt decided the United States might become a target from either the Pacific or Atlantic, or both. In 1939, he obtained a $300 million appropriation from Congress for building military aircraft. A war fought chiefly with air power, he reasoned, would cost fewer lives than one fought in World War I-style trenches or at sea. The approaching world conflict would prove modern air warfare to be more complex than the strike-and-retreat bombardment Roosevelt imagined, putting civilians in harm's way as never before. Yet, Roosevelt's optimistic view in 1939 revealed a president whose thinking had evolved tremendously since his tenure as assistant secretary of the navy twenty years earlier when he had dismissed airplanes as insignificant in combat.[33]

The thinking of South Dakotans also evolved, especially after the United States committed itself to the war in December 1941. The state no longer stood as part of the Great Plains bastion of isolationist sentiment. Don Smith was among 64,560 South Dakotans who entered military service just before or during World War II, the highest population percentage of any state.[34] Smith's upbringing in South Dakota led to the interest in flying that allowed him to make his own mark on the war, but an unsolved mystery also tinged his childhood.

Two young women, sisters who were visiting an orphanage in Sioux Falls, South Dakota, as part of their teacher training program in the early 1920s, stared hard at a young boy. There could be no mistake. The child was their cousin, Donald Gregory. They had no idea how long he had been there, but they knew his background. Their aunt, Don's mother Eva Streeter, married Chuck Gregory, and the couple had four children. Eva and Chuck had lived with her parents on the Streeter family farm outside Oldham, seventy-five miles north of Sioux Falls. Eva gave birth to Donald, the couple's fourth child, on 15 January 1918. A few years later, she became ill and died.[35]

Chuck's in-laws had work for him on their farm if he wanted it. But perhaps he found staying there surrounded by memories of Eva too painful, or maybe he did not think of himself as a farmer. Whatever the reason, he left, leaving his two daughters with Eva's relatives in Oldham and taking his two sons—George and Don—with him. Sometime later, Don arrived at the orphanage unbeknownst to extended family members. The Streeters never learned what became of Chuck and George.[36]

Within hours of hearing about Don's situation, an uncle drove to Sioux Falls and retrieved him. Ruth Streeter, a cousin eleven days younger than Don, later understood that the family had talked about taking him in to grow up with her at Oldham. But her grandmother lived with them in a small house that simply did not have room for one more. Everyone in town knew the story of the boy recovered from an orphanage, and a local veterinarian and his wife, A. W. ("Doc") and Laura Smith, stepped forward and offered to adopt him. Nothing, Ruth said decades later, could have been better for Don. "They did everything for him," she recalled. "He had all the love in the world." In the coming years, Ruth noticed that Don physically resembled his natural mother's family but mirrored Doc and Laura's quiet and cordial characteristics. After the adoption, Laura gave birth to a girl who died in infancy, leaving Don as their only child.[37]

Sometime in 1927, Doc Smith decided to relocate his practice 350 miles west to Belle Fourche, South Dakota, just north of the Black Hills and close to the Wyoming state line. Laura took a secretarial job there, the family settled in, and, except for Ruth, Don lost almost all connections to his Streeter relatives. In later years, Don always claimed Belle Fourche as his hometown. He knew it well because he came to understand and identify thoroughly with Doc Smith's work, helping livestock producers keep their cattle, horses, and sheep healthy.[38]

Belle Fourche claimed about sixteen hundred residents in the 1920s. It stood as the chief supply and services center for ranchers across vast sections of northwestern South Dakota, northeastern Wyoming, and a sliver of southeastern Montana known as "the tri-state area." The community sat on the banks of the Belle Fourche River, a waterway that originates in Wyoming and loops around the north end of the Black Hills on its way east to the Missouri River. For centuries, the river acted as a trade route for Plains Indians, which brought them in contact with French fur traders. The French traders bestowed its name, meaning "beautiful fork." By Don Smith's time, almost no one thought of the name as French, and there was certainly nothing continental in its pronunciation: "bell foosh." The town of the same name sprang up quickly in the late 1880s when Seth Bullock, former Deadwood lawman turned regional entrepreneur and rancher, offered a railroad right-of-way through his land, resulting in a depot right where Bullock thought a new town should take root. Regarded as Belle Fourche's founder, and a Black Hills character whose legend survives to this day, Bullock died a year after Smith's birth.[39]

As Smith grew up, the city's old-timers recounted stories of the town's rough-and-tumble era of the 1890s. Belle Fourche then was the end of the trail for cowboys who moved cattle cross-country. Up to twenty-five hundred railroad cars per month carried cattle from Belle to distant slaughterhouses, making the town one of the world's busiest beef shipment points. Coming in off the trail, cowboys collected their pay and sometimes spent it all in a dozen saloons along Fifth Avenue and in Madam Dora DuFran's brothel, where locals claimed that none other than Calamity Jane worked as a cook. The notorious Wild Bunch gang notched its mark in Belle Fourche history when they robbed the Butte County Bank in 1897, escaping with less than one hundred dollars.[40]

In 1918, Belle Fourche put its western heritage on display to raise funds for the Red Cross during World War I. The locals organized a Fourth of July rodeo, which proved a hit and soon became an annual fixture, eventually receiving the name Black Hills Roundup. The yearly rodeo became a significant part of Smith's world. As a boy, Smith competed in contests for youths, including trying to stay atop a bucking calf. Throughout his life, he boasted about the event to all his out-of-town friends. Today, the roundup is still a draw for those visiting the Black Hills and has become a major stop on the Professional Rodeo Cowboys Association circuit.[41]

The rodeo celebrated both an important industry and a proud lifestyle. By Smith's lifetime, the open-range cattle outfits were long gone. Some historians portray the contemporary beef industry as diminished, relegated to small fenced pastures. In fact, the fenced ranges of Butte County and neighboring counties were anything but small, frequently extending as far as the eye could see across mostly treeless prairies.[42]

Doc Smith traveled that region, visiting both cattle and sheep ranches, advising livestock producers, and handling their emergencies. Don often accompanied his father, helping to tote medicine bags and equipment. He treasured those memories forever. Far from home years later, on the eve of World War II, he wrote, "Wish I could be back home to go around with you like I used to when I was a little kid, Dad."[43] In the wide open expanses north of Belle Fourche, Don learned the names of landmark buttes that South Dakotans still use as orientation points: Deer's Ears, Castle Rock, Flat Top, Crow Buttes. He also grew familiar with the landscape and the much different agriculture immediately east of Belle Fourche. There, more than fifty thousand acres of formerly bone-dry land had been transformed into fertile farm country, thanks to an early United States Bureau of Reclamation project. One of the world's largest earthen dams at the time of its completion in 1911 had created Belle Fourche Reservoir. Five hundred miles of irrigation channels and laterals brought water to the dry farm country, allowing new crops, including sugar beets, cucumbers, and pinto beans, to thrive. Lush grain production in the irrigation district also meant high-quality feed for stock producers. All of it fascinated Smith. He seemed on course for a career in agriculture, his cousin Ruth would say, probably as a veterinarian like his father.[44]

By the 1930s, however, his dad's profession was changing dramatically. Veterinary science was about to evolve as never before with the development of antibiotic medicines, but the use of the horse, always a veterinarian's primary patient and professional concern, declined in agricultural operations thanks to technology. South Dakotans had reason to believe their state would keep abreast, or even lead, agricultural advancements in an age of new scientific knowledge and mechanization. The state claimed a well-respected school of agriculture at South Dakota State College in Brookings, far east of Belle Fourche near the Minnesota border. The Bureau of Reclamation also conducted agricultural research at state "experiment farms," including one just east of Belle Fourche at Newell, in the irrigation district.[45]

At the same time, many people began wondering whether South Dakota farmers and ranchers could ever rely on their skills and lands to earn a steady living. The first hints of approaching trouble had surfaced in the early 1920s when farm prices worldwide dropped sharply. Ironically, the improved efficiency that came with new tractors allowed farmers to plant more acres than ever before, which created surpluses that kept prices low. Then severe drought gripped the Great Plains in the 1930s. Winds whipped soil into the sky, creating "black blizzards" of dust, while tumbleweeds and thistles ravaged the prairies. Smith experienced those dirt storms, the worst of which occurred in 1933 and 1934. He also watched as the dry conditions led to a grasshopper infestation that finished off any vegetation left standing. Adding to these natural disasters, the nation continued to struggle through the financial calamity of the Great Depression. For South Dakota, that meant farm crops and ranch livestock brought next to nothing on the market. In lieu of cash, Doc Smith and other veterinarians often accepted produce and animals as payment for services, keeping their families better fed than many South Dakotans of the era.[46]

Even with the desperate conditions, there were days in Belle Fourche in the 1930s when it seemed as if nothing was amiss. The Smiths lived in a comfortable, two-story house on Day Street, a five-minute walk from downtown across the Belle Fourche River and up a hill. A contemporary of Don Smith's, Jack Wells, recollected that on Saturdays, farm and ranch families still drove into town to shop, conduct business, meet friends downtown, and maybe enjoy a café supper or a movie. Most spent less than in earlier years—sometimes much less—yet the Saturday ritual remained intact. The Black Hills Roundup still drew cowboys every Fourth of July, and, to keep attendance up, roundup organizers sometimes added seemingly incongruous yet popular personalities to the program, such as evangelist Billy Sunday.[47]

Belle Fourche's substantial size made it a good place to grow up, Wells noted, because the community could maintain a solid range of youth activities.[48] Smith, his cousin Ruth recalled, "was very much into Boy Scouting. . . . always into a different project," as he pursued merit badges.[49] The Boy Scouts emphasized experiencing the outdoors, and Smith had a head start there because of his family's love of the nearby Black Hills—especially Spearfish Canyon, a deep gorge at the northern end of the Black Hills about fifteen miles south of Belle Fourche. With high rocky cliffs, a swift mountain stream, waterfalls, and a forest of pine and spruce, the canyon felt a world entirely apart from the dust-ravaged plains.[50]

Smith entered high school in the fall of 1932, part of a freshman class of sixty-five students. Some of his classmates were new to Belle Fourche, having graduated eighth grade from Butte County's one-room country schools and relocated to town for secondary education. No matter their status as new or familiar faces, the students mainly identified each other with nicknames. Smith went to school with Baby Face, Tuffy, Mutt, Apey, Three Cow, the Pete and Repeat sisters, and even a Nudie. "Often," the high school newspaper observed, "teachers must pause before calling upon a student, in order to separate the nickname from their given name." Rather predictably, a young Belle Fourche man named Buck Pond became Duck Pond. As the son of a veterinarian, Don was rarely called anything in high school but Doc Smith.[51]

Belle Fourche High School prided itself in being big enough to offer an array of classes in the humanities, sciences, and manual arts. It also booked a series of assembly programs. A few weeks into his freshman year, Smith listened to Dr. No-Yong Park speak about recent tensions between the Chinese and Japanese. "Although he was Chinese by birth," reported the high school paper, "he seemed absolutely fair in his analysis of the problem."[52] As a junior, Smith heard an American missionary to Japan, identified as Dr. Cooper, describe the island nation as "not only a beautiful country, but [one that] also has attractive people." Perhaps aware that he was addressing youths who knew farming, Cooper stated that Japan had tillable acreage just half the size of Iowa yet needed to feed a population half that of the United States. The school paper summarized Cooper's presentation by repeating his closing statement: "We should all try to get a better understanding of Japan."[53]

Smith also had contact with a few of the forty-three South Dakota veterans of the Spanish-American War and subsequent Philippine Insurrection who came to Belle Fourche for a reunion. Three of them spoke at a school assembly, describing their deployment to the Philippines in 1898 and 1899, "marching and struggling through rice fields and thick forests or the muck and mire of jungle and swamp, fighting bravely on," a writer for the school paper reported. "They told of their experiences not as adventures, but as a grim form of work that had to be done. They spoke against war but praised patriotism and showed that it was necessary to every nation."[54]

Another assembly addressed the role of the military in American society. During his comments, the commanding officer of nearby Fort Meade, Colonel W. R. Pope, told students he did not know any "militarist" officers in the United States Army. Instead, he likened the armed forces to a life insurance policy for the nation. He went on to refute concerns about modern weaponry when he stated, "The popular belief that poisonous gas, machine guns, or airplanes could destroy a whole town or civilization is a lot of hooey."[55]

None of that talk seemed to have a direct bearing on day-to-day life in Belle Fourche in the mid-1930s, however. There was plenty else to think about. Although school kept him busy, Smith had a newspaper delivery route, and in season he packed just-sheared wool at a Belle Fourche warehouse. Apparently, much of the money he earned went toward acquiring and maintaining a car, "something along the lines of a Ford Model A or B," Harold Brost, the brother of one of Smith's friends, remembered. "I know it had a rumble seat."[56]

Although the Brosts lived eighteen miles from Belle Fouche down dirt roads, Smith regularly drove out to their place so he and Harold's older brother, Irvin, could go meet girls at dances. "In those days even if boys didn't like to dance, they had to learn for weddings and things," Harold Brost explained. "But Don really liked to dance. Lots of dances were out in the country somewhere with homemade bands. Don and Irvin might know about a couple of them, so they'd flip a coin to decide which one."[57]

Smith was physically coordinated, and the trait served him well on both the dance floor and the football field. The Belle Fourche High School Broncs football team played at the roundup grounds on the same surface where actual broncs bucked every Fourth of July. "They played on dirt," Brost recollected. "They just let the cow manure lay there until it became dirt, too."[58]

Regardless of the surface, the big wooden roundup grandstand gave team members a sense of playing in a stadium rather than the modest football venues common to western South Dakota and eastern Wyoming. Plenty of those grandstand seats were filled during Smith's sophomore season, when the Broncs did something remarkable. They played eight games and shut out all but one of their opponents. Rapid City scored twenty-seven points in its game against Belle Fourche, enough to give the Broncs their only loss and dropping them to a second-place finish in the Black Hills Conference. Smith did not see much action that 1933 season. He was small at the time and had, in fact, played on a junior varsity team with others who weighed 130 pounds or less the year before.[59]

But he grew fast. By the following season, his junior year, Smith showed prowess as an offensive guard and started his first game against Sundance High School from Wyoming. Belle Fourche won 32 to 2 and improved its early season record to 2 and 0, but the Broncs then dropped the next three games before closing the season with a 45 to 0 drubbing of Sturgis in a miserable game. That afternoon, extreme cold and a biting wind whipped the dirt into blinding clouds at the roundup grounds. The elements acted as a more formidable opponent for the Broncs than the Sturgis team.[60]

In his senior year, Smith played for a new coach, Coach Crakes. The physically imposing Crakes had played in professional football leagues in Ohio and Rhode Island and coached the freshman squad at the University of South Dakota a few years earlier.[61] Crakes had complete faith in Smith, who did not miss a single quarter all season, contributed to a coordinated team effort, and demonstrated leadership in a low-key manner.

Not that Smith was the team's star. That honor went to his pal, Lloyd Eaton, who was destined for a professional football career. Smith and Eaton would recall their senior season as disappointing. The Broncs finished 4 and 3 and could not get past mighty Rapid City, who beat them convincingly every year Smith and Eaton played. In 1935, at Rapid City, Belle Fourche fell 41 to 0 in a game where Smith suffered an injury that forced him out late in the contest. A few weeks after the season ended, he received a varsity letter for football.[62]

Although Smith won friends easily, he was quiet, an introvert. "Nothing of a showoff," his cousin Ruth said, recalling summer trips her family made to see Smith. He may have sought recognition indirectly through his cocker spaniel, Mugs, whom he taught countless tricks, and he enjoyed explaining to Ruth how the dog learned its skills. "I was very impressed because my dog at home couldn't do any tricks," Ruth said. The Smith family's chickens came up in conversation regularly, and Don explained his experiments designed to increase egg laying. "A chicken was a chicken to me," Ruth admitted, but Don recognized a wide variety.[63]

Given this interest, Smith probably knew all about a revolutionary chick-sexing system developed in Japan during the 1930s. It captured the attention of poultry farmers worldwide because of its potential to enhance their production efficiency. Just before World War II, the Zen-Nippon Chick Sexing School regularly drew groups of American farmers and agricultural school professors and their students, who hoped to observe and carry the knowledge home.[64] Smith certainly would have preferred a trip like that to Japan, rather than the one he eventually made.

At some point, Smith made the acquaintance of the remarkable Clyde Ice and added aviation to his already diverse interests. Born in Saint Lawrence, South Dakota, thirty years before Smith's birth, Ice first saw an airplane in 1914 in Huron, South Dakota. The experience set him on his ultimate career path, entertaining with stunts at air shows in addition to advancing flight mechanical systems and promoting practical and entrepreneurial uses for planes. Ice won national prominence in the aviation field. He befriended Smith's future commander, Jimmy Doolittle, as well as famed aviator Charles Lindbergh, who introduced him to Henry Ford. From that relationship, Ice occasionally advised the Ford Motor Company in designing airplane components.[65]

By the early 1920s, Belle Fourche was an important flight destination for Ice. He found he could make a thousand dollars during the roundup by offering plane rides to rodeo fans. In the early 1930s, Ice lived near Spearfish, a dozen miles from Belle Fourche, and managed the Black Hills Airport.[66] Ice likely gave Smith his first flying lessons, although no documentation has been found to prove it. Ice taught lots of South Dakotans to fly, and, Woodall said, "Clyde and Don became very close."[67]

Ice must certainly have told Smith what he himself learned from a

World War I veteran aviator who flew through South Dakota in 1919: "You just can't *make* an airplane do something it *can't* do."[68] It was vitally important that a pilot understand the machine's capacities and limitations fully. More than anything else, Ice modeled for young aviators the special responsibility that came with their skill. "He was always ready to help someone in need," wrote Joe Foss, a Medal of Honor aviator during World War II and later South Dakota governor. Foss first experienced flight aboard a plane Ice piloted. "He would risk his life when the weather was much too unsafe to be in the air if it meant fulfilling a mercy mission."[69]

Most of those missions involved getting medical supplies or a doctor to snowbound ranches or tiny towns where emergencies had developed. Spearfish osteopath George Betts made several wild flights with Ice, one to a distant ranch where a woman struggled in premature labor. Ice landed the plane safely despite intimidating winds. While Betts took care of the woman and her newborn, Ice and ranch neighbors held onto the aircraft to keep it from rolling away like a tumbleweed. Once during Smith's high school years, Ice's friends feared the worst when he flew off into a snowstorm with medical supplies and did not return. After nearly a week, Ice's plane finally approached Rapid City. On the ground, he explained that wind and near-zero visibility forced him down. He took shelter in a house, far from telephones or any other means of getting a message to the outside world, until the weather allowed him to fly again. In Clyde Ice, Smith met an aviator willing and capable of doing what most other pilots would not consider. Remarkably, Ice regularly flew through the most challenging conditions South Dakota could throw at him for sixty years, never seriously injuring himself or a passenger, and lived to the age of 103.[70]

In 1935, a South Dakota aviation adventure of a different type gripped the imaginations of millions of Americans, including Smith. Similar to the way broadcasters eventually covered NASA's early manned space flights decades later, NBC radio came to South Dakota for a live report describing the mission of *Explorer II*, a special balloon designed for high altitudes. It carried commander Albert Stevens and pilot Orville Anderson into the stratosphere to an altitude of 13.7 miles above the earth, higher than humans had ever before ascended. The National Geographic Society and United States Army Air Corps—the precursor to the United States Air Force—collaborated on the project. Stevens and Anderson sealed themselves inside a fifteen-hundred-pound gondola made of "Dowmetal," a magnesium alloy soon used universally in aircraft construction. National Geographic and the army declared that valuable scientific knowledge would stem from the risky mission, including how Dowmetal responded to extreme altitudes and frigid temperatures. Yet, it was the element of human adventure that especially fed the public's interest. The altitude Stevens and Anderson reached allowed them to shoot stunning photographs showing the earth's curvature for the first time.[71]

Explorer II lifted off from a unique Black Hills geological feature located sixty miles south of Belle Fourche. A 450-foot deep depression, the spot immediately became known as the Stratobowl. Explaining the formation's chief quality, Stevens declared, "There are few places in the world where it is safe to inflate such huge bags, for they tower into the air until they encounter strong air currents unless protected by a wall such as that of the natural bowl at Rapid City."[72] Even on calm days, Stevens noted, air movement could regularly reach speeds of six to eight miles per hour at three hundred feet above ground. As the cotton and rubber *Explorer II* balloon filled with helium, it stretched in height to 315 feet. At 7:01 A.M. on 11 November 1935, the mooring ropes were released, and, Stevens reported, the balloon "shot upward at a speed much greater than is given racing balloons on take-off."[73] *Explorer II* then stalled a hundred feet above the bowl's rim until Stevens and Anderson released lead pellets, much like buckshot, that weighted down the gondola. The action pulled *Explorer II* out of its stall, and it sailed into the early morning sky.[74]

Stevens and Anderson did not plan a long-distance overland course. Their mission was strictly about the vertical, to climb as high as possible. They rose to where "no sign of actual life on earth could be detected," Stevens later reported. "To us it was a foreign and lifeless world. The sun was the one object that commanded our attention. We were temporarily almost divorced from Mother Earth."[75] Those words, published in the January 1936 issue of *National Geographic Magazine*, read like romantic poetry to those fascinated by human potential in an environment free from gravity's pull, separate from earthbound perspectives.

At National Geographic headquarters in Washington, D.C., that November day, the society's officers and staff listened to NBC's coverage and studied a South Dakota map, guessing where *Explorer II* might land. Schoolchildren across the country did the same. In the afternoon, eight hours and thirteen minutes after takeoff, *Explorer II* touched down near White Lake, South Dakota, more than two hundred miles east of the Stratobowl.[76]

True to his love of scientific experimentation, Smith wondered if he might launch his own helium balloon and document its overland flight—perhaps as far as White Lake, or possibly beyond. Six weeks after the journey of *Explorer II*, Belle Fourche schools broke for Christmas vacation. It was a time of year he always loved, one for sledding down the hill near his home toward the Belle Fourche River and preparing small gifts for the neighborhood's little children.[77] Smith traditionally delivered the gifts himself, dressed as Santa. This Christmas, he had something else in mind. He acquired a sturdy balloon, found a way to inflate it with helium, and typed a note to attach to it. The note read: "Please return to Donald Smith[,] Belle Fourche[,] South Dakota[.] Sent aloft Dec. 23 at 4 P.M."[78]

He chose a gusty day to launch, and less than sixteen hours later, on Christmas Eve morning, a farmer named J. J. Guthmiller found the balloon three hundred miles to the northeast, near the town of Leola, South Dakota. "It was rather thrilling to find the blue balloon," Guthmiller wrote to Smith. "It was in the spokes of the threshing machine on the east side of our farm. The air was still in it and when I turned it loose in the house it immediately rose to the ceiling. My little girl is certainly getting a big kick out of it." She was not the only one. It appears Guthmiller himself got caught up in South Dakota's ballooning fever of 1935. He promised Smith he would return the balloon "after displaying it at Leola."[79]

In January, Smith turned eighteen, and in no time, it seemed, the gusty winter winds softened. With spring came high school graduation and then the countdown of weeks until his departure for college. He had decided to move to South Dakota's eastern edge and enroll at South Dakota State College's agricultural school. On the campus in Brookings, Smith knew, he would meet lots of classmates from farms and ranches hoping to return home someday with knowledge that could improve their families' agricultural operations. Though 1936 was another dry year, the rains returned beginning in 1937. Farming and ranching apparently would remain central to South Dakota's economy.[80]

Beyond its commitment to advancing agriculture, Smith knew that South Dakota State claimed a fine football team. In 1935, it upset the University of Wisconsin, 13 to 6. Smith hoped to join the team. Far from undersized now, he stood six feet and weighed about 190 pounds.[81] Broad shoulders suggested a remarkable upper-body strength that would serve him well in athletics and military endeavors. No one could miss the ruddy complexion that reflected a largely outdoors upbringing and lifestyle.

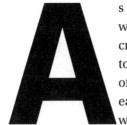**A**s the people of Tokyo tried to grasp what had hit them, Don Smith and his crewmates made their low approach toward Kobe in the *TNT*. All but one of the five men aboard were in their early to mid-twenties. Sergeant Edward Saylor, the engineer, was born in Jordan, Montana. Lieutenant Howard Sessler, from Arlington, Massachusetts, served as both navigator and bombardier. Before the war, he had played minor league baseball in the Boston Red Sox organization. Smith's co-pilot, Lieutenant Griffith Williams, the crew's youngest member at age twenty-one, hailed from Chicago. The old man of Plane Fifteen, Lieutenant Thomas R. ("Doc") White, age thirty-three, was born in Hawaii and studied medicine at Harvard, earning his medical degree there. Doc White held the dual roles of mission flight surgeon and gunner.[1]

The crew spotted Kobe, a long and narrow city, in the distance. They identified their chief target, Uyenoshita Steelworks, and Sessler dropped the bombs. "I know we hit our target," Saylor remembered. "Two fighters were on our tail, but they didn't close in on us, and there was a little anti-aircraft fire, but I don't think we got hit."[2] Smith reported that just after the bomb hatch closed, "a gun on the south edge of town opened fire at us, and we dove for the water, pulling out just above it, indicating 325 mph. We did not have an opportunity to see how much damage was accomplished."[3]

The crew had no way of knowing how the other fifteen planes fared. All had made it into Japanese air space and, in most cases, hit targets. While skill and planning accounted for much of the mission's success, luck entered the formula as well. Escaping Japanese air space required a second dose of it. When the raiders left the *Hornet*'s deck that day, they initially faced a strong west-to-east headwind, a force the fliers knew would eat away at their already precarious fuel supply. At one point, in

Doolittle's plane, South Dakotan and navigator Lieutenant Henry A. ("Hank") Potter did some calculations and projected they would likely run out of fuel about 135 miles short of the China coast. Gradually, the headwind shifted. Soon, a twenty-five-mile-per-hour tailwind pushed Doolittle and his raiders toward the southwest and the Chinese shore. Their escape, without the Japanese bringing down any planes, made the raid a complete success.[4]

At dusk—the original time slated for the planes to take off—Smith spotted the China coast. He could also see the coastal mountain range. Chuchow Field, the airstrip where Doolittle had instructed his pilots to land, sat on the other side of the mountains. But with the *TNT*'s gauges indicating all-but-empty fuel tanks, Smith and navigator Sessler believed the plane would not clear the mountains. The Japanese army occupied China's coastal lands, adding significant danger to a crash-landing there. Still, it would be nothing like being forced down over Japan itself. Rather than coming down alive in Japan, Doolittle had said, he would crash his plane—not that he necessarily advised pilots half his age to follow suit.[5] In China, Don and his crew believed, they would have a chance to elude Japanese soldiers if they encountered Chinese citizens eager to assist enemies of Japan.

Smith's journey to command of the *TNT* began during his years at South Dakota State College, known today as South Dakota State University, the state's largest institution of higher learning. Located in Brookings, fifty miles north of Sioux Falls and not far from Smith's birthplace, the school reflected the philosophy of the national land-grant college movement that took root in the 1860s. Under a federal act, states received lands they could then sell in order to establish colleges that differed from traditional institutions of the era, which emphasized classical or liberal arts coursework. Land-grant schools such as South Dakota State emphasized preparing their students for careers in agriculture, practical science, and engineering, while including liberal arts staples such as rhetoric, mathematics, history, and literature. Smith would list agriculture as his major when he arrived in 1936.[6]

Before leaving Belle Fourche, he grew familiar with that year's College of Agriculture and Mechanical Arts course bulletin, which noted, "Nearly a quarter of the graduates in Agriculture are practical farmers; or they are breeders of livestock and seed grain." Others, it added, found employment in packing houses, dairy plants, grain elevators, feed manufacturers, or as civil servants or researchers committed to advancing scientific farming.[7] Among the agricultural courses, one would keep Smith especially engaged—poultry culture. He excitedly reported to his father promising developments in increased egg production. Eventually, this interest led to his election as president of the campus Poultry Club.[8]

In some ways, soils professor Joseph Hutton was the heart and soul of the College of Agriculture during Smith's years there. An Indiana native, Hutton began teaching at State in 1911. For all the college's emphasis in the 1930s on agricultural science and technologies, Hutton reminded students that farming also represented something sacred and stood as a measure of civilization. He had become so popular with the students that they decided to include a poem he wrote in 1931 in their yearbook in 1940. Entitled *Life*, the verses reflected his views on the spiritual aspects of agriculture:

> In some misty eon past/The Virgin Earth conceived/And Life
> was born.
> Unto this day/Within her womb/The vital miracle recurs,/
> While from the Soil,/Maternal breast,/Redundant Life/
> Draws sustenance;
> But if it fail—/The Fount of Life—/Then: Hunger,/War, and
> Pestilence![9]

South Dakota State College had an enrollment of about eight hundred students when Smith arrived in 1936. During his four years, enrollment climbed dramatically as the state and region pulled itself out of drought and the Great Depression. South Dakotans made up most of the student population, but a good number also hailed from across the Minnesota state line, twenty-five miles east. The campus featured wide lawns, hardwood trees, and a dominant 167-foot bell tower, the Campanile. True to their mostly rural backgrounds, students in the 1930s dubbed it "the Singing Silo."[10]

The 1930 census counted 4,376 residents in Brookings, more than double Belle Fourche's population. Despite the larger size of the university town, the two places had many similarities. Both were county seats. The two also possessed tree-lined residential areas, businesses catering to agriculture, a downtown that came alive on Saturdays, and locomotives rumbling through town. The local commitment to a quality airport in Brookings especially impressed Smith. Two years before his arrival, the city received a federal grant for airport construction south of town. In 1935, a Works Progress Administration crew built a hangar. Support for the new airport emerged out of a growing interest in flying throughout the state. South Dakota, per capita, ranked as a leader among states in advancing aviation with twenty-seven airports, eighty-three registered pilots, and eighty-four registered planes in 1936. Just weeks after Smith moved to campus, Brookings staged an airshow, including Clyde Ice performing in a Travelair.[11]

Smith later described himself as reclusive in college. Yet, the evidence points to him moving easily among those who were part of three distinct social groups: "aggies," athletes, and army. As part of its land-grant status, South Dakota State required all freshman and sophomore men to enroll in the Reserve Officer Training Corps (ROTC) during Smith's tenure. Those planning to serve as officers in the military after college participated in their junior and senior years as well. At some point, Smith committed to the four-year ROTC plan and a postgraduate stint in the army. The program at State offered him the opportunity to learn more about aviation, culminating with time in the air at the controls of small single-engine planes, under the guidance of Civil Aeronautics Administration instructors.[12]

At State, Smith received an army uniform for ROTC functions. On it, he pinned the blue and gold shield of the Scabbard and Blade military fraternity. While active in that fraternity, he also joined another club called Blue Key. Both organizations engaged in service projects on campus and in town and placed considerable emphasis on social events such as box socials and dances, where the men brought dates, and smokers, where they did not. The two groups formed basketball teams to participate in a highly competitive campus intramural league as well. In high school, Smith had shown little interest in basketball, but he excelled as a forward in the intramural league. After a tournament in 1939 where 250 players took part, a committee selected Smith as an "honorable mention" for the all-tournament team.[13]

Varsity football remained Smith's main athletic passion and became a major part of his campus identity as he started at center for the South Dakota State Jackrabbits in his junior and senior years. The Jackrabbits played in the North Central Conference against college teams from both Dakotas, Minnesota, Nebraska, Iowa, and Wisconsin. The campus football venue, State Field, boasted a well-maintained playing surface that in no way resembled the dirt and manure mixture of the Belle Fourche Roundup grounds. In high school, Smith did not get his varsity letter until his senior year, but at State, he earned it as a sophomore. The honor made him eligible to join yet another campus group, the Monogram Club, known for its funding program for "needy athletes," a significant source of support for some of State's players.[14]

During the 1936 and 1937 football seasons, Smith gained important game experience and honed his skills with the junior varsity team. In 1938, his junior year, Jack Barnes took over as coach. Barnes liked what he saw in Smith and made Smith his center. To open the season, the Jackrabbits traveled to Rapid City for their matchup with South Dakota School of Mines. Throughout Smith's football career, Rapid City always proved a discouraging destination. His Belle Fourche Broncs never won when playing there, including the game when he suffered an injury in 1935. College football in Rapid City proved just as disheartening. The School of Mines spoiled Coach Barnes's debut with an 18 to 7 win, setting up a somber return to Brookings across four hundred miles of brown prairie.[15]

The Jackrabbits played better in coming weeks against Nebraska and Minnesota teams. South Dakota State had a 3 and 3 record going into the season's most anticipated game against their rival, the University of South Dakota Coyotes. The two South Dakota schools played annually for a "little brown jug" trophy. For the 1938 season, the battle for that jug took place in Brookings. Fans packed the bleachers at State Field, and the contest developed into one of outstanding defense and good kicking, but also profuse fumbling. In the third quarter, the Coyotes scored a touchdown that turned out to be the winning score in their 7 to 0 victory. A South Dakota State student sportswriter reached far to put the game in a positive light for Jackrabbits fans. "Except for heads-up playing displayed by the losers in recovering fumbles," he wrote, the Coyotes "might have easily rolled up a much larger score in retaining the jug."[16]

In 1939, the Jackrabbits again opened the season against the School of Mines, this time in Brookings. Smith's fellow ROTC men sold cowbells before the opener and urged State fans to keep up a clanging racket throughout the game. They did. Whether the cowbells figured into the game's outcome or not, the Jackrabbits avenged the previous season's loss easily, recording a 40 to 0 shutout.[17]

The next weekend, six thousand fans, all guests of local Brookings merchants, watched the Jackrabbits defeat a team of bigger players from Moorhead State Teachers College in Moorhead, Minnesota. The young season felt much different than the previous one as South Dakota State notched wins the next two weekends. A 3 and 0 record put the campus and community into an optimistic frenzy during homecoming week. Former heavyweight boxing champ Max Baer came to State as master of ceremonies for the festivities, also known as "Hobo Day."[18] The pre-game parade through the streets of Brookings, however, featured a strange, somber entry reminding spectators that a dangerous world awaited the students. The American Society of Agricultural Engineers, a campus club Smith had joined, created the unusual "stunt float." They had rigged a tractor to "gallop" and struggle for balance while pulling a low-slung trailer to illustrate, according to the float's sign, "European Balance of Power—Democracy vs. Totalitarianism."[19] Once the thought-provoking entry passed, observers shifted their thoughts back to football, and the game at State Field a few hours later did not disappoint. Against the University of North Dakota, the Jackrabbits scored two touchdowns in the first half and then held on for a 14 to 13 win.[20]

Smith and his teammates played in another homecoming game the next Saturday, one hundred miles south at Vermillion, where the University of South Dakota Coyotes ruined the Jackrabbits' perfect season and kept possession of the little brown jug with a 21 to 7 win. Smith and his teammates bounced back the following week with a 7 to 6 victory over Omaha University, setting up a must-win home game against Iowa's Morningside College on Armistice Day, 11 November. A victory in that contest would clinch a share of the conference championship with the University of North Dakota and University of South Dakota. The Jackrabbits scored early and won 34 to 14, making Smith a champion in his final season.[21]

The season ended with a train ride to Texas, a state Smith would soon come to know well, and a nonconference contest against West Texas State. Texas football employed a style that emphasized aggressive passing, as the Jackrabbits witnessed in 1939. Their hosts threw the ball

all over the field for a convincing 37 to 7 win. Easier to digest than the University of South Dakota loss, the defeat at the hands of West Texas State did not entirely spoil the season's end.[22] Back in Brookings in December, Smith learned the Associated Press had given him an honorable mention for the organization's Little All-America Football team. The *Daily Belle Fourche Post* made his honor front-page news. "For the most part," the newspaper explained, "the small college all-stars who comprise the team were scarcely known beyond their own immediate geographical territory, but their records indicated they could hold their own in any football company."[23]

With football behind him, Smith concentrated on fulfilling requirements for graduation in May 1940. He also kept busy with his fraternity activities and ROTC drills. Campus life at State felt remarkably vibrant in 1939 and 1940. A record thirteen hundred students crowded the campus, and the school opened a new four-story dormitory and a spacious student union to accommodate them. Still, developing international affairs in the late 1930s cast a shadow that even State's students could not escape. Campus and community leaders in Brookings stressed the need to stay aware of rapidly evolving developments. The Brookings Rotary Club, for example, sponsored on-campus lectures by two highly qualified speakers. German politician F. Wilhelm Sollman delivered an address titled "The Rise of Present Day Germany" and Austria's Prince Hubertus zu Loewenstein, an early opponent of Hitler, spoke about "The Changing Scene in Europe."[24] Whether or not Americans would go to war in the coming months and years, State placed considerable emphasis on preparing students to contribute in diverse ways should the need materialize. Pharmacy students, for instance, learned how to build "drug experimental stations" for developing medications in the event of wartime drug embargos.[25] Sixty-six men enrolled in a special two-year aviation mechanics course to prepare them for immediate industrial or military assignments.[26]

In his senior year, Smith was immersed in advanced ROTC training that included tactical problem solving, rifle marksmanship, and machine-gun operation. That school year, the number of men applying for the next round of advanced ROTC training was three times what the program could accept. Four commissioned army officers and three enlisted soldiers led the State ROTC program, which involved six hundred men at various levels during Smith's senior year. The ROTC classes and drills culminated in May when visiting officers conducted a two-day inspection, including classroom tests, a military parade across campus, and military and athletic competitions. The inspection marked one of Smith's last campus activities. When he graduated a few days later, he received his bachelor's degree in agriculture and the uniform bars of a second lieutenant in the United States Army.[27]

Eleven hundred miles south of Brookings, a beacon for American aviators stood above the south Texas plains. The 170-foot-high tower nicknamed the Taj Mahal after the shrine in India, or Taj for short, housed the administrative offices for the United States Army Air Corps' Randolph Airfield in San Antonio. Established in 1931, Randolph immediately gained a reputation as a futuristic "air city" with the moniker "the West Point of the Air."[28] At the time of its development, military and civilian leaders still disagreed about the significance of air power for modern combat, but few of them doubted that, at the very least, fliers would play major roles in transport and reconnaissance both in times of peace and war. Recognizing this importance, the army looked for a site to establish a first-class aviation training center. The terrain and temperate weather in Texas factored into the site selection, but the city of San Antonio's donation of twenty-three thousand acres northeast of town finalized the decision. The architecture at Randolph was anything but standard-issue military. Rather, it assumed a Southwest mission look, as if it stood in tribute to the state's fighting heritage, including valor demonstrated at the nearby Alamo. As a bastion for aviation, Randolph would remain as a part of the Texas landscape well into the future.[29]

When Randolph opened, the army reorganized local operations to create a new Air Corps complex. The branch incorporated the operations of two established airfields outside of San Antonio, Brooks and Kelly, both founded in 1917, into Randolph Air Base. They then used the three entities to launch a new system for pilot training. All cadets quickly came to understand that while Randolph served as the nerve center for the joint bases, the best aviators-in-training should shoot for an assignment at Kelly Air Field.[30]

Even with the development of the pilot training system at Randolph, Smith would not make his way to Texas immediately after graduation. By 1940, the large number of pilots needing instruction prompted the army to sign contracts with municipal airports (and later colleges) to serve as extension training fields aligned with Randolph's program. In fact, because the instructors at Randolph educated the instructors at the extension fields, a flier-in-training could succeed at one of the far-flung fields, get called to Randolph, and immediately enter specialized training at either Brooks or Kelly. The municipal airport in the Los Angeles suburb of Oxnard had just become one of those extension fields. Previously, the Oxnard Airport gained its reputation as a favorite airfield for eccentric aviation enthusiast and entrepreneur Howard Hughes. In the summer of 1940, the airport welcomed its first Army Air Corps fliers, Smith among them.[31]

The influx of soldiers and sailors reporting for training and civilians seeking work in newly developed defense plants substantially transformed southern California. Anyone who could sit down at a Los Angeles lunch counter and discuss aviation drew an appreciative audience as California embraced its role as America's chief airplane producer. Aircraft manufacturing was not new to the region, but the industry mushroomed between 1939 and 1941 with $150 million in federal defense funds invested into new and expanding factories in the state. Southern California airplane production companies working to win defense contracts in 1940 included North American Aviation, just months away from unveiling its new B-25 Mitchell bomber, as well as Douglas, Lockheed, Hughes, and Vultee. Additionally, parts suppliers and other subcontractors made the Los Angeles area home. Private investors added another $79 million, and sprawling plants emerged in Burbank, El Segundo, Inglewood, Long Beach, Santa Monica, and farther south in San Diego.[32]

Often, the architectural style of the factories worked as a type of camouflage, making them look like residential neighborhoods from the air. Californians clearly thought about the potential war differently than most of the United States. Of the Axis Powers—Nazi Germany, Fascist Italy, and Imperial Japan—most Americans viewed the two European nations as the prime threats. In California in 1940, however, Japan's motives in the Pacific caused the greatest concern.[33]

Some of Smith's experiences at Oxnard resembled his time in college, sitting inside for classroom instruction in flight science, aviation mechanics, navigation principles, meteorology, and Morse Code. Unlike South Dakota State, however, the culture at Oxnard, and later at the Randolph complex for those who advanced, was one of military precision and hazing—the stream of unreasonable demands and insults barked into everyone's face, all part of a unending quest to determine who could "take it." Loud bells constantly clanged to signal times for room inspections, in-class instruction, flight instruction, and everything else on a daily schedule that began with opening drills at 6:30 A.M.[34]

At times, Smith and his fellow air cadets had a hard time knowing where hazing stopped and official drills began. Superiors would spontaneously order an aviator-in-training to perform calisthenics that usually included hitting oneself hard at a specific point on the chest. All the trainees felt ridiculous marching to mess with their arms extended like wings, making turns in the direction of the downward-pointing arm with the opposite arm positioned upward. But both actions had a point. That spot on the chest? That was where they would find the ring to open a parachute should they ever bail out of an airplane. As for their mimicking planes, the men later said they never forgot how the wings of an aircraft should be positioned when banking. Beyond the practical value of some exercises, the continual drills and rigorous hazing signaled the Air Corps belief that there should be no easy path to or through the West Point of the Air.[35]

Smith and his peers found excitement in anything taught aboard an airplane, whether in the air or on the ground. Daily physical conditioning often felt invigorating after long periods of classroom instruction. Overall, they most hated learning Morse Code through headphones, though Smith left no record of his thoughts about the class. Some men also griped about marching drills, which they considered an antiquated practice with no relevance to flying. Their superiors disagreed. They embraced the philosophy of the commander at Randolph, Lieutenant Colonel I. H. Edwards: "Precision and snap on the ground can and does promote similar characteristics in the air."[36] When the time came for the fledgling pilots to take to the air over Oxnard, they and their instructors climbed into small single-engine P-17s that South Dakotans would call "crop dusters." During these lessons, Smith demonstrated an enviable quality. No matter the intensity of the maneuvers, he never suffered from air sickness.[37]

Not all of Smith's flight instruction happened in the air, however. He arrived in Oxnard knowing that some of a corpsman's training came in the form of "Link time." To increase the pilots' comfort in the cockpit, the Air Corps required them to log hours in a Link trainer, an early version of a flight simulator often called "the pilot-maker." The creator of the trainer, Ed Link, had admired the French "penguin system" for preparing World War I aviators. In this style of training, French pilots learned aviation principles and the workings of their aircraft while taxiing through fields, a technique that neither Britain nor the United States employed. Link believed he could improve on the French method by replicating and further enhancing the feel and functions of cockpits indoors, a step that would save fuel as well. Link had the ability to bring to fruition any mechanical device he dreamed up, thanks to a father who gave him free rein to experiment in the player piano and pipe organ factory he owned in Binghamton, New York. As the younger Link built his first pilot-maker prototype in 1928 and 1929, he borrowed a motor, bellows, and air hoses originally intended for musical instruments.[38]

Alan Shepard, two decades before becoming the first American launched into space, also experienced Link time in the 1940s and recalled the trainer as simple compared to later simulators. It resembled no particular aircraft and had no mission-specific functions. "However," Shepard would recall, "it *was* a *moving* base trainer and could simulate the roll, pitch, or yaw of a real airplane."[39] A moving base meant the student pilot sat above a pivot point inside a miniature craft that resembled an airplane carnival ride, while pneumatic movement controlled by an instructor simulated motions the pilot could expect in actual flight. An instrument panel displayed air speed, vertical air speed, rate of climb or descent, artificial horizon, and turns and banks. If the student failed to handle the stick or rudder properly, he felt the sensation of a nose dive, side slip, or beginning of a loop.[40] By 1934, the Link trainer had become especially effective in teaching pilots "to fly on instruments." During their instruction periods, an estimated half million World War II aviators in both the Allied and Axis nations trained in Link machines.[41]

With short fuselages and stubby wings, the Link pilot-maker did indeed look like an amusement park ride, and many of them ended up at carnivals in the early 1930s. Throughout the decade, carnival goers stood in line to test their aviation instincts. Many failed to keep the nose up or slipped to the side and "crashed." Chagrined, they climbed out of the trainer laughing and shaking their heads, muttering that there sure was a lot to think about in a cockpit. While a few private flight instructors quickly saw the trainer's potential for preparing actual pilots, the machine's popularity as a toy made it difficult for most aviators to take seriously. Still, the United States Navy bought one in 1931, liked it, and eventually ordered five more.[42] It took a national crisis for the Link trainer to capture the attention of the Army Air Corps.

The crisis came in February 1934, during Smith's sophomore year of high school, when the United States Post Office dropped airmail contracts with private aviation carriers. A congressional investigation into collusion and fraud in awarding federal airmail contracts revealed that just three corporations controlled twenty-four of the twenty-seven private companies that flew the mail. Small, independent aviation companies found it nearly impossible to make a successful contract bid. President Roosevelt ordered his postmaster to cancel all airmail contracts until the government sorted out the matter. Meanwhile, the Army Air Corps would take over.[43]

The last time the army flew the mail had been in 1927, when it set up a special route to the Black Hills, the site of President Calvin Coolidge's summer White House at Custer State Park. Major Henry H. ("Hap") Arnold, who would prove integral in devising and executing the Doolittle Raid fifteen years later as a general, headed the mission, which included an element of secrecy. President Coolidge wanted his mail every Tuesday and Thursday. Arnold, knowing the volatile Great Plains weather could sometimes delay his army planes, ordered a portion of each delivery of White House mail to be withheld at Rapid City. That way, Coolidge would have mail to read the following Tuesday or Thursday no matter the weather. Arnold's airplanes during that time were a far cry from those he commanded in 1942. The summer White House mail fleet consisted of single-engine, open-air cockpit biplanes flown by crews of two from the Sixteenth Observation Squadron and Third Attack Group. During that summer, one mail plane crash in Nebraska, which produced no fatalities, marked the only hiccup in Arnold's system. Even with that incident, Coolidge always got his letters.[44]

In 1934, the army assumed a much larger mail mission that saw a rash of fatal crashes and near accidents. Too many enlisted aviators at the time "flew by the seat of their pants," eyeballing terrain and horizon lines. Obviously, that method did not work at night or when the view was obstructed, and the hard winter of 1934 filled the skies with snow across much of the country. To deliver the mail on time, pilots had to fly through those turbulent conditions regularly. In response, Congress authorized an immediate appropriation, signed by Roosevelt in March, for equipping the army with Link pilot-makers. While the army's mail transport duty turned out to be short term, the Air Corps remained committed to ever-evolving Link trainers for pilots to practice in from 1934 on.[45]

In late 1940, because of the skills he demonstrated in the pilot-maker and P-17s and his solid classroom performance, Smith was selected for bomber pilot training. He had to report immediately to Randolph. While there, he would increasingly hear discussions about the use of airplanes as weapons and less as means for transportation.[46]

Once Smith arrived in Texas, he created a habit that went with him to each military post where he was stationed. He always found the "company typewriter" the airmen were allowed to use, before eventually acquiring his own, and kept his parents updated with letters every week or two. Usually, he closed with a standard line: "Your loving son, Don." In addition to describing both history as it unfolded and daily routines as drab as washing dishes, these letters reveal a young South Dakotan finding himself in a wider world. One question seemed to haunt Smith: Could he perform on a bigger stage? True, he had excelled in school, proved himself in college football, and learned to fly a plane. But away from small-town South Dakota, would life mirror that West Texas State game where men from other regions easily demonstrated more sophisticated prowess? At Randolph, Smith also saw the deeply ingrained hierarchy of the American military on display. Leaders at the West Point of the Air included officers who had graduated from the actual West Point of New York. The men who came from that school on the Hudson River were treated not only as superior officers, but as socially superior. In spite of his apparent doubt, Smith quickly decided he would measure up to others just fine. In 1941, he wrote his parents that "after observing the average type of man throughout this country, I still believe I am just as good as they are, and I certainly don't want to idle away my life."[47]

While Smith would know moments of professional triumph and personal joy in 1941, the United States faced unparalleled international danger. During one of Roosevelt's famed "fireside chats" that January, the president proclaimed, "Never before since Jamestown and Plymouth Rock has our American civilization been in such danger as now."

Roosevelt went on to reflect this concern in his legislative proposal to Congress later that month when he requested $10 billion for national defense spending out of a total federal budget of $17 billion. Washington observers noted the president's remarks warned Americans that they would have to make sacrifices for national security, including the possibility of American troops heading to combat. Roosevelt called the three nations of the Axis Powers "an unholy alliance . . . to dominate and enslave the human race." The Axis, the president declared, "not merely admits but proclaims that there can be no ultimate peace between their philosophy of government and our philosophy."[48]

Meanwhile, Smith marked his twenty-third birthday in Texas that January. "I don't feel any older, or notice any grey hair yet, but time is moving a lot faster than it did before," he wrote his parents. He was nearly finished with ground school and had accumulated 160 hours of flight time and expected to gain another 50 hours before receiving his wings at graduation in early March. "I am glad we finally started formation flying," Smith wrote, "as that was one thing I was a little worried about, as in the past some of the boys were unable to fly formation and were eliminated because of it." But, he added, "I got along all right, and think I can master it in a few more hours."[49]

By early February, Smith had completed half his formation flight instruction and instrument work. He still had to log fifteen hours of night flying, most of it on trips from San Antonio to Houston or Corpus Christi and back. He especially enjoyed night flights because he could "see all the large towns for 75 miles around" and "all the car lights moving slowly along." He also commented, "The air is so much smoother at night than it is in the daytime." So smooth, in fact, that during one three-hour night flight over Texas, Smith kept falling asleep as his instructor piloted the airplane, "and he had to bother me all the time or I could really have enjoyed myself."[50]

Smith also used calm moments during daytime flights to take in the Texas countryside. While studying the landscape below him during one flight, he noted manmade landmarks that few other Army Air Corps fliers gave thought to. "I had spotted a few poultry farms from the air," he wrote, "so drove out [in his recently purchased 1941 Ford] to look them over from the ground."[51]

During his flight instruction in San Antonio, Smith also learned about social expectations for Army Air Corps officers. Uniforms were important for public events, so he wrote his mother requesting shirts and his lieutenant bars from college, playfully indicating that his dog Mugs could help her find them. He also bought good civilian clothes, including a tuxedo.[52]

Though accustomed to country dances in South Dakota barns and community halls, Smith worried about how his dance skills would hold up to the more formal affairs of the army. He considered signing up for dance lessons, but his thinking changed one winter night when, at a party for a major, he "met a couple of girls that didn't mind having their toes stepped on so I just started learning that way." After that night, he "made up my mind to go to the Graduation dance for our class." A short time later, Smith recorded, one of his fellow trainees "who goes out with a 'deb,' asked me to go out with them on a blind date." To his relief, the young woman, Marie Crouch, "turned out to be all right, so I invited her to the dance."[53]

Crouch was from San Antonio. If friends found Smith generally reserved and cautious, those qualities seemed to melt away in her presence. She was a couple of years younger than Smith and less than three years out of San Antonio's Thomas Jefferson High School. They met in mid-February knowing Smith would likely transfer to a base outside Texas after his March graduation. By graduation day and the dance, it appears, the two had plans for an early summer wedding.[54]

As graduation approached, Smith completed in-flight instrument training and, back on the ground, underwent x-rays, blood work, and eye examinations to get certified as fit for duty. Smith understood that the Air Corps might select him for instructing novice pilots once he completed his training, but, more likely, he would be stationed with a combat squadron. The Air Corps also asked him to fill out paperwork indicating whether he had a stationing preference. He certainly did: Lowry Air Base in Colorado, as close to Belle Fourche as he could get. And if not Lowry, he requested any base in the Pacific Northwest.[55]

Wherever Smith's assignment took him, he hoped he would have a week's leave before reporting so he could visit Belle Fourche. The fact that the previous graduating class moved directly to assigned air bases dampened his optimism. To add to his uncertainty, Smith learned that he would have to move off base immediately after graduation, so he looked into short-term apartment rentals in San Antonio.[56] Searching for apartments soon became a familiar routine for the fly boy.

His parents could not make it to Texas for graduation but did send a congratulatory telegram. The graduation dance with Crouch as his guest "went over very nice," Smith recorded. By then, he still had not been given his new assignment, though he had found out he would not be a flight instructor. In the meantime, he rented a place in San Antonio with two other fliers who, like himself, had "nothing to do but wait and see where we will be sent."[57] They did not have to wait for long. Smith got orders in April 1941 to report to McChord Field near Tacoma, Washington. The timing gave him a few days to visit Belle Fourche after all. He said a temporary goodbye to Crouch and drove north. At Mc-Chord, Smith would join the Eighty-Ninth Reconnaissance Squadron, attached to the Seventeenth Bomb Group.[58]

n the growing dark of 18 April 1942, Smith decided a water landing offered the best chance for survival. While training the previous October, Smith's father had asked what he would do if forced to make an emergency landing. "Well," Don answered, "all you can do is leave the wheels up and skid it in on its stomach."[1] That night, he did just that. Smith and his crew were unharmed as the airplane came down several hundred yards from Tantou Island, just off the mainland in China's Zhejiang Province, but the *TNT* immediately began to sink. Smith and his men were not alone in losing their valuable B-25 that night. All sixteen crews lost their planes in one way or another.[2]

The five men had eight minutes to escape the sinking B-25. Usually, eight minutes would have given the men plenty of time, but Lieutenant White needed to retrieve his medical equipment and supplies. What good would he be as the mission's flight surgeon without the tools of his trade? Doc White, at "great risk to himself and with exemplary courage," Doolittle later reported, "remained inside the sinking ship . . . until his surgical instruments and medical kit could be salvaged." After White gathered his equipment and slipped out, "The plane plunged into 100 feet of water."[3]

White's effort was mostly for naught. To his regret in coming days, he lost much of his medical equipment soon after escaping the plane as the crewmen struggled against the tide, wind, and deflating raft to reach the Tantou shore. Howard Sessler got separated from the crew when he abandoned the raft to swim ashore. Once they pulled up on the sand, the exhausted fliers caught their breath then began searching for Sessler.[4]

The dogs of Tantou Island were the first to sense that something was happening on the beach. In his home nearby, a man named Ma Liagshui heard their barking and looked up from the hand of cards he was contemplating. Down by the water, he saw flashlight beams and recalled that pirates sometimes came ashore with flashlights. The possibility of Japanese soldiers added another threat. Ma ordered most of his family to hide behind the house. His father-in-law walked toward the beach and found four of the five fliers taking shelter in a goat pen. They did not know what had happened to the fifth member of their crew. Ma invited the men into his home, found dry clothes for them, and offered food. No one in the household spoke English, but someone produced a world map, and with it the four men established that they were Americans. At the first hint of daybreak, Smith, his crew, and the Ma family searched for Sessler. They quickly found him, cold but safe, not far from Ma's house. The family understood that Japanese soldiers were most likely hunting their guests and suggested the raiders dress as Chinese fishermen.[5] While the disguises might keep Smith and his crew safe for a time, they still had an arduous task in front of them. Smith knew that once he got his crew off the island, they still had to trek more than seventy-five miles cross-country to reach Chuchow Airfield.

The year before finding himself stranded on Tantou Island, Smith still had training to complete in his new assignment at McChord Air Field in Washington. For a young man growing accustomed to soaring over vast sections of the continent in just hours, the drive from Belle Fourche to Tacoma that spring was a blunt demonstration as to how most Americans traveled, especially in the West. "I stopped in Broadus (Montana) for gas, and asked about the road, and boy would I like to shoot that filling station man," he wrote. The man indicated that the road west was good, even informing Smith that a bus carried travelers over it daily, but what he found did not meet his expectations. Instead of a smooth highway, Smith drove over a rough Works Progress Administration project, "which was nothing more than a pile of boulders in the road sharper than razors, and larger than you[r] fist." To avoid a torturous ride for him and his car, he "pulled off the road and when [sic] across the parrie [sic]" at every opportunity.[6]

Later, Smith hit an intense snowstorm while crossing the Bitterroot Mountain range on the Montana-Idaho border and spent the night in Mullan, Idaho. Finally arriving at McChord Field and reporting to his superiors, he discovered the base did not provide housing or meals for the airmen. He and a fellow pilot found a furnished apartment in Tacoma, three blocks from the waterfront, "a pretty nice place, two rooms and a bath." Despite its comforts, Smith griped about the cost, "The whole town has raised its price on rooms so much the last year since the army moved all the air corps men in here, that we couldn't find anything very god [sic] for less than 50 [dollars] a month." He guessed that the going rate had doubled from the previous year.[7]

Still, he liked Tacoma. The steep streets reminded him of Lead, a Black Hills gold-mining town, and he especially enjoyed the view of Mount Rainier on clear days. As a fan of radio news and the *Jack Benny Program*, Smith appreciated Tacoma's clear radio reception. At McChord, he noticed with pride that he and other young lieutenants who had earned their wings were treated with respect, "like the officers we are." While Smith settled into a new life in Tacoma, he soon got to see other areas of the Pacific Northwest as his group in the Eighty-Ninth Reconnaissance Squadron frequently flew in and out of three bases in the region—McChord, Felts Field near Spokane, and one still under construction at Pendleton, Oregon.[8]

Shortly after Smith's arrival at McChord in April 1941, several British Royal Air Force pilots flew in to shuttle new four-engine B-17 bombers, commonly known as Flying Fortresses, back to Europe. The big planes left Smith a bit awestruck. Some of the war stories the British told him did so as well. He met two pilots who had flown in the battle over Dunkirk, where British forces barely escaped the oncoming Germans in northern France in May 1940. He observed that "for all the experience some of them have had they look awful young." That experience had taken its toll because a few of the men were on leave "to give their nerves a rest," from what Smith could gather.[9] His conversations with the British fliers seemed to bolster his emerging belief that airplanes would prove invaluable wherever the growing war played out and would serve as the main arm of defense in the future.

A typical day of training at McChord had Smith in ground school through morning, then flying in the afternoon. On 14 April, he wrote his parents, "I had my first ride Friday afternoon. We went up in a b23, which is a heavy bomber, a fairly late model, with a cruising speed of 210." In the two hours of flight, Smith split his time between observing and copiloting. He proclaimed, "It really is an interesting job flying the big ones. On the take off," he continued, "the co-pilot sets the throttles, and propellers, and keeps the motor and oil temperatures right by adjusting a series of hydro-flaps on the motor, opening them if they get too hot, and closing them if the ship's motors are cold." The copilot's job did not end there. Once the aircraft got off the ground, he would "change the prop pitch, and when the pilot signals with his hand we pull up the wheels and then go to throttling it back to cruising speed." In the air, the copilot had the responsibility of keeping the engines "together both in manifold pressure and in Propeller R.P.M." primarily to "keep the amount of vibrating down." He explained, "The first ten minutes are usually pretty busy ones, but after that we can look out and enjoy the country."[10]

The training also gave Smith a slightly skewed perspective on the pilot's job. They did "nothing but actually [fly] the ship," never touching any of the controls beyond the steering, he reported. "In landing[,] we drop the wheels, set the flapps [sic] in landing position, and start calling off the airspeed so the pilot won't have to look away from the runway as he is bringing it in." Once the plane "hit the ground," the copilot called "the tower to tell them you are O.K., and get the taxiing instructions."[11]

On 22 April, Smith got to handle the pilot controls of a B-18 Bolo while in flight. First introduced in 1936, the year Smith graduated from high school, the B-18 had become the standard bomber at McChord. Smith had little love for the aircraft. Even though the plane had been in production for only five years, he described it as "old." He found it so heavy that "it feels like you are wrestling with it and when it gets into a turn it just floats around like a flying boxcar." He told his parents that a B-18 weighed almost ten tons, "so you can understand how big a thrill it is flying one of them."[12] Army leadership seemed to share Smith's opinion as to the bomber's maneuverability. By 1941, the Air Corps had decided to scrap the B-18, considering it underpowered for modern warfare. Shortly after Smith reported to McChord, the branch prepared to reequip the Eighty-Ninth Reconnaissance Squadron with the newest bomber, the B-25 Mitchell.[13]

The North American Aviation Company manufactured the new planes. Originally established in 1928 to specialize in the trading of aviation stocks on Wall Street, North American began its aircraft assembly operations under corporate president Dutch Kindleberger in 1934. During World War I, Kindleberger qualified as a military flier but saw limited action. Still, warplanes were his chief interest. He trained as an aircraft engineer and worked for the Douglas Aircraft Corporation prior to joining North American. At the helm, he and designer

J. Leland Atwood turned their attention to building light bombers. An early prototype of the medium-sized B-25 first flew in March 1939. North American, not the army, dubbed the aircraft "the Mitchell," after the late General William ("Billy") Mitchell. Mitchell, who died in 1936, had angered some American military leaders as an outspoken advocate for increased airpower following World War I. His combative style and accusations of neglect on the part of army and navy leadership when it came to aircraft, in fact, led to a much-publicized court martial in 1925. Two decades later, at a time when the United States needed airpower as never before, production of a mighty warplane bearing Mitchell's name seemed like vindication for the late general.[14]

The army saw so much potential in the B-25 that it successfully thwarted the navy's efforts to procure the bomber, not wanting its own access limited. McChord pilots were the first to fly the aircraft regularly, leading operational trials. Among Smith and his fellow fliers, the Mitchell quickly won a reputation as operationally efficient and easily adaptable.[15] From Smith's perspective, the velocity at landing illustrated the main difference between the B-18 and the B-25. The B-18s "land at 90 [miles per hour]," he observed, "and our B-25s come in at around 125 m.p.h. and that is really tearing along when you're on the ground."[16] He added that a sloppy B-25 landing, where the plane might drop twenty feet to the ground, "about knocks your teeth out."[17]

Smith, who preferred calling the model simply a B-25, read through the pilot's manual once the planes arrived at McChord. It described the bomber as a mid-wing, land monoplane with two Wright Cyclone engines for power. "Propellers are the three blade type, hydromatic, and full feathering," the manual explained. "Hydraulically operated tricycle landing gear, wing flaps, engine cowl flaps, bomb bay doors, and brakes are provided." Comic-book style illustrations contrasted with the dry text. For example, a fuel tank depicted with a human face that looked exhausted and parched warned against letting "one fuel tank to run completely dry before switching to another tank!"[18] Another cartoon demonstrated how the B-25's emergency nose-wheel mechanism turned clockwise, just like the crank on a Model T.[19] The manual's section on water landings showed a tsunami-like wave tossing a ship at sea while an airplane soared high above. "The sea's not as calm as it appears up there," cautioned the caption.[20]

According to the manual, the B-25 had been designed for a five-man crew, consisting of a pilot, copilot, bombardier, radio operator, and photographer. Wars, however, have a way of changing standards. Once the Mitchell entered combat, a gunner manning one of the three sets of machine guns replaced the photographer, while the bombardier and radio operator took on dual roles and manned the other two sets. The crews would commonly have a designated flight engineer as well. Windows in the nose provided sight lines for the bombardier, who had to drop through a "tunnel" under the pilot's seat and then crawl forward to get there. The navigator, radio operator, and gunners usually took up positions in a crawl space above the bomb bay behind the pilot and copilot.[21] No crew member could escape the roar of the twin engines. Many, especially pilots and copilots who sat in close juxtaposition to the motors, suffered permanent hearing loss.[22]

The Air Corps at first gave little thought to armament or powerful guns for B-25 crews like Smith's. Commanders believed that the speedy B-25 would drop their bombs and quickly outdistance pursuing enemy planes. As 1941 progressed, however, Smith observed that North American Aviation increasingly fitted new B-25s with plate-metal armament and advanced gunnery. Although appreciative, he also realized that the change reflected the army's discovery of the increasing speeds of Axis planes.[23]

While piloting B-25s over Washington State, Smith closely observed the land and water below. One day, he soared just a hundred feet above the waves of Puget Sound. Of all the small islands below, one stuck in his mind. Smith estimated its size at forty acres, with a farmhouse that stood amid evergreens. Much of the land had been cleared and cultivated. As the sole occupant of an island, he noted, "One wouldn't have to worry about anyone else's livestock getting into your fields."[24] Though Smith had a particular passion for agriculture, even knowing the price Washington farmers got for eggs compared to what South Dakotans received, he had at least passing thoughts about another potential career after the army. Smith saw a major benefit to training in twin-engine planes. He understood that civilian airline and aviation transport companies would more likely offer jobs to pilots experienced with "two motored ships."[25]

In contemplating his future, Smith made it clear he had no desire for a career as an officer in the newly designated Army Air Forces.[26] Officers lived with social expectations he disliked, especially when too much liquor entered the picture and everyone tried to "put up a big front." Prior to the Royal Air Force pilots' departure, to Smith's dismay, his squadron threw a farewell party. He did not want to attend the event, but all squadron men would share drink costs whether present or not. "Being a Scotchman that kind of hurts," he observed.[27] Even worse, he believed, too much drink had a negative effect on his friends. "I have seen some very great changes in the different boys since we got together for the first time there in Oxnard last fall," he remarked. "I personally don't want to go the same way they are headed." While in the air though, Smith told his parents, he enjoyed the in-flight camaraderie.[28]

Shortly after the farewell party for the British fliers, Smith and his squad transferred to Felts Field outside of Spokane in eastern Washington for maneuvers. Before departing, he discovered that his old Belle Fourche football teammate and friend, Lloyd Eaton, was stationed nearby with the Marine Corps. Smith tried to look him up but was unsuccessful. With his new orders, Smith gave up the Tacoma apartment, packed items he did not need in his car, and parked it in a local storage garage. He and his squadron then flew east over the Cascades with "old Mt. Rainier . . . sticking up off to the right of our path."[29] The squad landed at Felts Field and received their new living quarters—army tents, with five men assigned to each. Stoves that proved tricky to handle heated their residences and, within days, one overheated stove burned one of the shelters.[30]

By the summer of 1941, Smith longed for a jaunt back to the Black Hills. He wrote his parents that he envied a trip they had just taken into Spearfish Canyon with his dog, Mugs. In the midst of his homesickness, Smith took pleasure in the arrival of three new P-17s, the little airplane he learned to handle at Oxnard the previous fall. While assigned to one for an afternoon, he enjoyed "tearing loose and doing a few acrobatics" after weeks of work keeping big bombers straight and level. During the brief assignment, he and a few fellow pilots assigned to the small planes each took an enlisted mechanic up with them. The mechanics, who were used to level flying in bombers, apparently saw nothing thrilling about the aerobatics. Some of them even got sick. Smith opined, "I have been lucky I guess and never have been air-sick, so I can't fully sympathize with them."[31]

Though he rated the food at his new station as only fair, he enjoyed Spokane's excellent radio reception and used it to keep up with Jack

Benny on Sunday nights.[32] On the evening of 27 May, however, he and sixty-five million other Americans listened to a more somber program. In President Roosevelt's radio address that evening, the commander-in-chief proclaimed that "an unlimited national emergency exists and requires the strengthening of our defense to the extreme limit of our national power and authority." Roosevelt also emphasized that he would not necessarily await Axis aggression before acting. "We in the Americas will decide for ourselves," he stated, "whether and when and where our American interests are attacked or our security threatened."[33]

In addition to preparing Americans for the possibility of war, Roosevelt expressed frustration with growing labor disputes, particularly those that affected the war industries. "When the nation is threatened from without, . . . as it is today," he said, "the actual production and transportation of the machinery of defense must not be interrupted by disputes between capital and capital, labor and labor, or capital and labor," especially when "the future of all free enterprise . . . is at stake."[34] That aspect of Roosevelt's address particularly caught Smith's attention, but, as he wrote the next day, "I am still wondering what the whole speech meant."[35]

As it turned out, the editorial staff at *Time* magazine wondered the same thing. They noted that few Americans would argue against the tone of the speech, but Roosevelt had not announced any plan of action to strengthen defense production. According to an American Institute of Public Opinion poll in June 1941, an overwhelming majority of Americans supported legally forbidding strikes in the defense industries. As a longtime advocate for organized labor, Roosevelt certainly would not have called for nor backed such a measure.[36] In the end, the *Time* editorial commented, "The full meaning of his speech would remain veiled until it was resolved in action."[37]

Smith's take on the situation was similar to those who answered the poll. He believed that striking against defense industries during a national emergency was "criminal," but that "no one seems to want to do anything about it." If national leaders had really wanted to avoid the disputes, he wrote, "They should have stopped the first few and they wouldn't have all this trouble now."[38]

Even with war and labor disputes dominating the headlines, Smith's thoughts focused on his impending marriage that June. Don and Marie planned to marry in Seattle or Tacoma near the end of the month.

Marie had not yet learned how to drive, but her parents planned on driving with her to Washington for the ceremony. Knowing that new orders for maneuvers or relocation could interrupt their plans at any time, however, neither Don nor Marie encouraged distant friends to attend the wedding.[39] The constant uncertainty of life in the Air Corps was something the married couple would need to embrace. Don predicted, "We will probably have to live pretty much of a traveling life the first few months." Although he had become acclimated to that lifestyle, he noted, "It will probably be hard for Marie at first."[40]

As the wedding approached, Smith's squad trained eighteen hours a day. The crews divided into three groups that alternated flying shifts, beginning at 6:00 A.M., 11:30 A.M., and 5:00 P.M. The pilots had discovered some "bugs" in the B-25 that needed working out. One day later that summer, for instance, one of Smith's colleagues discovered in flight that his landing gear would not come down. In such an emergency, the pilot was to continue flying to burn off fuel, then land the plane on its belly. This aviator took his B-25 to eight thousand feet and told his crewmates they could bail out instead of risking the crash landing. They all decided to remain on board. The landing went beautifully and, Smith wrote, "no one was even shaken." The plane suffered no damage until, Smith recorded, "some dumb guy" decided to attach a cable to the tail and drag it from the runway. The plane's tail ripped away, ruining the aircraft.[41]

Seeing that type of unnecessary damage must have caused Smith some pain because he had developed an affection for the B-25. He relished his time with the Mitchell while some of his squadron transferred to another outfit to learn dive-bombing maneuvers in single-engine airplanes, "something which is very hard on the men, both physically and mentally." On another occasion, when the B-25 was briefly recalled for retooling, he complained about having to fly the old B-18 once again, mentioning it felt as slow as walking.[42]

During a short break in the training, Smith's squadron briefly returned to McChord. While there, Don and Marie were married on 21 June 1941 in Seattle.[43] Having escorted the bride from Texas, Marie's parents were present, but Don's were not. He then arranged for three days off, and he and Marie spent the time buying "things like dishes and silverware" and preparing to drive back to Felts Field.[44] Don expected to remain there for several weeks. Shortly after the wedding, he wrote his parents thanking them for the sheets and blanket they sent as wedding gifts and informing them that Marie cooked well. Even so, he confided, she used more pepper than he was accustomed to, probably due to her south Texas upbringing.[45]

The countryside surrounding their new home of Spokane reminded Don of the Black Hills landscape near Belle Fourche. He hoped one day to show off his hometown to Marie. If the couple got an opportunity, he believed they could drive to Belle Fourche from eastern Washington in less than twenty-four hours. In late July, Don read about Spearfish preparing for a big air show. "I wish I could get a plane and come home for the weekend," he wrote his parents, "but the older pilots are always going somewhere with them." He envied a crew in his squadron who had flown deep into the Great Plains and passed Mount Rushmore on the way back. "They flew down the valley and one of the boys said they were so close to it they could almost count the whiskers on Lincoln's chin," he reported.[46]

By late July, the crews in Smith's squadron flew at altitudes requiring oxygen. Not paying attention to the altitude, oxygen equipment, or both, he noted, spelled quick trouble. One group had to abort its mission when an airman passed out at twenty-seven thousand feet. "I haven't been above 20,000 yet," Smith told his parents on 25 July, "but should draw one of the higher assignments any day now."[47] In addition to acclimating to high-altitude flights, the squadron worked at mastering gunnery skills—everything from pistols to airborne machine-gunning—something that did not come easily to Smith, but he had plenty of company. The Air Corps quickly learned that aptitude in handling aircraft had no connection to an individual's gunnery skill.[48] To compensate, the squadron spent much of its free time practicing, continually "firing the machine gun on the ground in our off hours."[49]

In the air, Smith also practiced flying the B-25 on one engine, "feathering one motor." The plane's handling in that situation impressed Smith. "I was surprised to find that you could get the ship to go 170 even on one engine," he recorded, "and after the controls had been trimmed it handled just as easily as if it had both motors on."[50]

During downtime on the base, Don taught Marie how to drive on the roads around Spokane. The lessons came just in time, as it appeared she would soon have to make a long drive. Word came that Don's squadron would spend most of the fall of 1941 in the southeastern states, flying mock warfare exercises. For a while, the couple planned on driving to San Antonio together, where Marie would stay with her parents, and Don would continue on to maneuvers headquarters. But, like much of his time with the Air Corps, "We never know one minute to the next what we will be doing." The corps initially granted him five days of "detached service" for the trip after denying a ten-day leave that would have made a visit to Belle Fourche possible.[51] Then in late August, the Air Corps assigned Don as a pilot to ferry a new B-25 to the southeast. About the same time, he received a promotion to "first pilot." Marie believed the promotion made her husband "very happy."[52] Don, however, noted something else: a bill moving through Congress that would extend soldiers' service by eighteen months. He lamented, "There is little hope of getting out of this service until the emergency is over."[53]

The last week in August, with two other army wives going home to Texas, Marie drove away in the Ford thinking Don would soon follow. She and her companions turned the long drive into a vacation, visiting Yellowstone National Park and Denver. Meanwhile, Don waited at the new Pendleton Army Air Base in Oregon for word about the plane from the North American Aviation factory in Los Angeles. Pendleton Field, he understood, would serve as his squadron's permanent home, where he would return after fall maneuvers and where he and Marie would have to acquire long-term housing—at least by Army Air Corps standards. While waiting, Don investigated the housing situation around the base. Because the Air Corps frequently changed an airman's assignments, he and Marie decided against buying, even though plenty of newly constructed homes were for sale in the town of Pendleton. When the squadron returned to Pendleton Field after the exercises, Don noted, most likely they would have to move to one of the "small town[s] around here," because Pendleton rent rates had skyrocketed. "If it gets too bad," he continued, "we are hoping the government will step in and make them come down to earth again with their prices."[54]

Development of both Pendleton Field and another in Walla Walla, Washington, prompted Smith to wonder why South Dakota had been overlooked. "That country north of Belle should be just wonderful for it," he wrote his parents, "plenty of cheap land for bombing and landing fields." He theorized that South Dakota being a Republican state in an era of a Democratic presidency did not help.[55]

By the time Marie arrived safely in San Antonio, Don remained at

Pendleton awaiting news about his assigned B-25. "We have nothing to do here but wait for orders, and play rummy," he wrote in the middle of September. In a break from the monotony, he attended Pendleton's annual rodeo but found it lacking. "It didn't compare at all" to the Belle Fourche Roundup, he reported. "They never even had a clown or any trick roping and riding."[56]

When word finally reached Pendleton that the airplanes were ready, Smith and his fellow pilots immediately departed for Los Angeles. While there, the Air Corps put the flyboys up in the luxurious Hollywood Plaza Hotel at the intersection of Hollywood and Vine. The South Dakotan described the accommodations as "really nice," adding, "I'm glad I didn't have to pay for it." Although near the heart of Hollywood, the men had no time for sightseeing. A North American Aviation representative drove them to the factory where they looked the aircraft over and received quick instructions about new gun turrets. With increased armaments, the planes began to feel like potent weapons. Smith noted that the addition of these B-25s brought his squadron close to its full strength of eighteen bombers, "and all of them new or only a few months at the oldest."[57]

He flew the airplane back to Pendleton, picked up a crew, and set out for Ellington Field in Houston. An enormous storm system that engulfed the nation's middle, with heavy rains as far north as Wyoming and Montana and a destructive hurricane pounding the Texas coast, complicated the trip. To avoid the rough weather, Smith flew south along the Pacific Coast, then east, but was ordered down for the night at Tucson, Arizona. When the hurricane forced an evacuation of Ellington Field, Smith and his crew were redirected to San Antonio until the base could reopen. In San Antonio, he got to spend an hour with Marie, and he met other fliers from his squadron who were waiting out the weather.[58]

News of the storms caused Smith's father to start thinking about aircraft safety, and he voiced his concerns to his son. The younger Smith assured his parents that the twin motors on the B-25 made it safe. He explained, "If something happens to [one of] our engine[s], we cut the switch and feather the prop, and continue on our merry way." With that theory in mind, Don later expressed an interest in getting "moved up" to four-engine bombers in 1942. "The bigger and the more motors" on the plane, he resolved, "the better I will like it."[59]

After arriving at Ellington, Smith and his squadron surveyed the hurricane damage. They also got assigned to a mock-warfare mission: fly northeast to locate and bomb the bridges of Shreveport, Louisiana. In place of live bombs, the Air Corps armed the crews with one-pound bags of flour. The commanders assured Smith and the other fliers that the bags could not hurt anyone if the B-25s swooped in low and dropped them from treetop height. During the exercises, P-40 Warhawk fighter planes occasionally pursued Smith and his squad after they hit their primary targets. Smith made sure to note that although the P-40s could chase the B-25s out of a confined area, they could not keep up for long distances. If no defending aircraft showed up after the crew accomplished their goal, they might elect to spend time "playing with the ground troops," which meant pelting their vehicles with flour.[60]

Though he had fun at the infantrymen's expense from time to time, Smith also expressed some pity for them. Unlike the flyboys who had a relatively comfortable base with barracks, the ground troops slept in tents and dealt with mud, dust, standing water after hard rains, and big southern mosquitoes. Still, Smith enjoyed observing their maneuvers from the air, especially at night. At times, he and his crew dropped flares to light up wide sections of countryside and watched the spectacle of the mock war spread out below. Sometimes, a line of headlights stretched for miles across the rural landscape as the infantry moved through the night for the next day's "battle." In Louisiana, the two-week-long military maneuvers involved about 400,000 soldiers, reportedly the largest training exercise in American military history. Within days, approximately 360,000 combatants, including Smith's squadron, began similar maneuvers across the Carolinas.[61]

Before the unit departed Ellington, Marie and two other wives, probably those who traveled with her from Washington to Texas, drove from San Antonio to Houston to join Don and the others. Marie and Don then set off for his next station at Savannah, Georgia. After settling into their new home, Marie wrote her in-laws that the trips between destinations took up "quite a bit of my time." Still, all the moves gave the couple an opportunity to see "a great deal of the United States." They tried to make the move from Houston to Savannah as quickly as possible. "We only slept four hours and stopped just long enough for our meals," she wrote. They were also able to spend "about an hour in

New Orleans and had supper in the old French Quarter." She called the experience "very interesting" despite being "unable to see a great deal as it was rather late." Having a chance to take in a bit of their new surroundings, Marie noted they were "not very fond of Savannah," but she did find it "nice to be in one place for a few weeks."[62]

Following the move, Don's squadron went back to work training for wartime scenarios. During these new exercises, the Air Corps squadrons primarily flew at night to prepare for similar runs against the Axis. Ground troops experimented with searchlights to determine how best to spot aircraft like Smith's B-25. In response, the Air Corps tried a variety of paint schemes to keep its planes as inconspicuous as possible. Some of the ground movement Smith enjoyed watching could have been Major General George S. Patton's tanks that had kicked up red dust while implementing some of his new strategies for the rapid movement of armored battalions.[63]

Army brass used the exercises as an opportunity to evaluate their current crop of officers. They especially watched for commanders who did not maintain troop discipline or showed indecisiveness in the field. After the Louisiana exercises, Lieutenant General Lesley McNair observed, "There is no question that many of the weaknesses developed in these maneuvers are repeated again and again." Mainly, he believed, the issues extended from incompetent or lackadaisical leadership. McNair expressed the frustration of many officers when he said, "A commander who cannot develop proper discipline must be replaced."[64] After the maneuvers in Georgia and the Carolinas, several officers found themselves out of command.

While training for possible future combat, Don kept an eye on the financial side of military life as well. He hoped Congress might soon see fit to increase army pay to cover living expenses adequately. In Savannah, Marie wrote, they had a "very nice room and private bath near the field for $5 a week but we have to take our meals out and food is very high here, 17 cents for a quart of milk."[65] Through the 1930s and into the 1940s, Don noted, the cost of living had climbed 20 percent while army pay remained frozen at a level set in 1929, which had been cut 10 percent from the previous year.[66] The lack of pay forced the couple to pinch their pennies. During the week, Marie recorded that "Don usually comes home for me at noon and we go out to the field for our noon meal," most likely to avoid buying groceries. On one Saturday evening after Don had a shift as the Officer of the Day, he took Marie to "a formal dance at the officer's club." While the pair "had a lovely time," Marie bragged that they were "very proud of ourselves as we spent only 20 cents the entire evening."[67]

The situation angered Don, especially when he heard of labor strikes in the civilian world that could hamper national defense. He fumed that the army could make an enlisted man "stay . . . for $21 a month," but no leaders could "make a man mine coal for four times that much."[68] In the meantime, Don and Marie moved to his next station at Augusta, Georgia, and once again hunted up a place to live. During the move, the couple questioned their practice of jumping from apartment to apartment. When they returned to Pendleton, they decided, they would examine their finances to see whether it made sense to buy one of those newly constructed houses on Don's pay.[69]

When not embarked on a training mission or dealing with finances, Don listened to sports on the radio to unwind. He wrote his dad about listening to heavyweight boxing champ Joe Louis make quick work of challenger Lou Nova at the Polo Grounds in New York. He also proclaimed that his South Dakota State Jackrabbits had lost too many good players to the army and—only two years after their conference championship—could not "beat their way out of a paper sack" in 1941. By mid-October, Don realized he had not attended a single football game that year, so he and some Air Corps friends tried to take in a Georgia Tech game against Notre Dame in Atlanta, but they could not obtain tickets.[70]

Maneuvers in Georgia and the Carolinas continued as fall turned to winter. From South Dakota, though, Don received some worrying news. Neither he nor his parents mentioned a specific illness, but Don expressed concern about a health problem his father had developed, which included discussion about a possible surgery. Don also learned that his beloved pup Mugs had injured a leg. Doc Smith assured his son that Mugs was on the mend and provided proof with a photograph of the dog resting comfortably on the family's front porch. Each worrying piece of mail turned Don wistful about coming home with Marie for several days at Christmas.[71] Marie told her in-laws that the two of them were "looking forward to it very much,"[72] although Don related to his parents that "it will seem very strange to her, being in snow and cold for Christmas." To give his new wife a full winter experience, Don wrote, "I will have to get ahold of a sled and give her a ride down our big hill next door."[73]

The maneuvers wrapped up in early December, and Marie, with her two friends, began driving to Pendleton. Meanwhile, Don had a scare on 3 December 1941 when landing at Maxwell Field near Montgomery, Alabama. Heavy rains pelted the South while he and his squadron flew into Maxwell. After two planes skidded off the landing field and received damage, Don's plane also began to slide. "It really made me feel helpless to have on the brakes, and the plane just kept sliding on," he wrote that night. Luckily, Smith brought his B-25 to a halt at the edge of the field. Recovered from his scare, he remarked on one of the similarities between Alabama and South Dakota. The field was so sloppy, he wrote, that it "reminded me of good old 'Gumbo' around Belle," referencing the thick, slick mud common across South Dakota's range country.[74]

Four days later, 7 December 1941, Marie continued on the road toward Pendleton while Don's squadron departed from Tucson, where they had spent the night. The crew initially experienced a routine flight on that clear winter day, but the calm soon shattered when Don and his crew received reports that Japanese airplanes had attacked the Pacific Fleet at Pearl Harbor. Don's B-25 landed at Pendleton at 4:00 P.M., and he found "everything going all right" there.[75] Everyone at the base, however, knew their lives were about to change drastically. The war that Don hoped his country might avoid was now inevitable. Early reports indicated that the attacks had killed approximately 1,500 Americans that day, but the number rose over the ensuing days to the official death toll of 2,403, mostly navy and army servicemen. The assault also crippled much of the Pacific Fleet.[76] "Within one tragic hour—before the war had really begun—the U.S. appeared to have suffered greater naval losses than in the whole of World War I," the staff at *Time* reported.[77] Don initially had a more personal take: "It looks like our chance of being home Christmas is all shot to pieces."[78]

While Americans came to terms with the initial shock of the death and destruction in Hawaii, Japan's forces demonstrated their reach across most of the Pacific. Within hours of striking Pearl Harbor, Japanese planes bombed Guam and ports in the Philippine Islands as well as the British naval stronghold at Singapore.[79]

The Japanese success created a "war of nerves" on the West Coast of the United States, the *New York Times* relayed, as residents of San Francisco reported "many planes," likely Japanese, flying over the bay the night of 8 December. Sirens wailed, residents received orders to black out their lights, and radio stations ceased broadcasting. Brigadier General William Ryan, commander of the Air Corps' Fourth Interception Command, theorized that the warplanes had followed "radio beams" toward the West Coast but lost track and turned back after stations went dead. No American aircraft jumped to the defense during the paranoia, he explained, "because you don't send planes up unless you know what the enemy is doing and where he's going." He also argued, "You don't send planes up in the dark unless you know what you are doing." Unable to verify rumors of Japanese aircraft carriers one hundred miles off the California coast, which would have explained the warplanes' presence, Ryan decided to keep his fighters grounded.[80] Japanese attacks on the West Coast in coming months, it turned out, were rare, small-scale occurrences. In the hours and days immediately after Pearl Harbor, however, panicked Californians would fear the opposite.

One South Dakotan certainly knew his political career had fallen into grave jeopardy as reporting from San Francisco made front-page news across the country. Senator William Bulow, the tobacco-chewing, sardonic isolationist Democrat from Beresford, had openly mocked the notion of San Francisco coming under attack three years earlier during a Senate debate over boosting the navy's budget. "I do not have any doubt my good friend the Senator from California [William G. McAdoo], if he were at home on his front porch gazing out upon the Pacific, might, in his imaginative fancy, see eight hundred or a thousand Japanese battleships approaching our western shore," Bulow said. He went on to guarantee that "this is not going to happen. If I were just as certain of heaven as I am that the Japanese will not invade the country in the next 50 years," he mocked, "I would feel perfectly safe. I do not believe I would even feel the need of going to church any more." All the talk from California at the time, he concluded, was simply a "mirage of battleships" that appeared every time an "appropriation bill for the Navy is brought before Congress."[81]

By 1941, few South Dakotans remembered how vigorously Bulow had campaigned for Roosevelt's candidacy in 1932, when the president carried the state in his first election to the White House. In 1936, the two men toured South Dakota together to observe how New Deal projects had brought renewed life to local agriculture. Not long into Roosevelt's second term, however, Bulow began backing away from the New Deal because of its costs. Reflecting his concern about strains on the national economy, Bulow declared in his speech on the navy's finances, "In my judgement, this country is in more danger of going to pieces by reason of the continuation of an unbalanced budget than it is in danger of defeat by all the navies of the world."[82]

Bulow's isolationist thinking extended beyond fiscal concerns. He believed it was the responsibility of those living under dictators to revolt against oppression, and he was confident they eventually would. Endorsing the long-held American "policies of isolation under which we became great," the senator voted against ending the federal embargo on selling war materials overseas.[83] "The cannons of war will soon cease booming if we refuse to furnish the cannons," he said in 1939. "If we furnish the cannons and powder to carry on the fight, those cannons will soon have to be fired by our men."[84]

In a flash on 7 December 1941, Bulow's philosophy seemed naïve and antiquated. Indeed, Gallup polling indicated that isolationist thinking had declined after the fall of Paris to the Nazis eighteen months earlier.[85] Deep into the night after the attack on Pearl Harbor, Roosevelt met with his cabinet members and congressional leaders from both parties. When speaking with reporters as they exited the White House, they left no doubt that Americans would immediately join the fight in defense of what the president would shortly term "justice and righteousness over the forces of savagery and barbarism."[86] The minority House leader, Republican Joseph Martin, declared, "There is no politics here. There is only one party when it comes to the integrity and honor of the country."[87]

The next day, President Roosevelt went to the Capitol to address a joint session of Congress. In a concise speech, just six-and-a-half minutes long, he requested a declaration of war against Japan. Thirty-three minutes later, both the Senate and House approved the declaration. The senators voted unanimously, while Representative Jeanette Rankin of Montana cast the only dissenting vote in the House to the accompaniment of boos and hisses. On 11 December, Germany and Italy declared war on the United States, and Congress responded in kind.[88] With that decision, the *New York Times* noted, "For the first time in its history the United States finds itself at war against powers in both the Atlantic and the Pacific."[89]

Senator Bulow's vote in favor of war on 8 December could not save his political career. He planned to run for a third term in the Senate in 1942 but did not win his party's nomination.[90] Meanwhile, Smith and his squadron prepared to employ their extensive training in combat. Little did Smith know that his piloting ability would put him in position to gain vengeance on the Japanese early in the war.

4 : The Special Project

On Tantou Island, Ma Liagshui's family and friends, despite the language barrier, confirmed what Don Smith and his crew had learned aboard the *Hornet*: the Japanese occupied large swaths of China's coastal lands. Smith, as *TNT*'s commanding officer, held the responsibility of leading his men to safety in Chungking. The five needed to escape the island immediately. If a Japanese boat patrol spotted the submerged *TNT* or even a piece of the wreck, their land units would tear the island apart. The Mas knew the owner of a junk, a type of Chinese sailing ship, that could transport the men to the mainland by way of a neighboring island called Nantien. With the Japanese presence on Tantou, however, the *TNT* crew would have to wait until nightfall for the transport.[1]

For the moment, Smith's men stayed put in the hut, greeted a stream of visitors, napped, and dried their clothes alongside a fire whose smoke floated up through the thatched roof. Rice, shrimp, and garlic greens filled their stomachs. Throughout the day, they received updates from the family about the Japanese soldiers searching for them. The Mas also disguised the five crewmen as local fishermen, giving them curious raincoats made of tree bark. At dusk, they were escorted to the junk moored in a nearby cove. The boatman had no nose, and Doc White guessed that leprosy had claimed the appendage. Across China, Doolittle's men noticed many faces lined in ways that suggested lifetimes of hardship.[2]

The *TNT* crew lay on the boat's floor, hidden under mats. Cold rain fell and only a little wind blew, making for a slow trip. At midnight, the junk reached Nantien, where a chorus of frogs drowned out any other noises. On Nantien, over lamplight in a little house, the crew met a guerrilla leader whose expression they found startling: strong, determined, almost cruel. Formally named Jai Foo Ching, he introduced himself as "Charlie" and informed the Americans that he already knew about them and their mission. The raiders found it amazing how quickly news spread through regions without telephones, calling the invisible communications network "the grapevine."[3]

Charlie used his limited English to inform Smith and his men that he had met another squad several hours earlier and helped get them off Nantien and onto the mainland. Using pantomime for the rest of the story, Charlie communicated that the men had crash-landed off the island and were badly hurt, with broken bones, shattered teeth, and bleeding wounds. A worried Doc White was determined to catch up with the battered crew. The *TNT* squad, Smith decided, would search for the men, but by this point leaving Nantien was no easy matter. Japanese soldiers searched the island aggressively, beating everyone they suspected of withholding information. Their discovery of Plane Seven, *Ruptured Duck*, flown by pilot Ted Lawson and now smashed in coastal waters, fueled their fury. Though difficult for them to accept, the *TNT* crew had no choice but to hide for a day in one of Charlie's huts. He also gave them chickens, which they butchered and ate.[4]

The fliers planned to start moving again after dark. That afternoon, however, Charlie notified them that Japanese troops were advancing toward their hiding place. He thought it best that the crew split up and move cross-country over tree-covered hills with one of his guerrillas guiding each airman to a rendezvous point. The men had a hard time agreeing to the arrangement because they had lost all of their guns except for Smith's .45 caliber pistol in the crash landing. Splitting up meant that four unarmed men would walk away with armed guerrillas. The imminent threat the Japanese soldiers posed, however, overrode such worries. The crewmen went separate ways, which gave them all a good look at their surroundings. Much like other areas of China they would see in the coming weeks, the island was lush, hilly, and naturally beautiful. Man-made structures, terraces, and gates looked ancient and often displayed intricate carvings. In contrast, the airmen could not miss the poverty. Families mostly survived on subsistence farming and fishing, traveled along narrow foot trails, and struggled with poor sanitation.[5]

Despite the crewmembers' fears, the guerrillas all led the men to the rendezvous at a canal, where local boatmen took them along in a skiff for several miles. They climbed out of the boat at about sunset, and the guerrillas led them through the dark to a Taoist temple. "The old priest," Doc White recalled, "had fine features, wild hair and beard and wore a black gown" and offered prayers for the airmen. Smith and his men later learned Japanese soldiers beat him and smashed the temple's religious symbols because they believed he withheld information about the Americans. The *TNT* crew marveled that no one on Nantien betrayed them in the face of ever-present brutality. White surmised the people's "sense of responsibility for us and their hatred of the [Japanese] were enough" to keep them quiet even when threatened and abused.[6]

The *TNT* squad spent a full day in the temple before someone led them to an unusual safehouse nearby that contained a secret passage connecting the structure to a hillside cave. Once in the cave, the fliers felt vulnerable, for the only route of escape lay through the opening back into the house. Before long, the men heard running, shouts, and blows coming from the building. The Japanese had arrived. The Americans watched the door start to open, and Smith pointed his gun at it as the other men backed away. They were relieved to see one of Charlie's guerrillas standing before them rather than a Japanese soldier. He let them know that the house and immediate surroundings were clear. It was time to move again.[7]

The *TNT* crew walked the rest of that day and into the night, heading for a mainland-bound junk. When they reached the boat, they had to say good-bye to their guerrilla escorts, but word of their movements traveling along the grapevine meant they had many people looking out for their safety. They landed on the mainland before dawn and found Chinese citizens who guided them up a river to a village where, according to the locals, the other flight crew received help. Once there, Smith and his men learned that the injured fliers had been taken to a hospital in Linhai for treatment. It was a full day's walk along the trail to Linhai, and local men offered to carry Smith and his men in sedan chairs. With blistered feet from their damaged boots, the *TNT* crew gladly accepted. They also accepted food, soap, and underwear but politely declined the service of prostitutes.[8]

Four months earlier, back in Oregon eight days after Pearl Harbor, Smith had written his parents that he did not expect to wear civilian clothes until after the war's end. He offered his dad "a good blue suit that I haven't worn over a dozen times, and I don't want to store it away, because by the time this is all over it will probably have gone out of style." In the aftermath of the Japanese attack, Smith certainly knew he would be sent overseas. Although he hoped to train on the larger, four-engine B-17 Flying Fortress, he understood he would probably continue flying the B-25 when first deployed. The Air Corps would not waste time teaching him to fly a four-motored plane when it needed B-25 pilots immediately.[9]

Shortly after Pearl Harbor, President Roosevelt instigated the first step in the plan to use the B-25 to attack Japan. The president expressed both anger at the navy for being blindsided that December day and concern about the assault damaging his presidential legacy.[10] As quickly as anyone, Roosevelt grasped the need to strike back at Japan, to show the enemy the United States would not back down. He now had popular support for the idea because, as *Life* editorialized, an instant change in thinking gripped Americans: "Divided and dubious on the morning of Dec. 7, the American people arose Dec. 8 united by a common enemy and common hurt."[11]

Roosevelt also knew the public mood could sour as Japan continued to expand aggressively in the Pacific. Without a response, finger-pointing among Americans would likely commence and consume time and effort better directed elsewhere. For American morale and as a demonstration of power, Roosevelt soon began considering how to take the war to the Japanese home islands. While the United States might have relied on a naval bombardment, it would have been difficult to mount under the best of circumstances. The loss of the fleet at Pearl Harbor made that option hard to discuss in a meaningful way, especially since manufacturing replacement cruisers and battleships took time. Losing the few remaining gunboats in a direct and risky naval attack could mean Japanese victory in the Pacific. Aircraft, on the other hand, were frankly more expendable.[12]

By the time Army Air Corps General Hap Arnold left a White House meeting on 21 December, he knew the president believed an air attack against Japan was the best option. For exactly how that might happen, Roosevelt would rely on his military men. On matters of air power, Arnold, with a long history in military and general aviation, was his key strategist. Well before the army officially recognized planes as part of its fighting arsenal, Arnold learned to fly from none other than Orville and Wilbur Wright. No other man had the experience and knowledge to bring together the larger plan Roosevelt envisioned.[13]

On Christmas 1941, when low clouds cancelled flight maneuvers at Pendleton, Don enjoyed a quiet holiday with Marie at their apartment. On the opposite side of the continent, Lieutenant Colonel Jimmy Doolittle did not have the same luxury. Don later described Doolittle as "one of those fellows who believe that unless they do 18 hours of strenuous work every day of the week someone will think they are slipping."[14] That Christmas Eve, Doolittle reported to a new post in Washington, D.C., thrilled to serve in an advising position with General Arnold. Shortly after arriving, Arnold asked Doolittle a strange question: What medium-sized bomber could best take off from a short runway—five hundred feet or less?[15]

Doolittle first flew an airplane in January 1918, the same month Don Smith was born. With the United States fighting in World War I at the time, Doolittle felt an urge to serve and to do so from the air. In the era before the Army Air Corps, he enlisted in the Aviation Section of the United States Signal Corps. The Aviation Section claimed just fifty-five planes, and most American military leaders saw little use for the group. Nonetheless, when Doolittle reported for training in San Diego in 1918, the moment represented the start of one of the most remarkable and unusual careers in American military history.[16]

Born in California in 1896, Doolittle spent most of his childhood in Alaska. With a new gold rush in the Klondike region, Doolittle's parents, Frank and Rosa, moved to the vast territory in the hope of striking it rich either through mining, supplying goods to miners, or embracing any other developing economic opportunities. The Doolittles and their only child settled in Nome, where riches and opportunities stubbornly eluded them. They primarily relied on dogsleds for transportation. Rosa usually steered the family sled while her son hung on as a passenger across two miles of snow and ice to a spring that supplied their water. While Doolittle later dealt with temperamental engines on his aircraft, none surpassed the unpredictability and nastiness of the creatures that powered the dogsleds. He and plenty of his young friends bore scars from the wild Alaskan huskies. They even witnessed an elementary school classmate whom a pack of huskies had attacked and killed after he stumbled and fell.[17]

Nome's reputation as a largely lawless town in the early 1900s meant those who passed through expected to have to protect themselves from time to time. As a boy in that environment, Doolittle learned to fight out of necessity. At the age of eleven, he and his mother relocated to Los Angeles where he would face struggles as the neighborhood's new kid. Though small with pretty, wavy hair, Doolittle had no difficulty demonstrating his tough makeup against the other kids. Later, while enrolled at Manual Arts High School, he met a teacher who helped him redirect his street-fighting skills into boxing. Doolittle eventually became so skilled that at age fifteen one amateur boxing organization listed him as the "fly-weight" champion of the entire Pacific coast. Observers noted he possessed important characteristics for the sport: strength, coordination, and absolute fearlessness. His fearless nature carried over to his interests outside the boxing ring as well. The teenage Doolittle loved speed and tore up and down the Los Angeles streets on a motorcycle until a collision destroyed his bike and sent him to the hospital for more than a month.[18]

Although he gained a reputation as reckless and a fighter, closer examination reveals a highly intelligent young man, especially when he applied himself to mechanics. He not only loved his motorcycle's speed but also working on its engine. In 1912, when he was fifteen, he read an old *Popular Mechanics* article that had instructions for building a personal glider similar to those of today. Doolittle used the instructions to construct his own glider from lumber, muslin, and piano wire and then tested the craft, once by leaping from a hillside and once by attaching it to an automobile for speed. Decades later, an organization of pioneer aviators who flew prior to World War I learned of his glider exploits and offered him membership. Doolittle declined.[19] Despite his valiant efforts, he admitted, by no means "could I claim that I had ever achieved controlled flight" as a teenager.[20]

Having an interest in engineering, Doolittle first started down a path toward becoming a mining engineer, spending two years at Los Angeles Junior College before transferring to the School of Mines at the University of California at Berkeley in 1916. He had spent one summer working at a mine that was part of the Comstock Lode in Nevada when the United States entered World War I, causing him to leave school before his senior year. Doolittle reported for flight instruction at San Diego, where a civilian pilot taught him to fly seat-of-the-pants style in a Curtiss JN4, a model known to all as "the Jenny." That type of training was problematic, as Doolittle and his cohort witnessed another student die in a mid-air collision during his first day of instruction. Less thorough than the training Smith experienced, Doolittle had to log only seven hours in the Jenny with his teacher before flying solo. Two months later, he was deemed a full-fledged pilot and commissioned as a second lieutenant. In his early military years, Doolittle was the antithesis of the disciplined Don Smith. Doolittle's superiors frequently grounded him or confined him to base for inappropriate stunts in flight, including chasing ducks.[21]

Eight months of war in Europe remained after Doolittle's commissioning, and he hoped for a swift deployment into aerial combat, but the orders never came. Instead, he found himself bounced around to different camps instructing new Signal Corps fliers—a tribute to his skill, but not a role he relished. In 1919, Doolittle had been transferred to Eagle Pass, Texas, where he mainly flew patrols along the United States-Mexico border to watch for smugglers and unauthorized immigrants. While not combat duty, the assignment contained an element of danger. One day, a smuggler shot at and killed one of Doolittle's close friends while in the air.[22]

That type of vulnerability to ground attack in the early 1920s was among the reasons most military leaders doubted whether airplanes could play significant roles in future conflicts. True, the actions of World War I aces like American Eddie Rickenbacker and Germany's Manfred von Richtofen, better known as the Red Baron, captured the public's imagination.[23] Although some army and navy officials acknowledged certain advantages to aerial observations, plenty of them considered fights in the air little more than jousts for honor with no bearing on the real battles raging below. The navy, especially, dismissed the possibility of planes changing the course of sea battles or determining control of the oceans. In fact, the assistant secretary of the navy at the time, Franklin D. Roosevelt, did not believe an "airplane or a fleet of them" could possibly inflict damage on naval vessels.[24] Army Brigadier General Billy Mitchell and the upstart Doolittle disagreed. In 1921, Doolittle flew in a widely publicized experiment in which aircraft bombed captured German ships moored off the Virginia coast. The mock attack sent the vessels, including a battleship considered unsinkable, to the bottom of the Atlantic. Although navy brass admitted the demonstration was impressive, they downplayed the success, noting that navy crews fire back during an actual battle.[25]

By then, Doolittle had joined the newly formed Army Air Corps. The branch engaged in an ongoing public-relations campaign that demonstrated a range of likely military uses for aircraft, which coincided with civilian efforts like those of South Dakota's Clyde Ice to win public enthusiasm for commercial flight. Both military and private fliers appeared regularly at public air shows or staged their own to demonstrate their machines' capabilities and safety. All the aviators sensed that people associated flight with speed, so their exhibitions included air races. In 1922, the army and Doolittle dreamed up an eye-popping stunt to illustrate the speed of air travel: a coast-to-coast solo flight in less than twenty-four hours.[26]

Doolittle had the honor of piloting his modified, open-cockpit DH-4. Having come to believe that pilots should know the mechanical workings of their machines thoroughly, he supervised the mechanical modifications, including installation of extra fuel tanks. With his plane prepared, he took it to Jacksonville, Florida, where a crowd of several hundred assembled on a beach in August 1922 to witness Doolittle launch himself into the record books. In his first attempt, however, the plane's wheels suddenly sank into the sand, flipping the craft into shallow water. When Doolittle freed himself from the cockpit and stood unhurt, after having thrashed around in knee-deep water, the crowd laughed. The scene was worthy of Buster Keaton, a popular movie comic of the period.[27]

Doolittle repaired the plane and a month later, on the evening of 4 September, took off successfully from Jacksonville. He flew through a massive overnight storm with rain streaming across his face for hours. After daybreak, he entered clear weather over Texas, the same airspace Smith would experience nineteen years later. Doolittle ate and rested at San Antonio for a little over an hour and took off again. Fighting fatigue, he sipped coffee, a drink he did not like, through a tube and landed at San Diego's Rockwell Field twenty-two hours and thirty minutes after leaving Florida. Not counting his stop in Texas, Doolittle covered 2,163 miles in twenty-one hours and nineteen minutes. The accomplishment made national headlines and thoroughly impressed Americans in 1922, a time when early pioneers who had ridden the wagon trails and laborers who had completed the first transcontinental railroad fifty-three years earlier still lived.[28]

Doolittle's transcontinental record created a loyal fan base who rooted for him as he won racing trophies and set speed records in Army

Air Corps planes. Few of those fans knew that the army had selected Doolittle to study aerial engineering at the Massachusetts Institute of Technology, where he earned a doctorate in 1925. He used his knowledge to help the army develop instruments that would allow pilots to fly through blinding weather conditions. In September 1929, Doolittle performed the first demonstration of "flying blind" when he took off, flew a course over New York's Mitchel Field for fifteen minutes using only the plane's instruments, and landed, all while seated in a hooded cockpit.[29] One *New York Times* reporter believed the flight "indicated . . . that aviation had perhaps taken its greatest single step forward in safety."[30]

For all his accomplishments, Doolittle did not earn much money. Now raising two sons with his wife, Josephine, he left the army, but retained the rank of major in the reserves, to work for Shell Oil in 1930. In the new position, he advised the company's efforts at upgrading flight fuels and opened doors for sales. He traveled around the air racing circuit and participated in the occasional air show with Shell-sponsored aircraft so spectators knew what product powered his machine. At one point, he accepted Clyde Ice's invitation to fly to South Dakota for an air show at Spearfish. There, he thrilled the crowd with one of his signature dives, which Ice estimated began at ten thousand feet, trailing smoke all the way. On that windless day, a great tower of smoke hung in the air as a testament to human daring and mechanical power.[31]

Shell also sent Doolittle abroad to perform similar exhibitions and keep abreast of technical developments. The international community of aviators tended to share knowledge with one another, regardless of nationalities. One trip in 1933 took him to Japan, China, and several European countries. In Europe, Doolittle witnessed commercial aviation beyond anything the United States could claim. He also sensed a commitment to advanced military flight, especially in Germany. After a return to Germany in 1937, Doolittle came to believe that under Hitler the nation could prove a military menace. Many in the United States did not support such ideas in the mid-1930s. Germany still owed the United States payments due to post–World War I loans to help them rebuild. Any official expression of anti-German sentiment could make gaining repayment difficult.[32]

During this period of restrained military thinking, Doolittle accomplished a breakthrough that would greatly benefit the Air Corps. He discovered that 100-octane airplane fuel, compared to the 90- or 91-octane fuel the Air Corps used in the mid-1930s, provided planes with significantly increased horsepower, possibly up to 25 percent more. Shell and other companies could produce this fuel, but at a high expense and with extensive engine retooling. Doolittle campaigned hard for the switch based on his testing. In 1936, the Air Corps embraced Doolittle's thinking and made 100-octane-compatible engines the standard for all their planes by 1 January 1938.[33]

World War II erupted in Europe on 1 September 1939 when Nazi forces invaded Poland. The next year, Doolittle returned to the Army Air Corps. At first, his assignments resembled some of his work at Shell, acting as a liaison between the military and private industry while the Air Corps expanded its inventory. He spent most of his time traveling to the various automobile company plants in the Midwest to inspect their operations as they transitioned into producing military equipment, airplanes included. Doolittle also went to England to study that nation's new warplanes in order to implement their manufacturing process in the factories at home. After Pearl Harbor, he requested a combat assignment rather than a stateside desk job. Air Corps commanders initially denied his request. As an older pilot, Doolittle envisioned being relegated to a non-combat role similar to his experience in World War I. Many of the men Doolittle met in the Air Corps, including Smith and his crewmates, were the same ages as his two sons, James Jr. and John, both of whom joined the army after finishing their college degrees.[34]

In December 1941 and January 1942, Smith patrolled the Oregon and Washington coasts, staring into mist and the grey waters of the Pacific, hunting Japanese submarines but rarely spotting any threats. During Christmas week, Edgar McElroy, one of Smith's fellow pilots, spotted and destroyed an enemy submarine near the mouth of the Columbia River, a unique adventure for the squad. Everyone else recalled days of monotony with nothing to report.[35] Smith's friend Thomas Griffin, who acted as navigator for Plane Nine in the raid, remembered, "The only thing I saw in six weeks was a whale. That was as exciting as it got."[36]

Smith and his crew usually flew for five hours and would then "come home for eats." Fridays meant fish at mess, sometimes one of the few indicators that helped Smith recall what day of the week it was. The patrols flew out of McChord, stranding Marie at Pendleton. By December, Don and Marie had important news to share: Marie was pregnant.

She remained in Oregon for a few weeks and then went home to Texas. As the wife of an officer, she was eligible for army medical care during her pregnancy. Because many officers made San Antonio their home, the army "arranged with a specialist to handle the officers' [pregnant] wives," Don explained. "So everything is working out all right."[37]

Back north, Smith faced a new challenge while flying—winter fog that often rolled in thick at McChord. He grew more proficient in flying on instruments, but the fog could still intimidate. Returning from flying search patterns one January day, he wrote that he "couldn't see the runway until I was about 300 feet off the end of it. I was a little to one side, but was able to get over it and set down all right. Good practice, but it made me sweat for a few minutes."[38]

While Smith dealt with these new experiences, Doolittle spent January in Washington, D.C., writing detailed plans for an air strike against Japan. Having chosen the B-25 as the plane for the mission, Doolittle wanted the fliers who had extensive experience in the bomber, the Seventeenth Bombardment Group's Thirty-fourth, Thirty-seventh, and Ninety-fifth squadrons as well as the Eighty-ninth Reconnaissance Squadron at Pendleton, as his personnel for what was then known as the B-25 Special Project. After receiving authorization, Doolittle worked quickly, insisting on strict secrecy for all parts of the project. In late January, he began the process of preparing the planes, ordering modifications at Minneapolis for eighteen B-25s to increase their fuel capacity. Meanwhile, he researched mission-specific gunnery, bomb-sights, and armament.[39]

On 3 February, the navy loaded two B-25s onto the deck of its newest carrier, the USS *Hornet*, at Hampton, Virginia, to test their takeoff capabilities. The *Hornet* steamed a hundred miles into the Atlantic, where Army Air Corps lieutenants John Fitzgerald and James McCarthy successfully launched from the deck. Although the bombers carried light loads, the test confirmed that medium bombers, just as Doolittle and other officers believed, could take off from an aircraft carrier and fly directly into combat. That same day, as the Seventeenth Bombardment Group and the Eighty-ninth Reconnaissance Squadron prepared to transfer to Columbia Air Base in Columbia, South Carolina, a call went out among the corpsmen for volunteers for a dangerous mission requiring several weeks of special training. By the time the men arrived at their new station, all who heard the call offered their services. From the volunteers, Major John A. Hilger, commander of the Eighty-ninth, selected enough men, including Don Smith, to compose twenty-four crews of five for specialized training at Eglin Air Force Base in Florida that spring.[40]

In mid-February, Smith flew ahead of most of his squadron, ferrying a B-25 to South Carolina. Essentially, he took the same route as the one he flew the weekend of Pearl Harbor, only in reverse, dropping south to Tucson and then east. Having to fly directly over San Antonio, he requested and received permission for a night of leave to visit Marie. Bad weather kept him in San Antonio an extra day, "which didn't break my heart," he noted.[41]

Smith arrived in South Carolina on 18 February 1942 and did not find the accommodations comfortable. "They call this the sunny south," he wrote shortly after landing, "but I am inclined to believe differently, as they have us quartered in tents, and it is really cold in them." Although the army equipped the airmen with wood stoves, "they don't burn all night," Smith reported, making it "a task to get up and build a fire" in the morning. "But we should[n't] kick," he explained, "the food is good, and it will be getting warmer as the time goes on."[42]

Smith primarily spent his thirteen-day stint in South Carolina getting less-experienced airmen into the sky, helping them accumulate the flying hours necessary for "fully qualified" status. While Smith took on some responsibility for instruction, Doolittle had selected Hilger as his deputy for the project, giving him greater authority and making him one of the few people who knew the full details of the upcoming mission. Hilger also would train rigorously as one of the raid's sixteen pilots.[43]

Doc White, the Eighty-ninth's well-liked physician, joined the detail in South Carolina and surprised everyone when he requested a spot with one of the flight crews. As valuable as a doctor might be in combat, Hilger told White, none of the planes could carry an extra man. His only option was to train as a gunner. White jumped at the opportunity and scored second highest for accuracy among all B-25 Special Project gunners. Meanwhile, he became a familiar face to all the project airmen as he inoculated them for bubonic plague, yellow fever, smallpox, and typhus, among other diseases. Some men got eleven shots in three weeks.[44] Everyone, including Smith, complained about the treatments: "They are still shooting us with vaccine, and by the time they finish with us, I don't expect to have any blood left, just a mixture of serum."[45] After fulfilling his role as doctor, White joined Smith's crew.[46]

Another South Dakotan, Lieutenant Hank Potter, also took part in the B-25 Special Project alongside Smith. Born in Pierre in 1918, Potter grew up and graduated from high school there, then attended Yankton College in southeastern South Dakota and transferred to the University of Oregon after two years. He enlisted in the Army Air Corps in July 1940. Eleven months later, he completed navigator training and was commissioned as a second lieutenant. Potter eventually served as the navigator for Doolittle himself.[47]

While Smith continued his stateside assignment, he heard news of South Dakotans, including those from South Dakota State College, who had already made their marks on the war effort. Smith was particularly impressed to learn of the role a former State professor assumed, procuring poultry and eggs as a civilian army quartermaster. In the same letter, Smith described the adventure of an unnamed "State boy" who escaped one of the battleships struck at Pearl Harbor. When the ship began sinking, the sailor leaped into the water and safely swam ashore.[48] One of his ROTC colleagues and football teammates, Willibald C. ("Bill") Bianchi, even received the Congressional Medal of Honor on 26 February 1942 for his actions while leading an assault on two Japanese machine-gun nests in the Philippines earlier that month. Bianchi destroyed one of the nests with a grenade but was wounded four times, twice in his left hand and twice in his chest. Unable to walk, he dragged himself to a disabled tank and fired its anti-aircraft gun into the second position until either a Japanese grenade or mortar round knocked him off the tank, rendering him unconscious. Bianchi survived the injuries and returned to action defending the Philippines shortly afterward.[49]

Back in the United States, on 27 February, Smith and the rest of the B-25 Special Project began transferring to Eglin Field on Florida's panhandle coast, about fifty miles east of Pensacola. To ensure secrecy, the men were assigned barracks apart from other personnel and ordered not to mix with the others. On 3 March, the project crews were assembled in a hall when a short man in uniform walked in with a sense of purpose and took the podium. "My name's Doolittle," he told the squads, though he needed no introduction. Most fliers knew the famous aviator the moment they spotted him, indicating to them the vast significance of their mystery mission.[50]

Smith apparently missed Doolittle's pitch. Unless he had his date wrong when he wrote his parents later in the week, something he continually struggled with while in the Air Corps, he flew into Eglin the following day, 4 March. Because several Mitchells were still going through fuel modifications, Smith most likely ferried a plane that had received its fittings after the others took off. Despite his delay, he soon knew the same scant details about the project as the other airmen. Doolittle avoided revealing specifics but suggested the men would get some sense of the mission as their training unfolded. The pilots, he divulged, would focus primarily on getting heavily loaded B-25s airborne in the shortest takeoff distances possible. The navigators, bombardiers, engineers, and gunners would also go through a rigorous regimen.[51]

Doolittle estimated the group had three weeks to prepare before attempting "the most dangerous thing any of you have ever done." Before providing any details, Doolittle promised, "If anyone wants to bail out, he can do so right now," with no questions asked. He then instructed the men not to share any information with "wives or buddies" or even to discuss it amongst themselves. If anyone outside the project asked questions, he wanted that person's name, which he would pass on to the FBI.[52] Thomas Griffin perhaps got the earliest indication about the nature of the mission. While the crews began their training at Eglin, Griffin and David Jones, who eventually piloted Plane Five, traveled to Washington, D.C., for "an interesting assignment." They went to the War Department and scoured maps from the Library of Congress, selecting those they thought best represented Japanese industrial sites and Chinese terrain.[53]

After 3 March, Doolittle remained at Eglin as much as possible, although he had to return to Washington, D.C., at times. In those instances, he turned command over to Hilger but never spoke to his deputy over the telephone about any aspect of the project, concerned that someone might listen in. If something developed in the Capital that Hilger needed to know, Doolittle would fly back to Florida to inform him. While Doolittle developed the details, he also worried that General Arnold would deny him the chance to lead the raid himself, something he desperately wanted. Arnold, however, feared that Doolittle's expertise was too valuable to risk in such a dangerous mission. Assuming he could eventually persuade the general, Doolittle trained at Eglin alongside Smith and the other pilots, mainly learning to master "kangaroo takeoffs" in which they launched their planes skyward at steeply vertical angles. To assist, Hilger suggested that Doolittle bring in a navy flight instructor, and Doolittle selected Lieutenant Hank Miller. His presence on the army base gave the project men an indication that their mission would also involve the navy, but they did not discuss it per Doolittle's orders.[54]

At one of Eglin's isolated landing fields, Miller ordered stripes painted across the runway indicating two hundred, three hundred, and five hundred feet from the spot where the Mitchells would begin moving for takeoff. He ensured the pilots that they could get airborne at a speed of just sixty miles an hour, less time and space than they initially believed. They simply needed to drop their landing flaps while generating a sudden burst of energy from their engines. Miller also cautioned them about the danger of the maneuver. Too steep an ascent could cause the plane's tail to hit the ground. Smith and his colleagues worked to perfect hitting the sweet spot. The demanding exercises made the seasoned pilots feel as if they had regressed to their earliest flying lessons.[55] Smith thought he "knew how to handle a plane pretty well," but after training for the kangaroo takeoffs he wondered "how I ever got around in one."[56]

Doolittle originally planned to put all twenty-four planes aboard the Japan-bound carrier, with fifteen B-25s making the raid and nine planes and crews sitting in reserve to join the mission if a plane crashed into the sea at takeoff. Training accidents at Eglin changed that plan, destroying two B-25s with no serious injuries and reducing the number of planes and crews to twenty-two.[57]

As the B-25 Special Project progressed, Roosevelt faced a new form of isolationist opposition. He dismissed policy critics who argued the United States should keep its military forces at home to defend American soil, derisively terming the concept the "turtle policy." Instead, he believed, the nation should "retain the eagle as it is—flying high and striking hard." If the southwestern Pacific fell to Japan, Roosevelt argued, then Japan would hold a stronger position for an attack on the continental United States. He proclaimed, "The object of the Nazis and Japanese is to separate the United States, Britain, China and Russia, and to isolate them one from another. . . . It is the old familiar Axis policy of 'Divide and Conquer.'"[58]

Hanson W. Baldwin, military and naval correspondent for the *New*

York Times, agreed, drawing upon recent events to illustrate his point. Writing in *Foreign Affairs*, Baldwin stated that a defensive mindset had been "proved fallacious" during France's defeat in 1940. He argued that "the third French Republic died because it was obsessed with the doctrine of the timid defense. Wars can be won only by carrying the fighting to the enemy."[59] Those who pushed for the defensive stance seemed to have forgotten that Japan's quick conquests in the winter of 1941 and 1942 were not due to its military strength alone. "The Japanese profited by surprise," Baldwin stressed.[60]

In late March, *Newsweek* reported that some high-ranking army and navy officials advocated taking the offensive against Japan. Their main motivation came from "Japan's successes," which had "made her almost blockade-proof" and forced the military to "abandon its long-held war-of-attrition plans." At the same time, frustrated Americans fretted about where the next round of Japan's offense would strike and demanded action. They especially worried that Alaska might make an attractive target as spring slowly thawed lands in the far north. Unfounded rumors circulated that Japan also had new surprises up its sleeve in the form of super-fast fighter planes, including one that approached five hundred miles an hour.[61]

No matter the direction of the war, government officials knew it would cost vast amounts of money, and the Treasury Department needed to find the funds. About the time the B-25 Special Project relocated to Florida, the department announced a tax increase to raise $9 billion for the war effort. Further, the department suggested that taxpayers would receive a credit rather than a refund when they overpaid. While a major change at the time, the necessity for the war effort offset any public anger. "Although it is perhaps unfortunate that the Treasury's war-tax proposal should have been announced at the moment when the average taxpayer was struggling with his 1941 returns, the new tax program is basically sound," editorialized *The Nation*. "Before weeping about the effect on the 'little fellow,'" the author pointed out that "under the new schedules" a man with three children and a house "would pay virtually no income tax on a $3,000 income." Obviously, the writer continued, higher-income families could "afford to bear the brunt" of the new policies while "taxes on corporations" would make up the rest.[62]

Even with unprecedented levels of new federal funds pouring into expanding war industries, Americans began to worry about production capabilities during the conflict. A new aspect of industrial production created the hottest controversy in March 1942 as Americans questioned the practice of the forty-hour work week, established as part of Roosevelt's New Deal. Many feared it would reduce the production needed in wartime. "Factories which can turn out 1,000 instruments of war a week are only turning out 500," according to the *Dallas Morning News*, all because "there is a law which says men should work only 40 hours a week." The author then asked sarcastically, *"Is there a law which says our sons must fight only 40 hours a week or die only 40 hours a week?"* The *Oklahoma City Oklahoman* even asked its readers to vote against any United States senators or congressmen who voted against "outlawing all strikes in every industry connected with defense" and the forty-hour work week.[63]

Roosevelt tried to defuse the controversy, reminding Americans that the labor law did not prohibit factory workers from logging more than forty hours per week but ensured them overtime pay if they did. In response, pundits scurried to estimate how much overtime pay might cost taxpayers over the course of the war. Other voices noted that factories already turned out more materiel than ships could carry to troops overseas and that strikes at defense industries were uncommon. Some even suggested that one could trace the whole controversy to Nazi propaganda.[64]

Although Smith did not mention this national debate specifically, he likely noticed the strife despite his isolation at Eglin. The labor controversy generated newspaper headlines and intense discussions on radio. He undoubtedly agreed with eliminating the forty-hour week, just as the previous year he had expressed worry, and even anger, over how labor could hurt the war effort. While citizens came together in many ways to resist the Axis, some divisions still existed, and Americans tended to express their far-ranging opinions with vigor even if it meant standing accused of being duped by enemy propaganda.[65]

On 18 March, exactly a month before the raid, Smith informed his parents that everything was fine, "though awful busy." He expected his squadron would leave Florida the following week, "after finishing the necessary work on the planes."[66] Some of the work involved replacing bottom machine gun turrets with fuel tanks and fixing any leaks. Doolittle thought little of the B-25's bottom turrets, finding them strangely complicated. "A man could learn to play the violin good enough for Carnegie Hall before he could learn to fire this thing," he stated, and gladly traded those guns for sixty more gallons of fuel.[67] To make the Mitchells appear more heavily armed and to discourage Japanese fighter pilots from pursuing them, Doolittle procured broomsticks, had them painted black, and ordered two installed on each B-25's tail to resemble tail guns. The airplanes retained the nose guns and a top turret that Doolittle found satisfactory.[68]

The most complex work on the Mitchells involved the carburetors, specifically fine-tuning them for maximum fuel efficiency at slow speeds and low altitudes. With Doolittle's background in aviation fuel, he believed he could wring more air miles per gallon from his planes than previously thought possible. To ensure that his modifications worked properly, Doolittle had his crews keep detailed records of miles flown and fuel consumed as they flew along Florida's panhandle and out across the Gulf of Mexico. When Smith learned one such flight would take him to Houston, he devised a personal mission objective: get Marie there for a rendezvous of just a few minutes. To accomplish the task, Marie's parents joined the adventure, driving their daughter across the Texas landscape as Don took off from Florida and sped across the water.[69]

Even on this journey, Smith followed Doolittle's orders for his pilots to make a habit of "hugging the deck." No matter the situation, the fliers were to cruise just above the waves at sea and just over the treetops on land, which made for exciting exercises but terrifying prospects for a bombing run. Crews sometimes dropped small bombs from five hundred feet above a Florida proving ground. The force of the percussion and its jarring effect on their planes surprised the crews. Though still unaware of their objective, this training, combined with the officers' continual reminders of the mission's danger and the fact that they could leave at any time, led the men to guess that they were preparing for a low-altitude attack, which could rip a plane apart and kill the entire squad. About the time of these practice runs, one pilot took up Doolittle's offer to drop out. Indeed, no questions were asked. Another pilot, Vernon Stinzi, fell ill, and Doolittle began filling in with his crew, including navigator Hank Potter.[70]

From the beginning, Doolittle stressed the importance of the five-man crews coming to know each other well and functioning as teams.

If any of Doolittle's crew for Plane One, which in addition to Potter included copilot Richard Cole and staff sergeants Fred Braemer and Paul Leonard, felt intimidated by the presence of an aviation legend, those feelings diminished quickly. Doolittle expressed interest in each man and tried hard to create a bond with them.[71] From early on in Florida, Smith worked closely with his crew consisting of Edward Saylor, Howard Sessler, Griffith Williams, and newly minted gunner Doc White. The crew, Saylor recalled decades later, respected their pilot for both his flying skills and his "straight arrow" personality.[72]

While Doolittle and the crew leaders bonded with their men, Doolittle also explored the B-25's capabilities in cold weather conditions. Doolittle had de-icing equipment installed on the planes in the hope that Soviet Premier Joseph Stalin might allow the aircraft to land in Siberia, the closest location for them to do so without encountering Japanese forces. Before finalizing the plan, the United States had to convince Stalin, who questioned what his country would gain.[73] Specifically, Doolittle informed General Arnold, they would get the Mitchells. "Should the Russians be willing to accept delivery of eighteen B-25B airplanes, on lease lend, at Vladivostok," he wrote, "our problems would be greatly simplified."[74] Even the lure of lend-lease did not convince Stalin, who was unwilling to risk Japanese retaliation.[75]

Doolittle also looked for an alternative to the highly regarded Norden bombsight fitted on the Mitchells. The army still considered the technology of the ten-year-old mechanism, which included the ability to lock onto a target and a function that released a payload automatically, top-secret. The Norden vastly improved accuracy from high altitudes, allowing a crew, as one myth suggested, to "drop a bomb into a pickle barrel from 20,000 feet."[76] Many officers involved in planning the raid feared that the Japanese might get access to the technology from a downed Mitchell. Doolittle had a more practical concern, however. Because Norden had designed the piece for high-altitude raids, it was not as effective for the low altitudes planned for his attack.[77]

Instead, Doolittle turned to Captain C. Ross Greening, the pilot of Plane Eleven who also specialized in gunnery and bombing, to develop a low altitude, rudimentary sight. In Eglin's own shop, at a cost of just twenty cents for the aluminum, Greening created a device he called "the Mark Twain," and what some others in the project referred to simply as "the twenty-cent bombsight."[78] Nothing more than a flat circle of metal marked with angle degrees and a metal sighting bar attached like a clock hand that extended past the circle's edge, the mechanism worked more efficiently for the raiders' purposes. The bombardier referred to the airspeed and altitude to set the sighting bar to the correct angle and simply waited until the target passed under the arm to release the bombs. Having tested the device successfully at Eglin, Doolittle had the Mark Twain installed on all the B-25s.[79]

As Smith's training at Eglin progressed into mid-March, Doolittle continued to make trips to Washington, D.C., to finalize plans with General Arnold. By then, they intended to land the B-25s in China after the raid if Chinese officials agreed to lend assistance. The raiders would set down at an airfield close to the coast, refuel, and then continue flying west over unoccupied Chinese territory as they proceeded home. General Joseph W. Stilwell, American commander of the China-Burma-India theater, had the task of winning Chinese approval and securing fuel for the second part of the escape. The mission's secrecy complicated Stilwell's job, for Arnold refused to share any information with either Stilwell or Chinese Generalissimo Chiang Kai-shek. Without that knowledge, Stillwell found Chiang far from enthusiastic about supporting the mysterious mission. Chiang had likely guessed the operation entailed a raid against Japan and feared retaliation from the Japanese occupiers. He informed Stilwell that the raiders could possibly land at either Kweilin or Chuchow airfields but never fully committed to assisting the bombers once they arrived.[80]

During the final meetings, Doolittle pestered Arnold about allowing him to pilot one of the planes. He felt comfortable arguing with his superior despite the difference in their ranks. The two had known each other since just after World War I, which made their relationship less strict than the typical superior and subordinate in the army. Doolittle did not hold back, arguing that his piloting one of the Mitchells made perfect sense. No one knew the mission better than he and, having joined the training in Florida, he had come to know and win the trust of the other fliers. Arnold finally relented and approved the move.[81]

Even though Doolittle was thrilled at the opportunity to fly into combat for the first time, he noted later that he would have stepped away immediately had Lieutenant Miller named a better pilot. Miller used the training runs to grade the pilots. As a result, flight crews came to think of practice missions as examinations, marking one near the end of March as their final exam. That day, all the crews were ordered to speed southeast to Fort Myers, veer sharply right, and fly low to the Texas coast. Once the crews spotted Houston, they raced back to Eglin, keeping records the entire time. Out of the practice runs, both the Smith and Doolittle crews received high marks from Miller, guaranteeing their places in the raid. While the men felt ready for their mission, they still had no idea as to its details or importance to the early war effort.[82]

On 23 March, twenty days after Doolittle first addressed the men, he called another assembly. If the volunteers believed they would finally learn the mission details, they were to be greatly disappointed. All they needed to know, Doolittle said, was that the twenty-two crews and planes would move out to McClellan Field in northern California. Again, Doolittle stressed the need for secrecy, noting that many lives depended on it. During the transfer, he directed, the crews would continue their training maneuvers, flying low and monitoring fuel consumption.[83]

Smith and the others did not know Doolittle had just received a coded message: "Tell Jimmy to get on his horse."[84] It meant the carrier *Hornet*, the same ship from which the two B-25s took off along the Virginia coast in February, had passed through the Panama Canal and now steamed its way up the coast toward the rendezvous point in San Francisco. Doolittle and the raiders moved fast, taking off and flying west in small formations. During the trip, the squads spent one night in San Antonio, giving Don and Marie, now six months pregnant, some time together before what could have been Don's first and final mission. In the name of secrecy, the crews had been ordered to stop writing letters, but Don told Marie she could mention he had passed through San Antonio the next time she wrote her in-laws.[85]

Once the twenty-two planes left Eglin, it became harder for the group to maintain secrecy. Army Air Corps personnel at Texas and California airfields naturally wondered about the oddly modified B-25s, with homemade bombsights, no bottom turrets, and phony tail guns, but the crewmen deflected questions about the planes or where they were headed with a curt "Mind your own business."[86]

The crews flew into McClellan without incident only to encounter a group of civilian flight mechanics who both expressed curiosity about the bombers and questioned their integrity for flight. In fairness, these mechanics performed the job for which the Air Corps had contracted them, thoroughly inspecting airplanes before they flew into combat. They especially objected to the carburetor settings, even with Doolittle's assurance they would work. The raiders later recalled heated verbal exchanges between their leader and the technicians, whom Doolittle told his crews to watch closely, only worsening the ill will. The operators performed final modifications, including installation of new propellers, but Doolittle grew frustrated with the pace of their work. He phoned General Arnold, who immediately told the commander at McClellan that he was to make the labor on the B-25s the base's highest priority until the planes departed on 1 April. When the group left, some of the airmen, perhaps even Smith himself, felt liberated.[87] Doolittle gave a succinct evaluation of the labor: "LOUSY."[88]

From McClellan, the squads made a short hop to Alameda Naval Air Station near San Francisco where they would meet the *Hornet*. Doolittle instructed Smith and the other pilots to stay aloft a full hour, testing everything during the trip and reporting any problems to him immediately upon landing. Smith reported his plane in perfect condition, and it was loaded aboard the *Hornet*. While the navy's crew brought the sixteen planes Doolittle determined fit for the mission on deck, 132 Army Air Corps men, 80 fliers and crew, and 52 support staff also stepped aboard.[89]

The airmen settled into their new sleeping quarters, some consisting of a spare cot in a cabin already full of seamen. Some of the sailors grumbled about this invasion of army fliers but complied with orders to ask no questions. Doolittle, after his men moved in, gave them leave for the night in San Francisco. Smith left no record of his evening, but several raiders made their way to the famous Top of the Mark Club. Late in the morning on 2 April, the *Hornet* passed under the Golden Gate Bridge with the B-25s fully visible.[90] Lots of pedestrians watched from the bridge, and the crews, Tom Griffin recalled, "were sure every tenth one was Japanese."[91]

Smith and his men met the battered crew of Plane Seven—*Ruptured Duck*—who had sustained cuts, broken bones, missing teeth, and deep bruises, at the Linhai hospital. Pilot Ted Lawson, who served with Smith in the Pacific Northwest and during the mock wars in Louisiana, South Carolina, and Georgia, recalled the arrival of the *TNT* crew: "You never saw five dirtier men, but God, how good they looked! They weren't a bit beat up—just worn out."[1] The recuperating airmen proceeded to tell their story to Smith and his crew.

The *Ruptured Duck* had followed Doolittle's plane to Tokyo, eventually getting a close look at the imperial palace. To Lawson's surprise, the city's sprawl reminded him of Los Angeles rather than the compact San Francisco, as he expected. Fires and a smoky haze rising from the imperial capital testified to the other raiders' successful strikes several minutes earlier. The *Ruptured Duck* crew never spotted their primary target, the Nippon Machine Works, but chose to hit one of several other industrial targets. Gunner David Thatcher saw a formation of Japanese fighters searching for them, but the group apparently never spotted the Americans. From fourteen hundred feet, Lawson made an east to west run through central Tokyo. Two bombs did little damage to the Japan Steel Piping plant and a second unnamed factory. A third hit a supply of coal coke next to a different steel factory, but the damage there also seemed minimal. Their final bomb sparked roof fires throughout the neighborhood.[2]

By then, anti-aircraft fire targeted the plane, and the crew ducked down as Lawson escaped the city. As they neared the Chinese coast, rain and cloud cover made it difficult for Lawson to see. He decided to try landing on a smooth beach on Nantien Island after making a pass to ensure it was clear of obstacles. Seeing none, he circled back over the sea to make his approach. Then, at one hundred miles per hour and a quarter mile short of the beach, both engines failed. The plane's wheels hit the water, causing the *Ruptured Duck* to flip. Lawson and copilot Dean Davenport, still strapped in their seats, were thrown through the windshield and found themselves fifteen feet underwater. Both managed to get free and make it safely to shore. Lawson emerged from the crash with the most severe injuries. When he launched from the cockpit, a metal clip in the pilot's compartment where his earphones hung ripped open his left leg near the knee. His teeth were bashed in—he eventually lost nine of them along with parts of his gums—and his lower lip was mostly severed so it hung over his chin. Davenport later told Lawson that his face looked as if it had been pushed in.[3]

Davenport, navigator Charles McClure, and bombardier Bob Clever suffered major injuries as well. Davenport had a deep wound on his lower right leg that eventually prevented him from walking. McClure's arms were swollen from his shoulders to his elbows. Clever had multiple injuries, including sprained hips and back and multiple cuts to his head and face, that prevented him from standing up or walking. Thatcher, the twenty-year-old enlisted gunner whom Lawson continually chastised for calling him "sir," came out relatively unscathed. A knock to the head left him unconscious for a few moments, making him the last to escape the upside-down plane. Though the lowest-ranking member of the crew, the native of Bridger, Montana, essentially became its commander, being the only man in shape to administer medical aid, interact with local civilians, and defend his injured comrades from any enemy threats.[4]

Once all the airmen managed to clear the wreck, they crawled onto the beach and lay there. Help soon appeared in the form of eight or so Chinese fishermen. These small men, the fliers recalled, were deceptively strong, lifting the injured squad members and carrying them to a mud-brick hut nearby. Thatcher spent the night dressing his crewmates' wounds with rags and helping the men shift their positions as shock wore off and acute pain set in. In the middle of the night, a man appeared and warned Thatcher of approaching Japanese soldiers, suggesting that he should hide elsewhere, but Thatcher refused to abandon the *Ruptured Duck* crew. Just before dawn, he returned to the crash site and searched for a medical kit but came back to the hut with only soggy cigarettes. Thatcher's last view of the smashed B-25 left him wondering how any of them survived.[5]

Shortly afterward, a local man who spoke broken English visited the men. He turned out to be the same Nantien guerrilla leader Smith would meet when he reached the island two days later, Jai Foo Ching, or Charlie. He informed the American squad that local men were offering to fashion makeshift litters from bamboo and rope to transport the fliers on the first leg of the multi-day journey to the closest hospital. Similar to the *TNT* crew's travels, the locals carried the *Ruptured Duck* men in a slow procession through rice paddies, over steep hills, and aboard a small boat that navigated a narrow canal. Each phase of the trip, especially being carried in the bouncing litters, increased the pain of the four injured men. The crew took comfort, however, in believing they were traveling deeper into unoccupied China. By now, Japanese patrols had almost certainly found their airplane, which Thatcher reported as clearly visible.[6]

Panic started to set in when the fliers realized they were not on the mainland, but on Nantien Island. Their anxiety worsened when a Japanese gunboat appeared near the rendezvous point for the junk to the mainland. Their rescuers quickly hid the Americans in a ditch while the Japanese soldiers questioned them before moving on, satisfied the Americans were not there. That night, Thatcher and the locals carried the injured airmen onboard the junk as rain fell. With the injured men desperately thirsty, Thatcher and their rescuers collected rainwater in bowls for them to drink. Thatcher had no time for sleep while caring for his mates, and Lawson fought off sleep, fearing that a doctor might appear and amputate his leg.[7]

After the junk reached the mainland the next morning, it continued up a river until docking at a small landing near a Chinese nationalist headquarters that afternoon. The Chinese assistants carried the injured men in while Thatcher ran to find a telegraph office and send word to Chungking (Chongqing) that all Plane Seven fliers were alive. Although in good hands, the men had no medication and no doctor, but one was on his way. Dr. Chen Shenyan owned a hospital in Linhai with his father and received word to come to the headquarters to care for the fliers. While they waited for Chen to make the forty-mile trip up a rough foot trail, caretakers at the headquarters bathed the raiders and gave them clean clothes. Chen arrived in the middle of the night and immediately checked the men's wounds. By then, he noted, Lawson was falling in and out of consciousness for long periods. Local

Christian missionaries and other volunteers, at Chen's request, agreed to carry the fliers to his hospital. Lawson was placed on a real stretcher, not one rigged with ropes, and Clever, Davenport, and McClure rode in sedan chairs.[8] Conscious as he and the others were carried out of town while receiving salutes from Chinese nationalist troops, Lawson wondered "if there was ever a more grisly parade."[9]

Lawson's pain grew so severe during this final phase of rescue, which was four days after the crash, that he considered asking the porters to abandon him and continue on to save his companions. After twelve hours, the party reached Dr. Chen's facility, En-Tse Hospital, first developed as an Episcopal mission clinic. The aviators were surprised to find sanitary conditions and real beds with springs. Still, medication was minimal.[10]

Smith and his crew appeared two days later. The fact that Lawson and Davenport had survived for that long amazed Doc White. He later described the scenario as "one of the many miracles which occurred on that memorable April 18!"[11] White immediately went to work, searching the hospital for any medicines that might help. He finally found sulpha drugs but knew they needed more. He then telegraphed the nationalist government requesting them to air drop better medications and supplies.[12]

White knew an infection could cost Lawson his leg or even his life. The Japanese troops had seized the best drugs for fighting infection long before. White still had a supply of morphine that he administered to Lawson to reduce his pain and prevent him from going into shock, but he had nothing to fight off the greater danger. Over the next several days, White treated Lawson as best he could under the circumstances, including using Smith's blood in a transfusion. Without the proper antibiotics, however, White had to amputate Lawson's leg above the knee to save his life.[13]

As the injured crewmen recovered under Doc White's watch in Linhai, Smith, Thatcher, and the other three members of the TNT crew decided to move out to their new destination, Chiang Kai-shek's temporary capital of Chungking. For the next few weeks, as Thatcher remembered, the five men spent long days walking along trails "on the levees through rice paddies." Sometimes, the fliers met young people who associated them with American sports. One day a teenage basketball team challenged Smith's group of five to a friendly game. The footsore Americans "didn't score many points," Thatcher recalled. He did remember that the "very polite" onlookers "cheered when we did score, but kept quiet when their own team scored."[14] Days later, word reached another Doolittle crew through the grapevine that Smith's squad had entered a Chinese village and been beaten. The other crew was relieved to learn the news meant a defeat on the basketball court.[15]

While the raiders tried to stay invisible to the Japanese occupiers, in an ironic twist, the Chinese population publicly celebrated their presence. Every village, it seemed, wanted to honor the Americans with banquets. In one photograph taken on their journey, Smith and his crew are seated on a high platform surrounded by Chinese citizens, including children, at a send-off from a village. A banner proclaims, "Farewell, brave American Aviator!"[16]

When the *Hornet* departed San Francisco Bay with Smith and the raiders earlier that April, seven other ships accompanied the carrier for defensive and refueling purposes. The entire armada, named Task Force 16.2, needed to stay on high alert as it hit the open Pacific. The Japanese navy and army continued to show their dominance in the world's biggest body of water, producing unwelcomed news in the United States. On the West Coast, for instance, a Japanese submarine shelled an oil refinery near Santa Barbara, California, in February 1942, causing panic in the Golden State. Americans also received grim updates from the Philippine Islands. On 9 April, American troops and their allies surrendered the Bataan Peninsula, where Smith's South Dakota State College friend and recent Congressional Medal of Honor recipient, Bill Bianchi, was taken captive. Bianchi survived the forced Bataan Death March but would remain a prisoner of the Japanese the rest of his short life. In this environment, Americans craved some positive headlines.[17]

Shortly after passing the mouth of San Francisco Bay, Doolittle finally divulged the specifics of the mission to his raiders. The crews would take part in the first offensive against Japan, bombing industrial and military sites at Tokyo, Yokohama, Nagoya, Osaka, and Kobe. "I guess I should have started worrying when we got the big picture but I had full confidence in the boss," wrote J. Royden Stork, Plane Ten's copilot. "He had that knack of giving everyone confidence in their own abilities and [convinced us] that we could all perform as he wanted us to."[18] The *Hornet*'s skipper, Captain Marc Mitscher, announced the plan to his crew over the carrier's loudspeaker, and they immediately broke into cheers. Now knowing the significance of their endeavor improved the relationship between army and navy personnel as their excitement over the prospect of avenging Pearl Harbor overwhelmed any rivalry. In the open Pacific about ten days after their departure, eight ships from Hawaii, known as Task Force 16.1, joined the *Hornet*'s group. The overall commander of the mission, Vice Admiral William ("Bull") Halsey, arrived with the new ships, including the flagship carrier USS *Enterprise*.[19]

For the next fifteen days before the raid, the personnel of Task Force 16.2 regularly conducted battle-station drills. The raiders went step-by-step through their takeoff procedures but did not start the engines. They also performed additional daily inspections on their Mitchells. First, they would ensure that the planes were securely lashed to the *Hornet*'s deck. The carrier had been designed for smaller aircraft, and the B-25s took up most of the deck space, with some of the planes partially hanging over the ship's sides. Then, to ensure the bombers stayed in flying shape, the raiders performed engine and mechanical systems checks on each plane. Harsh winds, corrosive sea air, and occasional pounding rains could affect hydraulic systems, brakes, and batteries. Although the flight engineers could make minor repairs, they did not have the facilities to remedy most major engine breakdowns. Under that scenario, the disabled B-25 would go into the Pacific, opening premium deck space. The abandoned plane's squad would then take on backup and support roles, something they all wished to avoid.[20]

The *TNT* crew faced that possibility one morning when Smith's engineer, Edward Saylor, thought he detected a catastrophic problem in the right engine. During a regular startup, a blower in the motor appeared to fail. Further inspection revealed that part of an engine gear had broken off, the equivalent of transmission failure in a car. Saylor, with Smith's and Doolittle's endorsement, decided to attempt a fix. He had never made this type of repair, let alone one on a rolling sea exposed to winds topping thirty miles an hour. The navy had installed machine shops meant for smaller fighter planes below deck, but the B-25's size prevented them from moving it there. They could, however, remove the one-ton engine and haul it below. Some of the navy crew assembled a tripod with a chain that lifted and moved the motor off the wing and onto an elevator. Although Saylor received plenty of help to move the engine, he was on his own to take care of the repair.[21]

Saylor carefully packed away the nuts and bolts that secured the engine to the wing and went below to take the engine apart. The machine shop fabricated the replacement parts, which Saylor then assembled. The process, he later remarked, "was just a matter of using your head, taking it apart and putting it back together again, getting everything just right."[22] After transporting the motor back to the flight deck, Saylor reattached it with the carefully organized nuts and bolts. Smith then jumped into the pilot's chair to test Saylor's work. To their relief, the big engine roared to life on the first try. They would find out if it would hold in flight during the raid on Japan.[23]

The preparations of Smith and the other raiders went beyond taking care of their Mitchells. The gunners continued their target practice on kites flown behind the *Hornet*. Various lectures also took place daily. Doc White prepared a series of talks for the airmen about possible health concerns if they did not reach Chuchow. Among other hazards, he warned them to watch out for a widespread and potent agricultural fertilizer in China called "night soil." Chinese farmers liberally spread night soil, a polite term for human waste, in rice paddies and on other crops to facilitate growth. Unlike local populations that had built up immunities to the bacteria and human-borne viruses in night soil, the fliers were susceptible to infections if they ingested it or absorbed it through open cuts.[24]

Another address reminded the airmen of the political realities across China that could affect their mission. Since the beginning of the war in 1937, Japanese troops occupied much of coastal China and would be the most prominent threat to the men's safety after the raid. To ensure the existence of his own regime, Chiang Kai-shek had moved his capital a thousand miles inland to Chungking. The United States recognized Chiang's Nationalist China, also called Free China, as the country's legitimate government rather than the regime of the Chinese Communist Party, which had independent control over some parts of the nation. Although the nationalists and communists maintained an uneasy truce while fighting the Japanese, the two factions rarely communicated with each other, creating another possible problem for any downed squad.[25]

On the ground, the men could also face difficulty distinguishing friend from foe. At times, local puppet authorities that existed under a tenuous agreement with the Japanese looked like the nationalist or communist-led units of the local Chinese government. Japanese occupiers granted authority to the puppet governments to handle day-to-day matters but retained control over larger issues. Countless bands of guerrillas claiming they were resistance fighters against the Japanese roamed the countryside as well. When encountering them, the raiders would have to question whether the bands were merely bandits, or if they were enforcers for a puppet government obliged to turn the Americans over to the Japanese. In any case, Smith and his fellow raiders would have to negotiate this environment as they moved through China.[26]

Navy officers also covered land navigation and Japanese and Chinese geography and ideology in their lectures. One officer's talk on what military intelligence knew about Japanese torture techniques became especially pertinent to the army fliers. Some of the raiders had decided to grow out their facial hair to try to look more masculine. The officer warned that their beards gave torturers a tried and true technique, that of plucking hairs one by one from tender facial skin. The information appeared to have little effect on the beard fad, however. In fact, the navy lecturers had trouble believing that Doolittle's men took their presentations seriously. While they did listen, many of the eighty men who would fly in the mission preoccupied themselves with the dangerous kangaroo takeoffs.[27]

The crews certainly took their meetings with Doolittle more seriously. Using the maps Thomas Griffin and David Jones had selected from the War Department, he let the squads choose the city they wished to hit and prioritize the targets within them. Smith's crew picked Kobe. Some of the squads following Doolittle to Tokyo initially toyed with bombing the Imperial Palace, but the commander immediately nixed the idea. Doolittle explained that the palace was not only a seat of government but a holy shrine. Any attack on it threatened to turn the conflict into a holy war, increasing the already strong resolve of the Japanese. Doolittle later called his decision to quash any talk of hitting the palace as one of the most important of his career.[28]

Only days before the raid, when the *Hornet* crossed the International Date Line, Doolittle lifted the ban on letter writing. Smith immediately took the chance to scrawl a note to his parents, careful to avoid anything the army's censors would black out. He informed them, "We have been authorized to write letters, as long as we are careful what we say, and if the censors pass it." Without giving away too much detail, he wrote, "I was lucky enough to get into San Antonio one night on the way" and had "told Marie the next time she wrote you, she could mention I had been there. We are still on the move, so I cannot give you any address where you might write me, but just as soon as possible I will write you again and give you my address." He then mentioned he had been promoted to first lieutenant prior to departing for the mission, which he believed would take "a little longer" than the original two-month time frame. After suggesting it could take longer than usual for the correspondence to reach Belle Fourche, he commented, "I wrote Marie a note too, and just wanted to let you know everything was all right here. Having a lot of new experiences to tell you about when I get back. Will close for now, and until you hear from me again, don't worry about me."[29]

The day after Smith wrote his letter, 16 April 1942, army and navy personnel came together to take part in an unusual ceremony on the *Hornet*'s deck. Having linked up with Task Force 16.1 two days earlier, Admiral Halsey delivered some souvenirs to the army fliers for their upcoming mission. After the Pearl Harbor attack, three navy veterans sent the secretary of the navy commemorative medals they had accepted from the Japanese government as part of a United States Navy visit to Tokyo in 1908.[30] They requested that the navy return their tokens to Tokyo "via bomb."[31] As the crews looked on, Doolittle attached the medals to a bomb, and some men stepped forward to chalk messages on the weapon. "You'll get a BANG out of this," one message read.[32]

Though the raiders were ready for the mission, Doolittle could only assume Chiang's forces stood ready at Chuchow airfield as well. Chuchow represented the brass ring, the exclamation point at the end of an almost impossible story, where the crews would refuel and escape Japanese territory before returning home. Doolittle's assumption, however, was wrong. Chiang Kai-shek regretted his earlier indications of support for the raid and begged for more time, suggesting a delay until May. By then, he argued, his soldiers could regain control in regions where Japanese troops might spearhead retaliatory action.[33]

For Doolittle and his raiders, Chiang's request came too late. As the *Hornet* approached the Japanese islands, Doolittle and his sixteen crews planned for a night raid on 19 April, but circumstances could change the desired takeoff time. After a smooth departure from San Francisco, it appeared they would reach their optimal launch position, four hundred miles from Japan, on Saturday, 18 April. Doolittle planned to take off that afternoon and hit Tokyo in the early evening. He hoped his strikes would ignite fires to illuminate the next round of targets for the raiders who followed. They were to launch around sunset, bomb their targets, and land at Chuchow in morning daylight on 19 April.[34]

Everything changed early on 18 April. On that rainy morning, between six hundred and six hundred fifty miles from Japan, the American ships spotted the Japanese trawler and destroyed it. Though the fleet had reacted quickly, those in charge feared the trawler's crew had already radioed in their position, putting both the mission and the armada at risk. Halsey wanted to protect his fleet and move out of the area as soon as possible. He had no choice but to order the B-25s to launch immediately.[35] Soon afterward, a voice echoed over the *Hornet*'s loudspeakers, "Army pilots, man your planes."[36]

After their months of training, Doolittle's men could get moving and into their airplanes almost without thinking, but the early takeoffs weighed on their minds. Japan was now six hundred miles away instead of four hundred, creating a strong possibility that all of the Mitchells would run out of fuel short of Chuchow.[37]

Thousands of eyes watched as the planes were positioned for takeoff. Lieutenant Hank Miller, the raiders' navy flight instructor, set up a blackboard near the point where the pilots would rev their engines immediately prior to launch and told them to look at the board for final instructions. After the bombers settled into position, Doolittle's plane rolled down the deck. The pilots in the following Mitchells watched with anticipation. They recalled thinking if Doolittle failed, they had no chance to get off the carrier. At 8:20 A.M. ship time, Doolittle glanced at Miller's board and then at navy Lieutenant Edgar Osborne, who signaled when the *Hornet*'s bow was best positioned for takeoff. To the relief of the observing raiders, Hank Potter recalled, "Takeoff was easy."[38] The lead plane cleared the deck with plenty of room to spare. Doolittle brought the landing gear and wing flaps up, banked to the left, and flew back over the *Hornet*, allowing Potter to synchronize the compass.[39]

Plane Two, piloted by Lieutenant Travis Hoover, gave Miller a scare.

Hoover kept the nose up too long, and the B-25 appeared to stall, sinking a bit just as it cleared the deck. Hoover recovered, but Miller wanted to avoid a repeat performance. He scrawled on the blackboard: "STABILIZER IN NEUTRAL."[40] B-25 stabilizers were adjustable tail surfaces, providing longitudinal and directional control, but when set they could make it difficult for a pilot to notice his plane sinking.[41]

Another South Dakotan, journalist Robert J. Casey, observed the takeoffs from aboard the *Enterprise*. A decorated World War I veteran from Beresford, Casey made a career of asking tough questions and crafting sharp observations in his writing. In the 1930s, he investigated Chicago's criminal gangs for the *Chicago Daily News*. He then covered both theaters of World War II for the newspaper. In addition to his reporting, he wrote features and books about the Black Hills. He had no knowledge of the role the Black Hills native Don Smith played on 18 April 1942. Whereas navy personnel from the *Hornet*'s task force knew about the mission, those on the accompanying vessels were left in the dark. Instead, the weather had Casey's attention that morning. "Went on deck to face the howling wind," he noted. "Sky gray. Sea pitching. . . . Water is rolling down the decks, sometimes a couple feet deep. It's hard keeping upright." Casey's curiosity rose when he saw the bombardment of the fishing boat and the "considerable activity aloft"—fighter planes flying off the *Enterprise* and B-25s off the *Hornet*. "I don't know what that proves except that an airplane will actually fly in this soup," he marveled. "I wouldn't have believed it."[42]

While the other fourteen bombers after Plane Two had smooth departures, a few mishaps occurred as the raiders got into position. A large wave hit the *Hornet*, and the sudden movement slammed the tail section of Plane Fourteen, piloted by John Hilger, into the nose of Smith's plane. The impact cracked a plexiglass piece in the *TNT*'s nose, damage that could possibly have put them out of action. A quick check, however, revealed the crack was not severe enough to hamper flight.[43] About fifty minutes after Doolittle's takeoff, it was Smith's turn. He received the signal to start and turned up his engine power, but the plane would not budge. Smith immediately "checked again to make sure the brakes were off, which they were." When he looked out to the tires, he found the problem. "The men had not removed the blocks away from the wheels," he recalled. Alerted to the problem, seamen hustled to move the blocks.[44]

Once the plane could move, Smith reported, "it took about three more minutes to taxi from my parking position to the takeoff posture. The carrier was rolling heavily and I could only advance as the bow dipped down and the water broke over it." Twice Smith got the signal from Osborne to increase the throttle to takeoff power. The first time he had to ease the twin motors back because, he explained, "The ship was listing too heavily, but on the second try, I received the signal to go."[45] The blast of air from Smith's launch probably contributed to navy seaman Robert Wall slipping on the wet deck and falling into one of Plane Sixteen's spinning propellers, an accident that cost Wall his left arm.[46]

In less than three hundred feet, Smith and his companions were airborne. Within a few minutes, the *TNT* caught up with Hilger's Plane Fourteen, destined for the city of Nagoya, also west of Tokyo, and flew off its wing for just over six hours, passing first over ocean and then well-cultivated lands south of Tokyo. For the entire trip, the pilots and copilots reset engine throttles and propeller pitch to adjust to less weight as the engines consumed the fuel. Other crew members poured gasoline into auxiliary tanks from the reserve five-gallon cans packed in with them. In a sign of the times, some of the fliers smoked cigars and cigarettes even while handling the fuel.[47]

After Hilger broke away toward his target, Smith stayed close to the southern coast, usually flying at a hundred feet or so. The only opposition the *TNT* encountered came in the form of four little boys who threw rocks at the plane. The fact that they moved unchallenged toward their target surprised the five fliers. They guessed that Doolittle had first struck Tokyo over an hour earlier, and they expected the attack to set off alarms to defend the skies. Smith and his crew watched for possible threats but only saw a passenger airliner bound for Tokyo fly above them. Smith reported, "We didn't bother him. He didn't bother us. But we heard him reporting sighting an enemy plane."[48] Still, no defenders scrambled to intercept the Mitchell. Trains and streetcars ran as usual below. The *TNT* zipped past colorful boats, almost touching the masts.[49]

As they approached their target, Smith pulled the plane up sharply to climb over the hills outside Kobe and get into attack position. He flew over the industrial city of Osaka, where thick smoke rose from factories and briefly reduced visibility. Twenty miles beyond the smoky city sat Kobe on the north shore of Osaka Bay, 260 miles southwest of

Tokyo. For ninety-one years, the port at Kobe had been vital to Japan's international trade. The city was also long known for a religious shrine and a hot springs resort. While having connections to Japan's ancient history, modern Kobe was not laid out until 1889, about the time of Belle Fourche's founding. In the twentieth century, Kobe prospered, attracting ever-evolving industries and claiming a population of one million in 1942.[50]

From two thousand feet, Smith's men spotted the landmark Koshien Stadium, home to one of Japan's first professional baseball teams, where Babe Ruth and Lou Gehrig's New York Yankees played an exhibition game in 1934.[51] "Everything looked very much as the objective folder had shown," Smith noted in his mission report.[52] Howard Sessler pointed out the steel foundries that marked the initial targets for their bombing run. Once Smith spotted the landmark, he lined up his plane. The bomb bay doors gaped open just as they flew at 240 miles per hour over the steelworks, and Sessler dropped four incendiary explosives, aiming for the Uyenoshite Steelworks, Kowasaki Dockyard Company, Electric Machinery Works, and Kowasaki airplane factory. Some confusion occurred as Smith sped on because a red light on his instrument panel indicating the payload had dropped never lit up. Sessler assured him that all the bombs were on their way. The *TNT*'s targets stood in the middle of residential neighborhoods, and those homes took the brunt of the attack. One person was killed and five injured, while twenty-one homes were destroyed and fourteen damaged. In the days following the raid, the Japanese claimed that the *TNT* crew had bombed a hospital but gave no supporting evidence. Just as the bombs hit, Kobe's defenses awoke. Smith dropped his Mitchell to an altitude just above the bay's waters and roared off toward China.[53]

At sea a couple of hours later, Robert Casey joined the navy officers from the *Enterprise* who clustered around a radio to listen to a Japanese report. He recalled the voice exclaiming that "bombs had been dropped on numerous nonmilitary objectives. Children had been killed. Temples had been blasted. . . . And all the customary indignation." Still having no knowledge of Doolittle's mission, Casey was left "wondering if our journey up here might have been synchronized to this raid for some purpose."[54]

Fog, rain, and nightfall challenged Smith as he piloted the B-25 toward China. As he approached the coast, his engine power suddenly seemed compromised, convincing him the plane would not get over the coastal mountains to land at Chuchow. With the beach on Tantou Island in sight, Smith announced to the crew, "Brace yourselves. I'm going to set her down in the water."[55]

He did so perfectly at about eighty-five miles per hour. The airplane's tail gently glided into the choppy sea first, then, with the smallest of jolts, the nose. By the time the plane hit the water, the four crewmembers had donned life vests. Smith quickly pulled his vest on just as water began filling the cockpit through a crack the impact from the landing had made in the nose window. White scrambled to gather his medical equipment while Smith grabbed an inflatable raft. Climbing out of the top hatch, Smith pulled the raft's inflation ring as he entered the water. Saylor, Sessler, and Williams were already in the water, the plane's landing lights illuminating the area. They began calling for White, who emerged gripping his equipment not long before the plane began going down nose first, taking the light with it. In the dark, the men heard hissing and realized a wing flap had penetrated their raft. Without a way to make a repair, the five men could only hope the tear was small. The dinghy stayed afloat, but the loss of air on one side made it unbalanced, causing it to capsize three times. Sessler, believing the deflating raft could not hold the weight of all five men, began swimming to shore a few hundred yards away.[56]

Smith, Saylor, Williams, and White took turns pushing the raft, briefly climbing back in to rest. After two hours, they crawled onto the beach, worn out and cold as a shrill wind pierced their flight uniforms. They began calling for Sessler but heard no reply. After a few minutes, they walked up a steep bank and saw a light in the distance. They made their way toward it, not knowing whether they might encounter potential friends or established enemies. Finally, they laid down in a relatively dry goat pen that offered protection from the wind. Soon after, fisherman Ma Liagshui emerged from his home nearby.[57]

Like Smith, Doolittle ran low on fuel as he approached China earlier that evening. Still, he took pride in the success of his carburetor strategy. He had been airborne thirteen hours, he wrote, and "still had enough gas for half hour flight." More important, he had dropped the first bombs on the Japanese homeland, hitting a highly flammable industrial section of Tokyo. After the bombs fell, Doolittle reported anti-aircraft fire as "very active but only one near hit." Hank Potter, he stated, "plotted a perfect course to pass north of Yaki Shima," where the crew spotted "three large naval vessels just before passing west end of Japan."[58] From their low altitude, the men could see another potential danger in the water: sharks. Doolittle later recalled that he "didn't think ditching among them would be very appealing."[59]

Upon reaching the Chinese coast, Doolittle tried to radio the Chuchow airfield but received no answer. None of the B-25s would reach Chuchow that night. Potter guessed that Doolittle's plane came closest, getting within sixty miles. Not that getting to Chuchow would have done any good. Had any of the raiders made it, they would have found the landing field unlit and unprepared to help them.[60]

Unaware of the situation, Potter believed he had Plane One right on course for Chuchow as it crossed Mig Po Bay. Even with Potter's confidence, Doolittle began looking for landmarks. Overcast skies complicated matters, so Doolittle dropped lower. "By the time we got down," Potter reported, "either the clouds hid the lights or they were turned out by the residents, thinking an air raid was coming." Having no way to see where they were going, Doolittle and the crew were "basically lost and ended up bailing out around 9:30 pm."[61] Doolittle pulled the plane up to eight thousand feet, and he and the crew jumped from the bottom hatch. As they fell through the darkness, they could only guess what waited for them below. Landing in Japanese-occupied China would be their worst scenario. Coming down in communist-held territory or landing amongst bandit groups could also turn out poorly. Their best hope was that they had bailed out over territory that Chiang's nationalists still controlled.[62]

Potter jumped second and Doolittle last. As he neared the ground, he brought his knees up to lessen the possibility of breaking bones in his feet and ankles, which were weak because of injuries dating back to his motorcycle wreck as a Los Angeles teenager. Doolittle's landing was soft, into a mushy rice paddy thick with the dreaded night soil. Luckily, rain fell as he pulled himself out of the paddy, washing away some of the filth. After a short walk, he came across a farmhouse and knocked while stating in Mandarin that he was American, but he got no answer. Doolittle then started down a small lane searching for any shelter to protect him from the cold wind and rain. Coming upon a crate propped on two sawhorses, he climbed in, only to discover that he had just clambered into a coffin and was now closely acquainted with a deceased elderly man. More bothersome for Doolittle was the fact the casket did little to block the wind. Still freezing, the commander climbed out and continued down the lane until he found shelter in a watermill. Although out of the rain and wind, he had no source of heat and spent the sleepless night doing calisthenics to increase his blood flow. In the morning, he met a farmer and drew a picture to communicate his desire to find a railroad. Instead, the farmer led him to Nationalist China military authorities loyal to Chiang.[63]

All of Doolittle's crew—Potter, copilot Richard Cole, bombardier Fred Braemer, and engineer-gunner Paul Leonard—survived their jumps. Potter hit the ground hard and injured an ankle but could still walk. Early in the morning, he limped through a village and spotted an elderly woman who appeared to be praying. Potter remembered that he decided to walk on "by her because, frankly, I didn't know her as Japanese, Chinese, or what." Other people appeared, including a small child who tugged at Potter, "and when I couldn't talk to them it made it even worse." Indeed, Chinese phrases the raiders learned aboard the *Hornet* were in a dialect few of the locals understood. Eventually, Potter came across Braemer, also trudging along, and the pair ended up being "followed and under the control of five people with guns for a while."[64] The five seized both men's weapons and army identification. Suddenly, a young Chinese man, a teacher who spoke English, appeared. Potter never forgot this savior who talked to him and told the captors that they should gently escort the Americans to a nearby government building.[65]

There, all five Plane One fliers were reunited in good health. While his crewmen were making their ways to the building, skeptical nationalist officers interrogated Doolittle. He had alarmed the officers when he refused to surrender his .45 caliber pistol upon arriving. To ease the tension, Doolittle led one officer and some of his soldiers to the spot where he had landed after bailing out. When the troops found his parachute in the farmhouse he had first approached the night before, they began scouring the countryside to help find the other American airmen. They also took Doolittle and Paul Leonard to the site where their B-25 had crashed on a hill eight miles away. The commander surveyed the wreckage from what he considered at the time a failed mission, believing he may have lost sixteen B-25s just when his country needed them most. Doolittle predicted the raid would garner him a court-martial and time in the United States Disciplinary Barracks at Fort Leavenworth.[66]

Worse yet, for all Doolittle knew, most of his men were dead or captives of the Japanese. He eventually learned that three raiders died on 18 April. Nine of the crews bailed out over China, and all but one man, Leland Faktor, engineer/gunner from Plane Three, survived their jumps. Faktor died either due to a parachute malfunction or from hitting the plane when he bailed out. Griffin experienced the easiest jump of the night out of Plane Nine. After feeling twigs slapping his face as he approached the ground, he landed gently on his feet with his parachute hung up in a tree. He unbuckled and walked away. "You have to live right to have a landing like that," he noted years later.[67] Like Smith's *TNT*, four other planes crash landed. Plane Six came down in coastal waters, and its engineer/gunner and its bombardier, Donald Fitzmaurice and William Dieter, both drowned. The other three crewmen made it to shore where the Japanese captured them. The five airmen from Plane Sixteen also ended up as Japanese prisoners, an outcome Doolittle had warned might be worse than death.[68]

One of the crews had an easier time that night. Plane Eight's pilot Edward J. ("Ski") York and his crew—far from seeking shelter in an unknown land or shivering in wet clothes after a water landing—dined on caviar, meat, cheese, and black bread, washing it all down with vodka. They had landed at a Russian military post near Vladivostok, Siberia, where Soviet officers and airmen gave them a friendly but confused greeting. The Soviets were naturally curious about what a United States Army bomber was doing in Siberia. After some hesitation the Americans told the truth, or at least part of it. They said they had just bombed Japan, a common enemy of the two nations. York's crew did not reveal, however, that they had taken off from the *Hornet*. The Soviets congratulated them on their successful strike, and more vodka flowed. While the Americans appreciated the hospitality, they let their hosts know that they really needed fuel to fly for a rendezvous with their commander and the mission's other fliers, not vodka. The groups would discuss the fuel situation later, the Russians replied. The five went to bed intoxicated and optimistic they could head to China the next day.[69]

They awoke to a much different situation. Word of their landing quickly reached the Kremlin. Joseph Stalin, fearing that any news about American fliers landing in his country would trigger Japanese repercussions, communicated with the American ambassador to the Soviet Union, William Standley, hoping the two nations could keep Plane Eight's landing quiet. In a later meeting between the two, Stalin denounced the actions of York and his squad, declaring they had broken international law when they flew to Siberia without permission, and interned the five men. Although Standley understood Stalin's position, he disagreed with his decision and immediately used diplomatic channels to try to smuggle the raiders out of the Soviet Union, but with little luck.[70]

News of the raid quickly began to circulate internationally. At first, Japanese propaganda spread false reports that the American attack purposely targeted civilians and that Japanese gunners exacted revenge by shooting down eleven of the bombers. The disheartening story reached York's crew through the Russians, who had seized their Mitchell and pilfered all the crew's candy and cigarettes. The American fliers began to fear they, too, would remain in the Soviets' possession for the duration of the war. They also did not know that Doolittle considered their landing a grave error that could both endanger the Soviets and damage United States relations with Stalin's government.[71]

Back in China, Doolittle's newly won friends in Chiang's army began searching for the fifty-nine raiders who were alive and free in the country. All of them would need help from Chinese soldiers and civilians to evade Japan's occupation soldiers while finding their ways to Chungking, their new destination after Japanese forces overwhelmed Chuchow airfield. When reunited with the boss, the surviving crew members from all but one of the planes could report hitting their targets. Plane Four, having experienced electrical problems and leaky fuel tanks, had to jettison its bombs into Tokyo Bay to escape tailing Japanese fighters. In the coming days, the United States would finally have the first good news coming from the War in the Pacific.[72]

Dressed in his Boy Scout uniform, a young Don Smith poses with his mother, Laura Smith, around 1930. *Tri-State Museum*

Smith treats his dog Mugs to ice cream during a family outing in Spearfish Canyon. *Tri-State Museum*

Smith appears here in 1936, the year he graduated from Belle Fourche High School. *Tri-State Museum*

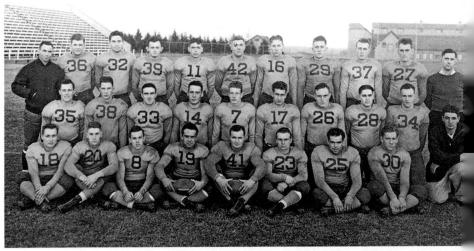

In this undated photograph of a South Dakota State College football team, Smith appears at center right wearing number 26. *Tri-State Museum*

During his senior year at South Dakota State College in 1939, Smith started at center and was named to the Associated Press Little All-America Honorable Mention Team. *Tri-State Museum*

Nicknamed the Taj, the central building at Randolph Air Force Base housed administration offices. The tower encloses the base water tower. *Air Force Historical Research Agency*

The Doolittle Raiders strapped their B-25 Mitchells to the deck of the
USS *Hornet* to prevent them from falling overboard. Smith's plane, the *TNT*,
is second to last in line. The USS *Nashville* sails in the background.
U.S. Naval History and Heritage Command

Aboard the *Hornet*, Lieutenant Colonel Jimmy Doolittle ties a Japanese
medal given to a navy veteran in 1908 to one of the bombs destined for Tokyo.
National Archives

One of the Doolittle Raiders prepares to launch his B-25 on the morning of
18 April 1942. *National Archives*

Hornet crew members watch as a raider becomes airborne over choppy seas. *National Archives*

A photographer on an accompanying ship captured the takeoff of the B-25 at right. At left, some of the bombers' tails hang off the rear of the carrier, illustrating the limited space on deck. *National Archives*

Local Chinese civilian and military leaders in Sanmen County, Zhejiang Province, honored Smith and the *TNT* crew with a farewell ceremony. Seated at front center, from left, are Edward J. Saylor, Thomas R. ("Doc") White, Don Smith, Griffith Williams, and Howard Sessler. *ww2db.com*

The other Doolittle Raiders experienced crowds like the one that gathered in Sanmen County to see Smith and his aviators. *ww2db.com*

Smith and his parents, Laura and A. W. ("Doc") Smith, take in the Black Hills Roundup from their seats in the grandstand on 4 July 1942. *Tri-State Museum*

Prior to the roundup festivities, Smith was honored as one of the Doolittle Raiders. *Tri-State Museum*

In this portrait, Smith wears the Distinguished Flying Cross and the Chinese Medal of the Armed Forces A-1 Class awarded for his role in the Doolittle Raid. *Tri-State Museum*

Smith flew a B-26 Marauder like this one during his final stint with the
Army Air Corps. *pwencycl.kgbudge.com*

The day Smith's crew reached the Chinese mainland, President Franklin D. Roosevelt met with reporters at the White House to confirm the attack on Japan three days earlier. Roosevelt also wanted to address the false rumors spread by Japanese propagandists. When asked where the bombers had started their mission, Roosevelt quipped that they had taken off "from our new secret base at Shangri-La," referencing a fictional land high in the Himalayas from James Hilton's 1933 novel *Lost Horizon*.[1] The president's Shangri-La remark had more bite to it than simple off-the-cuff banter with reporters. He also meant to create confusion and concern among Japanese leaders. While they worked on determining how medium-sized bombers had invaded Japan's skies, they would have to be on the alert for another attack from Shangri-La. *Time*, with a nod to the CBS radio quiz show, *Take It or Leave It*, noted Japan would have to "sweat over the $64 question: Where did they come from and where did they go?"[2]

In China, the route for Smith's men continually changed as their guides learned of Japanese movements that made certain towns dangerous. Hank Potter provided a description of the myriad ways the raiders made it through and out of China: "We walked, went on rickshaws, sedan chair, rode a horse, went on a boat on the river, some sort of a car, a so-called bus which was a truck we sat on, a train and finally a C-47 airplane at Chungking."[3] Smith, with Edward Saylor, Howard Sessler, Griffith Williams, and David Thatcher, slogged around rice paddies, through bamboo forests, and into villages that first felt small but stretched for miles.[4]

They also heard of the atrocities that followed them as Japanese troops stormed into villages suspected of aiding the American fliers. Anyone found with American souvenirs—coins the men distributed to children and other friends, for example—faced immediate execution. Sometimes, the Japanese troops wiped out entire villages. In other instances, they released biological weapons, spreading diseases such as anthrax and cholera. The news distressed the raiders terribly, but it also strengthened their resolve to contribute to the destruction of Prime Minister Hideki Tojo's government.[5] The raiders, including Smith's crew, continued to receive Chinese assistance despite the dangers of Japanese retaliation.

Even with help from the locals, Smith's men faced numerous threats in the course of their journey. In the city of Heng-yeng, the squad experienced a full-fledged air raid as Japanese bombers pounded the town for three days. The Americans took cover in an unassuming pagoda on a hillside to try to stay out of harm's way. Soon after the men left, Japanese planes returned and targeted the pagoda with bombs and machine-gun fire. This turn of events must have left Smith's crew wondering whether someone in Heng-yeng had turned informer, perhaps striking a deal to spare the city in exchange for the American aviators' whereabouts.[6]

After almost a month spent crossing the Chinese countryside, Smith's crew reached Chungking in mid-May. The massive city, with a population in the millions, sat above the Jialing and Chang Jiang rivers. Steep streets climbed from the old city's position on a rocky ridge to the capital's newer sections. Here, Smith and his companions met or learned the fate of the other crews.[7]

By time they arrived, Doolittle had already departed China, having been ordered back to Washington, D.C. Instead of facing a court-martial as he had feared, he was hailed as a hero and promoted to brigadier general. Shortly after hearing the news about their commander, Smith's group boarded a C-47 for India, far away from the threat of Japanese soldiers.[8]

On 21 May, from the War Department in Washington, D.C., Doolittle wrote a letter to Dr. A. W. Smith to notify him of his son's status. "I am pleased to report that Donald is well and happy although a bit homesick," the newly minted brigadier general wrote. After informing Doc Smith that Don had participated in "a very hazardous, extremely important and most interesting flight and the air raid on Japan," he noted that Don had "comported himself with conspicuous bravery and distinction. He was awarded the Distinguished Flying Cross for gallantry in action," Doolittle continued, "and was also decorated by the Chinese Government." Due to extremely poor "transportation and communication facilities" in the region, he told Doc Smith, "It may be some time before you hear again from Donald directly." He would, however, "probably be returning home sometime in the not too distant future." Doolittle concluded that he was "proud to have served with Donald, and hope that I may have an opportunity to serve with him again."[9] Once Smith arrived in India, the Air Corps likely put him back into a plane as soon as possible to get him comfortable with flying again after his crash landing in China. For the next three weeks, he ferried aircraft to regional hot spots from Karachi, a stopover point where the Air Corps prepared the machines for combat.[10]

While hindsight makes India seem far removed from military action in the Pacific in 1942, the subcontinent could easily have become a war zone that spring and summer had the raid failed. Prior to that April, Japanese officers had begun planning an invasion of India, believing the nation would give Japan a strategic advantage in the South Pacific and Indian Ocean. They needed, however, to consider carefully the possible outcomes. On the one hand, a growing undercurrent of resentment against British rule could draw popular support for overthrowing the government and make it a simple operation. On the other hand, the Indian population could see an invasion as an attack against them as well, boosting support for the British. The unpredictability left few in favor of a quick offensive.[11]

Smith and the other raiders caused Japanese leaders to shelve the Indian discussions as they searched for the source of the attack on their homeland. Anxious to avoid another such assault, Japan's military looked to expand its already extensive empire to create a protective barrier. At the edge of this imaginary line lay tiny Midway Atoll, a mere speck in the Pacific where the United States had airstrips and had started constructing a submarine base. Some Japanese military officials believed Midway was Roosevelt's "Shangri-La." Recognizing its strategic importance, Admiral Isoroku Yamamoto, architect of the attack on Pearl Harbor, planned a trap that he believed would put the aircraft carriers that had escaped his grand assault the previous December out of commission and finally destroy the Pacific Fleet. He wanted to lure the three carriers, the *Hornet*, *Enterprise*, and *Yorktown*, to Midway and then attack with two battleships, four aircraft carriers, twelve destroyers, three cruisers, and 248 carrier-based planes before the United States was prepared. A Japanese victory at Midway, Tokyo believed, could force the United States to surrender the Pacific, handing Japan control of territories as distant from one another as Alaska and India.[12]

While Yamamoto and his fleet prepared their assault, the United States Navy created a ruse of its own. The United States had intercepted and broken a series of sloppily coded Japanese radio communications —something Germany had warned its ally about previously—that laid out Japan's entire battle plan. With that information in hand, naval operators sent out a false radio message concerning a water-supply problem at the atoll that was designed to lure the enemy into position while the Americans were at a supposed disadvantage. Meanwhile, the navy sent an armada consisting of the three carriers with 233 Douglas Devastator dive bombers and Douglas Dauntless torpedo bombers as well as fifteen destroyers, eight cruisers, and sixteen submarines to join the 127 land-based planes already at Midway.[13] "If we can sink a couple battleships and four carriers," journalist Robert Casey wrote, "the sea road to Tokyo is open, and to dominate the Pacific we won't need much more equipment than what we happen to have on hand. Of course, the dice may not roll that way. But somehow optimism has replaced the casual gloom of yesterday's outlook."[14]

The battle began when American scouting planes first spotted the Japanese fleet about six hundred miles southwest of the atoll late on 3 June 1942. Early the next morning, after the American bombers from Midway failed to inflict any damage, the Japanese carriers launched their bombers, which hit the Midway airfield. The Japanese, however, remained unaware that the American aircraft carriers were approaching. By midday, the *Hornet* was in the thick of the battle, and another South Dakotan, Lieutenant Commander John C. Waldron, would fly a single-engine fighter off the same deck Smith had used seven weeks earlier.[15]

Born in Fort Pierre in 1900, Waldron was Oglala Lakota on his mother's side. He possessed remarkable aviation instincts, graduated from the United States Naval Academy in 1924, and made time to study law. The navy recognized his skill as a natural leader and placed him in command of Torpedo Squadron Eight in 1941. The squadron flew the outdated Douglas Devastators, which the navy loaded onto the *Hornet* shortly after the Doolittle Raid.[16]

Aboard the *Hornet* on 3 June, Waldron saw a contact report indicating Japanese carriers to the northwest of their position. He wrote up a plan for his squadron to attack the next morning, but Captain Marc Mitscher, the carrier's commander, opposed it, instead wanting Waldron's squad to find the Japanese support carriers he believed were approaching from the west. The hard-headed Waldron defied the orders, and he and his fifteen Devastators veered northwest toward the known position of the Japanese carriers. As the Americans approached, the carriers launched their Mitsubishi Zero fighter planes, which quickly outclassed the Devastators. They shot down all but one of Waldron's squad. None of his planes registered a single hit, and Waldron's men, except for George Gay, died. In the end, only four out of a total of forty-one Devastators launched from the *Hornet* survived the battle.[17]

Despite the heavy losses, the American attack forced the Zeros out of position while the Japanese ships changed course, leaving an opening for the first strike from the quicker, more agile Douglas Dauntlesses. Over the next three days, the Dauntless squadrons hammered the Japanese vessels. By the battle's end on 7 June, the United States Navy had destroyed four of the six Japanese carriers, all of their airplanes, and one destroyer. The United States, in comparison, lost the *Yorktown*, one destroyer, and 150 planes. More than 3,000 Japanese personnel died as opposed to 307 Americans.[18]

Although the war continued for three long, bloody years after Midway, the fight marked a turning point in the Pacific. The United States Navy and Marine Corps used the victory as an offensive springboard. Starting in August 1942, they hopped from island to island in their approach to the Japanese home island. The Japanese also lost most of their best pilots, turning air superiority in favor of the United States, and the defeat at Midway strained Japan's industrial production beyond its breaking point. The nation had difficulty replacing the planes lost in the battle and built only two more carriers during the remainder of the war. Meanwhile, the United States increased its airplane production and manufactured another seventeen carriers between 1942 and 1945.[19]

In time, Midway became known as the battle that marked the passing of the era of battleships and introduced aircraft carriers as the vessels central to naval warfare. In its aftermath, Casey wrote incredulously about how the great ocean battle had been won from the air. As much as anything, the Doolittle Raid, by prompting the Japanese to change priorities in the Pacific, set up the history-altering clash.[20]

The day the Battle of Midway ended, Smith boarded a Boeing C-75 Stratoliner for his trip home. Having arrived in India about three weeks after Smith, John Hilger, Doc White, and C. Ross Greening, who enjoyed the satisfaction of knowing his twenty-cent bombsight had exceeded all expectations, joined him, along with the recovered fliers from the *Ruptured Duck*. Ted Lawson, still in immense pain and minus his left leg, was carried aboard as well. All of them had miraculously escaped the Japanese squads ransacking the Chinese countryside after having left the hospital in Linhai.[21]

From India, the plane flew west over the Middle East and landed at a base in Egypt, where Smith visited the Great Pyramid and Great Sphinx of Giza. During the layover, he and his companions picked up the 1 June 1942 issue of *Life*. Though it featured movie star Hedy Lamarr on the cover, war news and photography—the magazine's specialty during World War II—dominated the inside pages. On page twenty-nine, they saw a full-page image of Brigadier General Doolittle at the White House, with President Roosevelt pinning the Congressional Medal of Honor on his uniform while Doolittle's wife Josephine and General Arnold looked on.[22] The facing page featured portraits of twenty other raiders, including Smith, with an accompanying article that began, "Here are the faces of Americans who bombed Japan." The twenty rectangular portraits resembled a collection of baseball cards. Of Smith's companions in Egypt, Lawson, Hilger, and Greening also appeared in the layout. For the first time, Smith and the other men understood the true impact of their mission for Americans at home.[23]

The essay provided a succinct description of their commander's actions that April day. Doolittle had "swooped astonishingly down out of the Far Eastern skies at the head of his volunteer squadron and spread destruction along a 40 mile swath in the very heart of the remote island empire." The author also noted, "Where these fliers came from and how they returned from their perilous mission are secrets known only to few in the U.S. High Command."[24] Doolittle used some hyperbole to enhance the tale of heroism for the American public. *Life* quoted him as saying that he had flown low enough to read the expressions on the faces of Tokyo residents. When asked to describe that expression, Doolittle replied, "It was one, I should say, of intense surprise."[25]

In South Dakota, future senator George S. McGovern, then a student at Dakota Wesleyan College, took special interest in news coverage of the Doolittle Raid as he prepared to enter the Army Air Corps. "Before it was Japan hitting us," McGovern said of the raid. "It was imperative that we strike back." When full details became public, McGovern expressed amazement: "I didn't believe twin engine planes could take off from a ship's deck, and I thought it was miraculous. It was such a bold plan. I don't think anyone but Americans would have tried it." McGovern eventually piloted the four-engine B-17 Flying Fortress in the war's final year, taking part in thirty-five bombing runs.[26]

From Egypt, the Stratoliner flew to Nigeria, where Smith briefly reunited with his raider copilot and navigator/bombardier, Griffith Williams and Howard Sessler, who were both assigned there. The group then continued to the African Gold Coast and across the Atlantic to Brazil and then Puerto Rico, eventually landing at Bolling Field in Washington, D.C. There, in a ceremony on 27 June, General Arnold presented the Distinguished Flying Cross to Smith and twenty-four other raiders.[27]

Granted two weeks leave after the ceremony, Smith expected to spend most of it in San Antonio with his pregnant wife, but first he planned to visit his parents. Many other Belle Fourche residents, some old friends and classmates as well as strangers, hoped to see him to express their admiration and affection. The situation was awkward for a man well-practiced in avoiding the spotlight, especially when thousands of other South Dakotans were also fighting, but Smith would shake every hand, thank his well-wishers, and answer every question he could without revealing any military secrets.[28]

Before heading home, he stopped in his former college town of Brookings. During a talk at the Dudley Hotel, he told the members of the Brookings Rotary Club, "You see a lot of the world on a trip like that." He also mentioned that he had become well acquainted with General Doolittle, who was aboard Smith's plane during the final equipment check prior to the raid. His mission on 18 April, Smith explained, "was to pilot our plane over Kobe, Japan, one of the largest airplane manufacturing centers, so that the other four fellows in the plane could deliver presents to the Japs." When asked about the whereabouts of Shangri-La, which the press now called "the mythical point of embarkation," Smith described it simply as "very beautiful."[29]

In the student union at South Dakota State, a group of students presented him with a sharp kitchen knife so he could carve his name into the cafeteria wall. After visiting former professors and other friends, he boarded an overnight train to Rapid City, arriving early on the morning of 2 July. His parents and two members of a Welcome Home Committee that the Belle Fourche Commercial Club had set up greeted him. After the five arrived in Belle Fourche, Smith had a couple of hours to greet his dog Mugs and wash up before a luncheon at the Don Pratt Hotel. His mother, Laura, spoke first. She urged those present to remember "other mothers whose sons are giving valiant service to our country and for whose safe return home we are all praying."[30]

Lon Newell of the Welcome Home Committee then formally introduced Smith. As he walked forward, a writer for the *Daily Belle Fourche Post* noticed that Smith had changed. Although his outward appearance, minus some of his "ruddy complexion," had remained the same, the writer observed that his eyes reflected the "look of a man who has seen what war can do, the eyes of a man who will carry on till the job is done." Once Smith stood in front of the crowd, he related the few details of the raid he was allowed to discuss. He compared it to "the old sleeper play in football. We caught them napping and got away with it." Before reaching his target, Smith recalled for the audience, his crew faced "the stiffest resistance we had," the children who threw rocks at the *TNT*. He also described how his crew "spread a path of incendiaries 300 feet across those factories." With the mission accomplished, "we nosed the ship down, headed for water and Shangri-La."[31] Finally, Smith addressed the Japanese propaganda that claimed he and his crew had bombed a hospital. If they had, he quipped, it was "the first hospital where airplanes came out of it," referencing Kobe's prominence as an airplane manufacturing center.[32]

Smith's homecoming coincided with the roundup rodeo, and organizers decided to make it a war benefit, just like the original rodeo in 1918. Because so many men were away fighting, there were fewer competitive cowboys to make the summer circuit throughout the West. To compensate, coordinators streamlined the event from the traditional three days to one and emphasized "home-grown" competitors. The change did not hurt attendance, for observers spotted cars from as far away as California, Texas, and Indiana. As the attendees settled into the grandstand, the out-of-staters had no idea that one of "Jimmy Doolittle's boys" was joining them. As soon as Smith strode into the arena in his dress uniform, the crowd broke into thunderous applause. After he took a seat with his parents, a photographer captured him watching the rodeo action through aviator sunglasses.[33]

If the Pendleton rodeo had disappointed Smith a year earlier because it lacked a clown and trick roping, Belle Fourche had those departments well covered. Like many of the competitors, the clown was home-grown and got the crowd laughing with a miniature pony as his sidekick. An expert trick roper drove in from Lame Deer, Montana, and members of the Belle Fourche High School band demonstrated some rope twirling of their own. During a break between contests, roundup chairman W. F. Thomas introduced Smith to the appreciative crowd of four thousand.[34] On Sunday, 5 July, he boarded a bus bound for Denver and Lowry Air Base. Although his stay was short, he made sure to let his parents know he "really had a great time at home, even though we were going most of the time."[35]

By the time Smith headed toward Colorado, he likely knew that his next overseas assignments would be in Europe and North Africa, joining the fight against Nazi Germany and Italy. Before deploying, he would train with the B-26 Martin Marauder, a medium bomber similar to the B-25 in some respects. Those prospects, however, paled in comparison to what could happen in Texas at any moment: the birth of a son or daughter. The bus trip was the first leg in a race to reach Marie in time. Once he got to Lowry, Don hoped to find an open seat on a flight to Randolph Air Base, but first he would have to wait a day. Even then there was no guarantee he could get on. Wanting to reach San Antonio as quickly as possible, Don climbed aboard another bus instead. On 6 July, as he bounced across the plains of Colorado, Oklahoma, or Texas, Marie gave birth to a healthy girl.[36]

Don arrived the following day and rushed to the hospital. He then wired his parents with the news of their new granddaughter, mistakenly telling them that the baby's name was Dianna Marie Smith. He corrected himself in a follow-up letter. The little girl was Donna Marie, named after her parents. Not only was she "the biggest baby in the hospital, . . . fat as a pig and so good humored," she was also the cutest.[37]

Almost immediately an avalanche of baby gifts began pouring in to the new parents, many from Belle Fourche. Don took note of each gift so he could eventually acknowledge them all. In the middle of everything else happening in his world, he wrote his mother to ask about the real name of a Mrs. Roberts's husband, widely known by a nickname: "I didn't believe it would be correct to say babe."[38]

The Air Corps granted Don a few weeks of temporary duty at Kelly Field. Marie and Donna Marie stayed in the hospital for several days, and then Marie's parents welcomed the three Smiths into their home. Don relished the time he spent with his wife and daughter, including "helping with the housework." All the while, he prepared for his new assignment with the 439th Bomb Squadron, part of the 319th Bomb Group. Before service overseas, he would once again train rigorously in the skies over Louisiana and other southeastern states. While taking part in his own training, Don would also instruct newly minted pilots.[39] He would do all this drilling as Captain Smith, a promotion that made him proud. He found humor in being addressed with his new rank, telling his friends not to mistake him for the Captain Smith of Pocahontas lore and having telephone operators identify him as Captain Smith in his long-distance calls to Marie.[40]

By late July, the new captain resided at Barksdale Air Field in Louisiana. "We are whipping a new squadron together," he wrote. "I am the second ranking officer, and there are only three of us with much experience at all." The other pilots were "fresh out of training school."[41] Smith's workdays usually started at 7:30 A.M. and continued until 6:00 P.M. On the occasions when he participated in a night flight, he could expect to return to quarters some time after 11:00 P.M.[42]

In August, the squadron moved to Harding Field in Louisiana, and Don arranged for an apartment nearby so Marie and the baby could join him. Marie booked a Pullman berth, and the mother and daughter arrived to find Don even busier than he had been at Barksdale, often leaving the apartment at 6:00 A.M. and returning at midnight. The long days did not matter to Don, who simply enjoyed having his little family "all together again."[43]

On 21 August, shortly after Marie and Donna reached Louisiana, two airplanes from Harding Field had fatal crashes, reflecting the ever-present dangers of flying even outside of combat. Don wired his parents as soon as he could, so they would not "worry as [the Air Corps] didn't put the names in the paper, and I imagine it went all over the country." When the news broke, he explained, "Everyone was calling their sons all day long."[44]

By the time the crashes occurred, Marie's mother had arrived to help her daughter prepare for a move back to Texas, as word had come that Don's squadron could expect to deploy overseas at any time. Marie had been in Louisiana for just a couple of weeks and found it "very hard to have to give Don up again for a while." Still, she wrote it was "wonderful" to spend as much time as possible with him and was "thankful Don was able to be home for a while and see his little daughter." Marie noted that Donna "does not look like an infant anymore. She is a little miniature of her Daddy. . . . I am so happy I will have the baby to keep me company while Don is away."[45]

On 29 August, Marie, her mother, and the baby left for San Antonio. Over the next few weeks, Don waited for his new deployment, which was not as imminent as everyone thought. Instead of battling Nazis, he swatted Louisiana mosquitoes "as big as day old chicks, and once they find you they give you little peace."[46] Well into September, he and the other officers continued to shape the squadron. "It seems like the more promotion you get the more is expected of you," he noted. In typical understated fashion, he mentioned that "I have sort of taken over the responsibilities of the operations officer," such as managing runways and acting as a liaison between crews and officers.[47]

Smith was not the only South Dakotan stationed in the Deep South. He always enjoyed encountering others from his home state and hearing stories of friends and familiar places. He met an engineering officer who had graduated in his class from South Dakota State and wrote, "We have a lot of fun talking over old times, and keeping track of the rest of the boys from school."[48] It was one of South Dakota's United States senators, however, who attracted the most attention on the southern bases that summer, although there is no indication Smith crossed paths with him.

Senator John Chandler ("Chan") Gurney from Yankton supposed that he logged seven thousand miles driving from army base to army base through the South and then back to South Dakota during the summer of 1942. He had a dual purpose for doing so. First, he visited his two sons, Lieutenant Deloss Gurney and Staff Sergeant John Gurney, who had both enlisted in the Air Corps. Second, he used the opportunity to gather the opinions of both civilians and military personnel about a key question floating around the halls of Congress: Should the government amend the Selective Service Act and draft younger men, ages eighteen and nineteen? Secretary of War Henry Stimson argued it had to happen, but most senators and representatives wanted to avoid the matter until after the November elections. Following his trip, Gurney urged Congress to take the bold step of approving the amendment so that it could be implemented in short order. On his travels, he learned that "the American people want to win the war in the shortest possible fashion and will do what it takes to accomplish that."[49] Along with Representative James Wadsworth of New York, Gurney stood as the congressional leader in amending the draft policy.

Meanwhile, Smith continued to fly maneuvers in the new B-26 bomber. He mailed his parents a photograph of a B-26, explaining an easy way to differentiate it from the B-25. "They only have one tail," he explained, "where the B-25 had two tails, that is the main way you can tell them apart."[50] Up close, other differences stood out even for casual observers. The B-26, produced by the Martin Aviation Company of Baltimore, had multiple nicknames, including "the Rolls Royce of combat planes." Its interior incorporated more modern features, such as the use of plastic and electronic gadgetry. The airplane's exterior looked smooth, thanks to the use of larger aluminum plates with fewer rivets holding them in place than on the B-25. Additionally, the process of baking, or heating the plates to eliminate any wrinkles in the metal, smoothed out the skin to increase top speed. The plane appeared sleek and mighty, with two massive three-blade propellers, powered by twin Pratt and Whitney engines, that nearly touched the runway. To the company's owner Frederick Martin, appearance mattered; so did glowing press releases, one of which dubbed the B-26 the "Marauder."[51]

Air Corps brass loved the new bomber from the beginning. In fact, Doolittle most likely would have recommended the B-26 for the raid had it been capable of kangaroo takeoffs. The B-26 first flew in November 1940 and quickly proved it would fulfill the Army Air Corps' request for a bomber capable of speeds topping 300 miles per hour. The first plane off the assembly line hit 323 miles per hour while showing off its capacity for heavy bomb and fuel loads. Impressed with the display, the Air Corps initially ordered about 140 planes and established a B-26 bomb group in California and a training school at MacDill Field in Florida.[52]

The pilots of the new bomber had a different take on the plane, as design problems appeared immediately. The short sixty-five-foot wingspan combined with its power to make it difficult to handle, especially when landing. Pilots hit the runway at more than one hundred miles per hour, similar to modern fighter jets, to avoid the plane's stalling speed of ninety miles an hour. The tricky landings caused several fatal crashes in the bomber's early days, including taking the life of the Air Corps' representative to Martin, Lieutenant Colonel Elmer D. Perrin. Further, without a balanced cargo, the B-26 could be nose-heavy. At times, the mighty engines spun the propellers at different speeds, which could cause the bomber to go into a spin and dive if the pilot did not correct it quickly enough. The plane's difficulties and crash record led Air Corps fliers to think up another nickname: the Martin Murderer. So many B-26s crashed off Florida's west coast that the mantra "one a day in Tampa Bay" echoed throughout the corps. Records show that about one crash a week was more accurate but still far from acceptable.[53]

Not all those who flew the B-26 disliked the aircraft, however. Doolittle himself tested the Marauder early on and approved of its capabilities despite its being "unforgiving" of pilot error.[54] In a move Frederick Martin's public relations team certainly appreciated, one Women's Air Service Pilot (WASP), Jacqueline Cochrane, called the men who feared the B-26 "sissies" after having a chance to test it out.[55] She eventually volunteered her WASP squadron to deliver new Marauders to Air Corps bases, to the shock of many of the male pilots who considered the bomber unflyable.[56]

It took an astute pilot to feel entirely comfortable in the early version of the plane, a fact that forced General Arnold to question keeping the B-26 in the Air Corps. He believed practice would lead to competence but still appointed a board to determine whether to drop the Marauder. The board endorsed keeping the plane with modifications, while Arnold and Doolittle pushed to implement an extensive training program for the novice Air Corps fliers who were climbing into the Marauders' cockpits.[57] Martin began their modifications immediately. The next generation of the plane had six feet added to the wingspan and more powerful but consistent engines. Despite its rough start, the B-26 eventually made key contributions to the Allied war effort, beginning with the Twenty-second Bomb Group's operations out of New Guinea, which commenced the same month Smith and the raiders struck Japan.[58]

While training in the Southeast, Smith heard the news that Rapid City, on the eastern edge of the Black Hills, had won an army air base. He hoped to fly there sometime but saw little chance of that happening before his European tour. In September, he asked his parents about the progress of construction on what would later be named Ellsworth Air Force Base. It had just become operational. The crews there, including the 398th Bomb Group that eventually served under Doolittle late in the war, trained to fly the mighty four-motored B-17.[59]

The bombing range that Smith had earlier envisioned for placement on land north of Belle Fourche never materialized. Rather, the federal government proclaimed eminent domain over three hundred thousand acres east of the base, taking a large portion of the Pine Ridge Indian Reservation. Landowners were told to leave and received payments that they considered less than the property's value as grazing land.[60] To this day, scattered pieces of tin mark the remnants of the World War II-era "dummy bombs," two-foot-long shells filled with sand and used for training. Although not explosive, they could still cause significant damage. During one exercise, a "bomb" crashed through a church roof in the town of Interior after a flight navigator apparently miscalculated his plane's position—something that was easy to do on the vast and sometimes featureless Great Plains.[61]

More dangerous, though, were the .30-caliber machine gun and tracer bullets employed for gunner training. Some bursts of aerial shooting sparked grass fires below. After the war, the federal government warned that the possibility of live shells made the land unfit for grazing or human habitation. As a result, it offered the South Dakota National Guard use of the land for gunnery training for much of the Cold War. Eventually, the army transferred some acreage to the Department of the Interior for the south unit of Badlands National Park. Three decades after World War II, during a period of increased awareness about tribal sovereignty, a few members of displaced families were able to buy back their lands.[62]

That fall, Smith's squadron moved north to Baer Field in Indiana, the first step in their deployment to England. He wrote on 25 September 1942 that an autumn chill in the Indiana air let the group know that "winter is coming." He also wished they could stay "long enough to go up to South Bend and see a good football game," but he knew the assignment at Baer would be brief. The season always made Smith nostalgic for home. He lamented not being able to have a family Thanksgiving in 1942 but held out hope for the following year's holiday. At the same time, he worried that his long absence would cause Mugs to forget him.[63]

One day later, 26 September, his squadron landed in England, and several weeks passed before he could get any of his mail from home. In fact, receiving any news from the United States was difficult. About a month after landing in England, he did learn about one personally disappointing event. Having grown up a New York Yankees fan, Smith had been able to celebrate eight World Series victories since the age of nine. But in October 1942, the Yankees fell to the Saint Louis Cardinals in five games. "Guess the old Cards were just too fast for them," Smith mused. In the same letter, he implied that sports might be one of the few topics he could cover in his future communications, as his mail would be censored. Because of the limit on how much he could say, he would have to save "all the good news" for his parents "until I get back again."[64]

Six days earlier, three of the captured raiders wrote heartrending letters to their family and friends telling them they would not return home. In late August 1942, all eight raiders held in Japanese-occupied China had received death sentences after Japanese officers held a mock trial. By the middle of October, only Lieutenant Dean Hallmark, pilot of Plane Six, and Lieutenant Bill Farrow and Sergeant Harold Spatz, pilot and engineer/gunner of Plane Sixteen, had not had their sentences reduced to life in prison. No one has ever determined why these three were chosen for execution.[65] The captured men themselves struggled to find an answer. "I can hardly believe it," Hallmark wrote his mother about his imminent execution. "I did everything that the Japanese have asked me to do and tried to cooperate with them because I knew my part in the war was over." Farrow asked his mother to remember that "God will make everything right, and that I will see you again in the hereafter." Spatz sent his father his love, wished him God's blessing, and assured him he "died fighting for my country like a soldier."[66]

Late in the afternoon of 15 October, Japanese guards drove the condemned men to a cemetery outside Shanghai where three small wooden crosses had been erected. Each man knelt with his back to a cross, and his arms were lashed to the beams. Blindfolds covered the men's eyes. The Japanese then placed black smudges on the Americans' foreheads as targets for the executioners. From twenty feet away, the riflemen aimed and fired. The three raiders died instantly.[67]

Eleven days later, the United States lost another player in the Doolittle Raid—the *Hornet*. During the Battle of Santa Cruz, coordinated attacks from Japanese bombers and torpedo planes severely damaged the aircraft carrier. Even after the thirty-five-minute onslaught, the ship remained afloat, but without power or communications, the crew had abandoned it. Vice Admiral Halsey tried to tow the *Hornet* to safety but decided to scuttle the vessel as enemy ships approached and it sank into the Pacific's depths. One hundred thirty-three crewmen died in its final battle, only one year and six days into its service.[68]

Just before the loss of the *Hornet*, on 23 October, Smith wrote his parents an unusually melancholy letter:

> Dear Folks;
>
> Another short note, just in case the other letter didn't arrive yet, or will be delayed and I wanted you all to know everything is going well for your Son. Haven't been able to receive any mail yet, but expect to in a few days, so from Marie's letters you will know better than I how your Grand Daughter is growing.
>
> Wish we could all be together for Thanksgiving, but guess we will have to wait until next year after we have settled everything with Adolph + Co.
>
> Have they started calling married men from around home, like Harry + Kennedy? Suppose I wouldn't know the old town, most of the old gang in the Army, or out on the coast working in plane factories.
>
> Not much more news, will close for now, when you write, let me know how everything is at home. Slide Mugs across the dining room floor once for me.
>
> As ever, your loving Son.
> Don.[69]

It was the last the Smiths heard from Don. News of the airplane crash that claimed his life reached Marie first in San Antonio early on Sunday, 15 November 1942. She then immediately contacted her in-laws.[70]

Tom Griffin believed he was the last man on the ground to see Smith alive, having driven him and his crew to the plane on 12 November. Griffin recalled that Smith's squad was executing a routine flight in a B-26 over the English countryside that day. He speculated, "They hit bad weather, or something else went wrong."[71] Whatever the problem, it caused the Marauder to crash near London, claiming the lives of Smith and his crew.[72] Griffin had lost a friend he fondly remembered as "a South Dakota boy, a wonderful man, a wonderful father."[73] No one associated with Smith during the last half of 1942 could miss the fact that he was a doting dad.

Four months after joyfully covering Smith's homecoming, the *Belle Fourche Bee* reported his death on 19 November, although the entire town already knew. "In a short period of time," the obituary read, "he had gone from our midst as a youth, attained his education in the flying corps and made for himself a world wide reputation for initiative, gallantry and devotion of duty."[74] That same day, South Dakotans gathered at the Belle Fourche High School auditorium for a memorial service, as the Air Corps had initially interred Smith's body in an American military cemetery in England. Reverend Harry Blunt of the Congregational Church recalled Smith's boyhood in Belle Fourche, and C. L. Carter of the American Legion reviewed his army career. The service closed with the playing of "Taps."[75]

The day after the memorial service, South Dakota Congressman Francis Case wrote the Smiths from Washington, D.C., expressing the sentiments of many: "I doubt if you will realize how much the people of South Dakota, generally, will feel a share in the loss which has come in the death of your son, who has given his life for his Country and for the freedom of people everywhere." He continued, "I say that because in this office when the word came, it was received as no similar news since the war began." Although neither he nor any of his staff had met Don, "each of us thought he belonged to all of us."[76]

Friends who had attended the memorial observed that Don's death seemed to overwhelm his father. The stress, most likely, became too much for Doc Smith to bear. About a month after Don's fatal crash, his father suffered a stroke that paralyzed him. He died shortly afterward on Christmas Eve.[77]

Smith was gone, but the war raged on for another three years. Even after his untimely death, Smith continued to have an indirect influence on the conflict when the squadron he helped "whip together" with the rest of the 319th Bombardment Group began making low-altitude strikes in North Africa on 28 November 1942. They mostly targeted the German and Italian transportation infrastructure, initially taking heavy losses due to their low-altitude approaches. Once the B-26s started attacking from higher altitudes, the casualty rate dropped. Seven months after the Americans joined the Allies in North Africa, they swept the two Axis forces out of the region and secured a staging area for reaching across the Mediterranean Sea and into Italy.[1]

In the early days of the North Africa campaign, Air Corps pilots, no matter the type of plane they flew, might find Jimmy Doolittle joining them for the day's mission. Now the commander of the Twelfth Air Force, Doolittle wanted firsthand knowledge of aircraft performance and to show his men that he shared their fighting spirit. The practice ended abruptly after General Dwight D. Eisenhower, Doolittle's superior and overall commander of American forces, could not reach him because he had taken a new British Spitfire for a test flight. "I want my airmen available when I want them," an angry Eisenhower told Doolittle. "You can either be a major and fly Spitfires or you can be a major general and be my senior air officer down here." It was Eisenhower's way of telling Doolittle to stay out of the aircraft, as well as the fact that he had received a promotion.[2]

Doolittle sensed a resentment in Eisenhower that he felt elsewhere in the army as well. It seemed that other officers had pegged him as an opportunist who left the military to make money with Shell Oil only to return to grab headlines as a war hero. That resentment faded among many as the war progressed and Doolittle successfully led the Twelfth, Fifteenth, and Eighth Air Forces.[3]

Doolittle's raiders were never far from his thoughts, even in his new assignments. As the first anniversary of the attack on Japan approached, he arranged for a reunion of the raiders stationed in North Africa, and the group gathered on 18 April 1943, in what the press described as a farmhouse but what Doolittle called "an Arab's old barn." Doolittle rounded up champagne and coffee cups for himself and eight other raiders, along with a handful of the mission's support staff to toast "those who couldn't be with us because of other assignments and those who would never be with us."[4] On that first anniversary, sixty-five of the eighty raiders were alive. Of the fifteen dead, nine had been killed in combat or training crashes around the world in the months following the raid.[5]

The pragmatic Hank Potter, on one of those "other assignments," did not understand the reunion fuss when he read about it in a newspaper. After all, he thought, he and the other surviving raiders were still fighting the war. Yet, the get-together initiated what became an annual postwar tradition that extended well into the twenty-first century and included a visit to Smith's Black Hills. Goblets, each engraved with a Raider's name, eventually replaced the coffee cups. When a raider passed away, the reunion attendees turned his goblet upside down in its specially designed, portable display case, and he became one of the airmen toasted at future reunions.[6]

A year and two days after Doolittle's Raid, the War Department revealed the details of the mission to the public in a communiqué. "In practice for the great venture," the document read, "the planes in training swept in over the American coast and fanned out as they would have to do over Japan." During February and March of 1942, the fliers had traveled "exactly similar geographical distances" over the United States as they would during the raid itself. Officials decided to maintain secrecy after the mission both in the hope of getting all the crewmen home safely and as part of their larger military strategy. "As long as this secrecy could be maintained," they informed the public, the Japanese would not be able to pin down where the planes had originated and would be "obliged to set up defenses against a number of possibilities." By causing paranoia in Japan, that nation could not "know when the attack might be repeated," forcing it to "tie up part of their military strength during crucial months."[7]

With the truth exposed, the War Department knew that Americans would crave literary and dramatic interpretations of the mission. Officials hoped to exert some control over such accounts, especially the portrayal of the Chinese who assisted the raiders. While the many Chinese citizens who helped the squads at great risk to themselves were central to the story, military leaders feared renewed Japanese retaliation against China if Japan's leaders believed the Chinese government was tied to any aspect of the raid.[8]

Despite these concerns, entertainment companies moved quickly. By the end of 1943, Metro-Goldwyn-Mayer (MGM) Studios had a movie in the works, *Thirty Seconds over Tokyo*, based on Ted Lawson's book of the same title. The movie focused mainly on Lawson's life and his role in the raid, but the War Department urged MGM to remember also "the heroic exploits of the Army Air Force as a whole in relation to the 'Tokyo Raid.'"[9]

The studio tapped Mervin LeRoy, who had helped produce *The Wizard of Oz* in 1939, as the director and cast Spencer Tracy as Jimmy Doolittle, Van Johnson as Ted Lawson, and Bill Phillips as Don Smith. Metro-Goldwyn-Mayer gained permission to shoot some of the scenes at Eglin Base in Florida and built an interior set, big enough to hold three real B-25s, to represent the *Hornet* at its Hollywood studio. California's cities and countryside stood in for Japanese and Chinese locales, and LeRoy worked brief footage of the takeoffs from 18 April 1942 into the movie.[10]

Phillips's casting as Smith was a curious choice. Short, stout, balding, and looking every day of his thirty-six years, Phillips in no way resembled the tall, broad-shouldered Smith. He created a likeable, competent character, but one louder and more demonstrative than the real man. Had Smith lived, however, he might have been pleased to see himself portrayed as a smooth dancer at the Eglin officers' club. The movie also included a love story about Ted and Ellen Lawson's marriage that could have been transposed for Don and Marie Smith. The Lawsons, like the Smiths, married in 1941 and were expecting a baby at the time of the raid.[11]

With *Thirty Seconds over Tokyo*, LeRoy joined a list of distinguished American filmmakers who made quasi-propaganda movies that, they hoped, conveyed the American values for which the soldiers fought. From the start, these filmmakers had in mind their German counterpart, Leni Riefenstahl, and her 1935 movie *Triumph of the Will*. Considered artful in its imagery despite its racist overtones, Riefenstahl's propaganda film depicted the German people as superhumans assured of eventual world domination. Other German filmmakers pointed to American movies that failed to match the power of Riefenstahl's films as evidence, at least in this field, of German superiority.[12]

Hollywood directors such as John Ford and Frank Capra, however, rejected Riefenstahl's pageantry and overt symbolism. Instead, they emphasized the everyday Americans who had been plucked from happy lives and found themselves on the front lines, where they prevailed through grit and sacrifice. Many American filmmakers also saw power in authentic combat footage for their movies, a sharp contrast to Riefenstahl's stylized cinematography. Ford enlisted in the navy, where he filmed parts of the Battle of Midway at great personal risk. In one instance, a Japanese bomb blast knocked him down as he filmed. His resulting work, *The Battle of Midway*, won an Academy Award for best short subject documentary in 1943, perhaps due to the real-time footage. Meanwhile, Capra directed *Prelude to War*, the first in a series of popular documentaries collectively titled *Why We Fight*. To convey the threat the Axis nations posed in this initial installment, he employed archived foreign footage, including some pirated from Riefenstahl. Like Ford, Capra won an Academy Award for best documentary in 1943.[13]

Thirty Seconds over Tokyo ranked high among contemporary war movies. It premiered simultaneously in New York City and Chungking on 15 November 1944. The next day, *New York Times* film critic Bosley Crowther called the film "nigh the best yet made in Hollywood" regarding the war and lauded MGM for handling "the thrilling material with restraint and in a realistic style." He believed that the "facts were so much wilder than most fiction and the evidence of courage so plain that a less discreet treatment might have made this a stupendously distasteful film," something that would have been "most unfortunate, considering the importance of the deed." Crowther appreciated that the filmmakers were "permitted to use the actual names of the principal participants in the 'Doolittle raid,' for [the movie] is a fitting tribute to all of them."[14]

As audiences lined up to see *Thirty Seconds over Tokyo*, the war in the

Pacific raged on. After the Doolittle Raid, the Imperial Japanese Government tried to prepare the island for future assaults. They directed their prefectural governments to build public air raid shelters in the cities. Shortages of steel and concrete limited the construction efforts, leaving less than 2 percent of the population protected. Recognizing the problem, government officials encouraged individual citizens to build their own shelters, most of which were little more than trenches. Locals also attended government-sponsored firefighting instruction, to cover for the lack of fire departments in the cities, and pledged an air defense oath, promising to aid others during American raids.[15]

Starting in 1943 and increasing in 1944, the air and naval forces of the United States kept up a constant stream of air raids on Japan. Initially, the Air Corps used "carpet bombing" techniques, bombing cities indiscriminately, in both theaters of war. With their predominately wooden buildings that quickly went up in flames, Japanese cities were particularly vulnerable to these types of attacks. By 1945, some cities created firebreaks by tearing down neighborhoods, displacing more than six hundred thousand people. The exercise failed to create the cushion of protection the government intended. To reduce the number of civilian deaths, the imperial government recommended moving older people and children into the countryside.[16]

In addition to carpet bombing, the American military looked to weaponize fire to maximize the potential damage. They developed an intensely flammable, sticky gel called napalm that could be used in both flamethrowers and incendiary bombs. Shortly after Smith and his fellow raiders left Eglin Air Base in early 1942, the new substance proved destructive in several tests, especially one against a mock village the Air Corps called "Little Tokyo," constructed at Eglin with plywood, pitch pine lumber, and other materials common in Japan. The napalm ignited multiple fires that eventually consumed the entire model town and yielded new insights. Whereas conventional bombing used powerful blasts to knock down targeted buildings, napalm dropped in smaller bombs could increase destruction, as the substance would seep through building cracks and start fires that would quickly spread into wide, long-burning conflagrations. While the firebombing of Dresden, Germany, in February 1945 first illustrated the true potency of the new incendiary bombs, Japan's primarily wooden structures stood far more vulnerable.[17]

As the United States experimented with new firepower, it also developed a new bomber that bore little resemblance to either the B-25 or B-26 of Smith's time to deliver the horrific cargo. The B-29, also known as the Superfortress due to its size and massive armaments, was a four-engine bomber with a 141-foot wingspan that carried crews of twelve, compared to the five-man crews of Smith's missions, and could deliver twenty thousand pounds of explosives at a time. The airplane could reach a top speed of nearly 360 miles per hour at twenty-five thousand feet, and it had a range of about four thousand miles, initially making airfields in India or China ideal launching points. Commanders in the Pacific Theater clamored to get as many B-29s as possible, causing Boeing to rush a large number off the line.[18]

Despite its terrifying power and size, the B-29 saw only limited success in a handful of raids against Japan in mid-to-late 1944 due to a lack of pilots trained to perform at high altitudes. Initially, the Air Corps thought its ability to strike from an altitude of three miles or higher would be an advantage, but the pilots learned something in 1944 that Doolittle and his raiders never faced. Clouds obscured targets from the high-altitude positions, and strong winds could push bombs far off course. Still, the United States was determined to find a way to put B-29s and napalm to destructive effect. Doing so, officials believed, could keep the United States from committing to an Allied land invasion of Japan and almost certainly high casualties.[19]

While the United States increased the frequency of the raids in 1944 and into 1945, some B-29 pilots noticed orbs, thirty-three feet in diameter, rising into the sky during their missions that winter. The fliers initially thought they were a form of anti-aircraft defense. Yet, the objects rose high into the stratosphere where no airplane could fly. In reality, they were rice-paper balloons on their way to the North American continent. Drifting with the prevailing west-to-east jet stream, the balloons carried payloads of up to sixty-five pounds of explosives meant to cause random destruction throughout the United States. Japan launched more than six thousand balloons between November 1944 and April 1945, but the exact number of balloons that reached North America is unknown, for they typically self-destructed. Some remnants and some full balloons and gondolas were found as far north as Alaska and as far south as northern Mexico. One made it as far east as Michigan.[20]

At least eight balloons came down in South Dakota but caused no damage. One landed on the Waring family ranch thirteen miles south of Ree Heights. They immediately called the county sheriff, but he never responded, most likely thinking it was nothing more than a downed weather balloon. Weeks later, the family contacted the state attorney general's office, which investigated and took the gondola.[21] Because the federal government had requested the press not to report on the attack balloons, stories such as the Warings' rarely came out, leaving most Americans in the dark. Reporters' silence on the matter had its intended effect, frustrating Japanese agents in the United States who had been assigned to monitor news reports to determine how many attack balloons successfully crossed the Pacific.[22]

President Roosevelt's Joint Chiefs of Staff referred to this strange attack strategy as "the robot bomb threat."[23] Indeed, the gondolas housed mostly useless robotic atmospheric pressure gauges that triggered detonation functions at low altitudes. The only known fatalities from the balloons were those of a woman and five children who chanced upon a downed balloon near Bly, Oregon, on 5 May 1945. A bomb packed within the gondola exploded when one of the six touched it. Some American military leaders considered the balloon bombs so ineffective overall that they assumed the launches in 1944 and early 1945 were test runs for a deadlier onslaught. One theory held that the Japanese might weaponize anthrax, which they would then drop into sheep-grazing country in the western United States. Contact with infested sheep could cause rapid pulmonary fatalities in humans, a condition commonly called woolsorter's disease, rare but not unheard of in South Dakota. Even if the Japanese had developed plans for germ warfare, they likely would never have had the chance to carry them out, for American air attacks in winter 1944 and spring 1945 essentially terminated any system for such an assault.[24]

During this time, the Allies gained a significant advantage for their air raids on Japan when they captured the Mariana Islands in the summer of 1944. Now only thirteen hundred miles south of Tokyo, the American forces immediately began construction on six airfields that eventually allowed B-29s to strike the Japanese home island and return without refueling. In early 1945, General Curtis LeMay—a grim-faced, cigar-chomping aviator—took command of the army's B-29 operations against Japan just as the Mariana Island fields opened for service.[25]

Considering it his duty to pound Japan until the population realized the absurdity of continuing to fight, LeMay took some Doolittle-like actions to gear up for his strategy of unrelenting attacks. He ordered the armaments removed to reduce weight, freeing up the planes for heavier fuel and bomb loads. He offset the need for defensive weapons by planning for night raids, using darkness to cover their approach and escape, as Doolittle had originally planned. To increase the accuracy of the bombers, his pilots would attack from low altitudes—usually five to ten thousand feet rather than twenty thousand feet or higher. Like Doolittle, LeMay also instructed his fliers to steer clear of the emperor's buildings. On 25 February 1945, LeMay's squads carried out their first assault when 172 B-29s wiped out a square mile of Tokyo's industrial section with incendiary bombs. Apparently, Japanese air defenses had not improved much in the three years since the Doolittle Raid, and Japan's citizen firefighting efforts proved futile.[26]

Encouraged by his success, LeMay prepared another, larger strike on the imperial capital for the night of 9–10 March, one that would leave witnesses astounded at the level of sudden urban destruction. The night was cold and windy, sending most Tokyo residents inside and to bed earlier than usual. Few noticed the "pathfinder" B-29s that marked large target areas of Tokyo with magnesium, napalm, and phosphorus shortly after midnight. Thirty minutes later, the first wave of B-29s unleashed their payloads on the unsuspecting inhabitants. For the next three hours, 279 Superfortresses hammered the city with 1,665 tons of incendiary bombs, filling in the dark spaces between the lines the pathfinders created.[27]

The firebombing practically leveled Tokyo. War industries were severely damaged, and more than one million residents were left homeless. Almost eighty-four thousand people were killed and just over forty-eight thousand injured that night. So many people had been burned that the B-29 crews recorded gagging as the stench of burning human flesh rose into the sky. Within days, American bombers began dropping leaflets that urged the Japanese people to overthrow their government or face additional deaths. Even then, LeMay's crews did not relent. They firebombed the cities of Nagoya and Osaka only days later. Then, on the night of 16–17 March 1945, they hit Kobe, the same city Smith had targeted in 1942. The death toll at Kobe topped eight thousand, and nearly a quarter of the city burned. Throughout the spring and summer of 1945, the B-29 squadrons bombed sixty-six

Japanese cities, killing 330,000 people, injuring another 476,000, and leaving more than 8 million homeless.[28] The bombs leveled nearly 160 square miles of urban Japan, prompting Doolittle to remark that Japan could become a nation without cities and its people "nomadic" once the war ended.[29]

Still, Japan's citizenry failed to revolt as the American pamphlets urged. The government did not surrender, and the Japanese military aggressively pursued a new aviation tactic unveiled the previous fall. Pilots, many wearing replicas of the headbands Samurai warriors wore into battle in ancient Japan, deliberately crashed their planes into Allied ships in suicide missions called *kamikaze*. That desperate maneuver, combined with increasingly bloody island campaigns, such as Iwo Jima and Okinawa, indicated the extent to which the Japanese would resist an invasion of the home island.[30]

In mid-summer, an entirely new weapon emerged to save the United States from launching a land assault on Japan. Early on the morning of 16 July 1945, scientists from the Manhattan Project detonated the first atomic bomb, "possessing more power than 20,000 tons of TNT" and a force equal to "the load of 2,000 B-29s."[31] With two functioning devices remaining after the initial detonation in the White Sands area of New Mexico, the new president, Harry S Truman, authorized their use against Japan.[32]

Piloting his B-29, *Enola Gay*, Colonel Paul Tibbets flew over Hiroshima on the morning of 6 August, and bombardier Major Thomas Ferebee aimed for the Aioi Bridge in the center of the city. With a blinding flash, the bomb flattened Hiroshima. Any person caught in the city's center was vaporized. In an instant, almost eighty thousand people perished and tens of thousands more would die from radiation exposure and other injuries. Three years and four months after Doolittle's raiders made the first United States strike on the Japanese homeland, another air attack on Japan ushered in an entirely new age of warfare.[33] Smith's fellow Raider, Tom Griffin, sometimes called the attack in 1942 "a pin-prick of a raid."[34] Although historically incorrect, in comparison to the death and devastation of 1945, Griffin's statement rang true.

President Truman spoke that day, confirming the destruction of Hiroshima and the power of the new weapon. He also referenced the recently issued Potsdam Proclamation, under which the Allies assured

Japan that upon surrendering, its soldiers "after being completely disarmed[,] shall be permitted to return to their homes with the opportunity to lead peaceful and productive lives." Truman further promised that at no point would the Japanese people be "enslaved . . . or destroyed as a nation." He explained that Japanese officials had initially rejected the ultimatum meant to "spare the Japanese people from utter destruction" and went on to warn, "If they do not now accept our terms, they may expect a rain of ruin from the air the like of which has never been seen on this earth."[35]

On 9 August, the United States having received no response to Truman's ultimatum, Major Charles Sweeney piloted his B-29 named *Bockscar* toward Kokura, Japan, carrying the second atomic bomb. Finding that haze obscured the city, he continued to his second target, Nagasaki. In the blink of an eye, much of Nagasaki and approximately forty thousand people disappeared, with thousands more left to die of radiation poisoning. Even in the wake of devastation from the atomic bombs, the Air Corps continued its incendiary bombing runs for the next few days. Although he commanded the Eighth Air Force in Okinawa at the time, Doolittle decided against participating in those final raids, thinking it unreasonable to risk the lives of his men with the war effectively over. Five days after Nagasaki, on 14 August, Japan's Emperor Hirohito announced the nation's surrender. Japanese officials then signed the surrender documents on 2 September 1945 aboard the deck of the battleship USS *Missouri*, formally bringing the Second World War to a close.[36] The final terms, wrote *New York Times* reporter and analyst James Reston, reduced Japan "to little more than the territory she occupied when Commodore Perry introduced her to the western world in 1853."[37]

More than three years after the raiders' first strike, surviving American service men and women returned home. Lloyd Eaton, Smith's Belle Fourche football teammate who had been stationed in the Seattle area at the same time as Smith, was one of them. After the war, he returned to South Dakota to begin his career as a football coach, working his way from the high school to college ranks. Eaton eventually took over as head coach at the University of Wyoming and led the team to a victory in the Sun Bowl in 1966 and an appearance in the Sugar Bowl in 1968. After eight years with Wyoming, he moved up to the National Football

League where he was director of player personnel for the Green Bay Packers from 1970 through the mid-1980s. After retiring, Eaton settled in Idaho where he lived until his death in 2007.[38]

Many of Smith's fellow South Dakotans never made it home. His South Dakota State College classmate and Congressional Medal of Honor recipient, Bill Bianchi, died in the war's closing months. Having survived the Bataan Death March and three years of imprisonment, Bianchi perished while aboard an unmarked Japanese prison ship. The "hellship," as such vessels came to be known, was off the coast of Formosa when Allied bombers attacked it, unaware that it contained prisoners of war. Similarly, Smith's high school classmate, Bob McGee was a lieutenant with the army's Thirty-first Infantry who arrived in the Philippines just days before the Japanese seized the Bataan Peninsula. McGee survived the death march only to face years in prison before dying aboard a different hellship. Most likely, Bianchi, McGee, and their fellow prisoners were being transferred to be used for hard labor on the Japanese home island. Another Belle Fourche High School graduate, Frank Williams, a trumpet player in the Cowboy Band that performed annually for the Black Hills Roundup, also died in Japanese custody. Like Bianchi and McGee, he survived the Bataan Death March, but Williams never left the prison camp, dying a few weeks later. Another of Smith's classmates, Fred Stankey, perished while working for the Army Corps of Engineers.[39]

In all, at least forty-six men and women from Belle Fourche and the farm and ranch country immediately surrounding it died during World War II. Out of those forty-six, seven others in addition to Smith perished while flying for the Army Air Corps: Earl Brammer, Lon Brown, Joe Donahue, Douglas Levee, Leslie Raber, Lewis Sisson, and Frank Williams.[40]

In August 1948, Smith's body came home from England for re-interment next to his father at Pine Slope Cemetery in Belle Fourche.[41] By then, most Americans knew the story of the Doolittle Raid. At the dawn of the Cold War, the raid seemed to have acquired special significance as a model for bold action and self-sacrifice. When news spread of the fallen raider's homecoming, Smith's mother Laura received notes from across the country expressing gratitude, including one from New York City Mayor William O'Dwyer. He wrote on behalf of all New Yorkers to articulate their "heartfelt sympathy to the family of Capt. Donald G. Smith, who so honorably gave his life that others might enjoy peace and freedom. I trust and pray his sacrifice will not have been in vain."[42]

Not all the raiders had known about Smith's death, having lost touch with others during the conflict. Ed Saylor, Smith's flight engineer on *TNT*, for instance, heard the news only after the war.[43] The raiders who did survive had their own unique experiences to relate after the conflict.

The five crewmen from Plane Eight, who drew Doolittle's ire by landing in Siberia, escaped the Soviets after thirteen months of living a bizarre wartime adventure. As the Soviets slowly moved them westward across the vast nation, they forced the Americans to perform menial labor such as salvaging bolts and screws from wrecked machinery. Their imprisonment in multiple locations allowed the crew to observe the country, which copilot Robert G. Emmens described as "a nation kept in complete ignorance of world affairs, whose borders are closed to outsiders and outside things."[44] With most Soviet men away desperately fighting the Nazis, women often guarded the Americans, at least minimally. The men were typically left in tiny villages surrounded by great empty plains and had the run of the town. Indeed, the raiders even watched a 1937 Deanna Durbin musical, *One Hundred Men and a Girl*, five times in Soviet movie theaters. They paid no admission because the Russians thought them penniless.[45]

Despite that perception, pilot Ski York kept hidden a few hundred dollars he had won playing poker aboard the *Hornet*. When near the Russian-Iran border one day in May 1943, York used $250 of his winnings to buy the men the services of an Iranian smuggler, Abdul Arram, who took them into Mashhed, Iran. After sneaking past additional Soviet guards at the edge of town, they received a warm welcome at the British consulate. To Doolittle's amazement, the Soviets sent monthly bills to the United States government for the fliers' room and board prior to their escape.[46]

After the war, Shell Oil Company offered Doolittle his previous position, at a salary three times that of a general. He declined in order to take part in the establishment of the newly christened United States Air Force, now an independent branch. While remaining in his leadership position, Doolittle did his best to make certain his raiders were safe and adjusting to postwar life, even fighting with the government when needed.[47]

One specific case highlighted Doolittle's loyalty. At the war's close, Japan confirmed the executions of Bill Farrow, Dean Hallmark, and Harold Spatz in October 1942 as well as the later death of Lieutenant Robert Meder, copilot of Plane Six, from the disease beriberi, caused by malnutrition. In August 1945, American paratroopers from the Office of Strategic Services—the precursor to the Central Intelligence Agency— liberated the final four Raider prisoners: the lone survivor from Plane Six, Lieutenant Chase Nielsen, and Corporal Jacob DeShazer, Lieutenant Robert Hite, and Lieutenant George Barr of Plane Sixteen. Barr suffered severe mental trauma from his wartime experience. A native of Brooklyn, New York, Barr had enrolled in college in Wisconsin and then enlisted in the Army Air Corps to train as a navigator. He completed that training at McChord Field only weeks before Smith reported there. On 18 April 1942, Barr was navigator aboard Plane Sixteen, dubbed *Bat Out of Hell*.[48]

In a real sense, the raid proved to be a trip into hell for Barr and the rest of the crew. From the start, Barr never shook the image of seaman Robert Wall's left arm being torn off by his plane's propeller just before takeoff. Seventeen hours later, after bombing the city of Nagoya, the crew bailed out over Japanese-occupied China, near Nanchong. Japanese soldiers quickly seized Barr and the others. They proceeded to throw the eight airmen from Planes Six and Sixteen into maggot-infested jail cells, beat them, and subjected them to torture later called waterboarding. Barr believed he would drown before that torture ceased. A transfer to Japan did not improve prison conditions. His captors withheld food except for sparse rations for the next three years. When released after Japan's surrender, Barr believed it was a cruel Japanese ruse, and he panicked when separated from the other fliers for treatment.[49]

Americans assigned to treat Barr found him uncooperative and intimidating. The medical assistants ended up beating him, as well, in an ill-considered attempt to calm him. Indeed, one medical corpsman knocked Barr unconscious when he tried to run away from the airplane that would transport him back to the United States. With no records or even identification, medical personnel struggled to figure out Barr's status, and no one believed he had been a Doolittle Raider as he claimed. Mentally and physically exhausted, Barr attempted suicide at San Francisco's Letterman General Hospital. Shortly afterward, the army moved him halfway across the continent to Schick General Hospital in Clinton, Iowa, putting him in a straitjacket for the entire three-day train ride. Barr's friends located him there, lost in the veterans hospital system, and immediately contacted Doolittle.[50]

The general soon showed up in Clinton, where he listened to Barr's story beginning with the raid and going through his mistreatment in the army hospitals. He later recalled that he had "never been so angry in my life as I was when George told me what had happened to him."[51] True to character, Doolittle turned his anger into action. The infuriated general stormed to the office of the hospital's commander and demanded Barr's release. He also ordered a new uniform for the despondent man and promised him a promotion to first lieutenant. Doolittle then pushed the army to get Barr three years' back pay—more than seven thousand dollars—and arranged for him to receive proper treatment.[52]

Under psychiatric care, Barr slowly recovered. By February 1946, he had begun to put weight back on and reported fewer nightmares. He later worked as a management analyst for the army, married, and had four children. The man Doolittle considered the last raider to come home died of a heart attack at the age of fifty on 12 July 1967. Afterward, Doolittle became the Barr family's advocate in their dealings with the United States Veterans Administration. Initially, the Veterans Administration denied the family the benefits they would have received had Barr's death resulted from combat or another wartime ailment. The organization backed down, however, after Doolittle argued that Barr did indeed die because of his war experience, which had a "permanent deleterious effect, in this case on his heart."[53]

Mental health difficulties after the war affected Doolittle even more personally through his eldest son, James Doolittle, Jr. The younger Doolittle served through the war and stayed in the Air Force as a career officer while simultaneously battling depression. He eventually succumbed to the illness and took his own life in April 1958 after being passed over for a promotion.[54] The elder Doolittle observed, "Jim may have suffered personal stress all his professional life from being easily identified as my son because of his name." As a result, "there may have even been commanders senior to him who saw it as a way to get back at me for imagined injustices."[55] Doolittle struggled with the situation for the rest of his life.

Over the years, the senior Doolittle's relationship with General Eisenhower improved, and he eventually considered the future president a friend. Despite his lack of interest in becoming involved in politics, Doolittle publicly supported Eisenhower's political aspirations, endorsing him for president in 1952 and for reelection in 1956.[56]

Doolittle became a regular visitor to the White House in the four decades during and after the war, beginning with President Franklin Roosevelt's presentation of the Congressional Medal of Honor to him in 1942. Presidents Truman, Eisenhower, and John F. Kennedy appointed him to various presidential commissions and advisory boards. Ronald Reagan pinned the hardware of a four-star general on his uniform in 1985, and George H. W. Bush awarded Doolittle the Presidential Medal of Freedom in 1989.[57]

From time to time, the general also enjoyed trips to Smith's home state. An avid hunter, Doolittle joined another World War II Medal of Honor pilot and former South Dakota governor, Joe Foss, along with sportscaster Curt Gowdy and actor Robert Stack for a pheasant hunt south of Oldham, Smith's birthplace, in 1962. Gowdy hosted the ABC television series *The American Sportsman*, and the broadcasting company filmed the hunt for an early episode of the show.[58]

Then, in 1978, Doolittle and his raiders gathered in Rapid City for their annual reunion. Hank Potter, who had not seen the point of the wartime reunion, now took charge of the event planned for his and Smith's home state that April. As preparations began, the raiders took a special interest in locating Marie Smith and getting her to Don's Black Hills for the affair, which proved a difficult task. Her association with the world of the Air Corps had long since ended, and there was no listing for Marie Crouch Smith in San Antonio. Laura Smith had died in 1964, closing a likely avenue for information about her daughter-in-law and only grandchild, Donna.[59]

A break in the situation came when Hoadley Dean, a Rapid City businessman and Black Hills promoter who assisted Potter with arrangements for the event, discovered that Don had a biological sister, Dorothy Stevens, living in Miller, South Dakota. Dean took a shot, hoping Stevens had been in contact with Marie. Despite their never having met in person, Stevens had stayed in touch with Marie, who had remarried and was now Marie Zimmerman of San Antonio. After Dean contacted her, she agreed to attend the reunion with her daughter Donna, also married and living in Arlington, Texas. Both women looked forward to meeting Don's *TNT* crewmates. Having never been to South Dakota, Marie used the opportunity to visit Belle Fourche and Don's grave for the first time as well.[60]

Raider William Bower, the pilot of Plane Twelve who lived in Boulder, Colorado, transported the eighty goblets from the United States Air Force Academy in Colorado Springs to Rapid City. A local savings and loan bank put the goblets on public display for two days before they went back to the raiders for their official toast. Twenty-eight of the remaining raiders, including Doolittle, attended the Rapid City reunion, although fifty-six goblets remained upright in 1978. The group, Doolittle's copilot Richard Cole erroneously told a reporter, had not lost a member since 1964, forgetting about George Barr's death in 1967. Before the official ceremonies began, the raiders came together on Thursday evening and enjoyed some light-hearted conversation about which two would survive to make a final toast to the other seventy-eight. Doolittle, who was eighty-one at the time, joked that he expected to attend the final reunion and wondered only who the second man would be.[61]

By 1978, according to Jack Hilger, the passage of time had mellowed both the raiders and their reunions. First, most of the men had passed the age of sixty, the age Smith would have been at the time of the Rapid City event. Second, the gatherings had become family affairs, which was not the case originally. "It's mostly just seeing old friends," said Hilger. "But a lot of us talk about our grandchildren now."[62] Still, the men looked back on their mission and swapped stories about how naïve they had been in 1942. Richard Knobloch, Plane Thirteen's copilot, for example, recalled that after he bailed out over China and broke through the clouds, he spotted what he believed was a road but was actually a river. He remembered, "My first thought when I was still floating down, and I was hungry, was here's a highway, and I'd walk a few miles and find a hamburger stand. That's how much I knew about China."[63]

Doolittle, long retired from the Air Force, said he stayed active and was committed to remaining useful in his eighties. His main concession to age, he added, were hearing aids, blaming his hearing loss on years spent piloting noisy aircraft.[64] In response to one interviewer, Doolittle also discussed the difference between the B-25 and B-26. "There are forgiving airplanes and there are unforgiving airplanes," he said, sounding rather professorial. Forgiving aircraft correct a pilot's mistake, whereas unforgiving ones amplify them, he went on to clarify. In Doolittle's opinion, the B-25 was "one of the most forgiving airplanes that I ever flew." Although he considered the B-26 an excellent aircraft, he acknowledged that, due to the Marauder's unforgiving nature, it "took a good deal more training before you could handle it." In any case, he concluded with a thought similar to the sentiment Smith expressed before the raid: "I'm sure we all loved our B-25s."[65]

The raiders also batted around theories about the dark airfield at Chuchow but never came to a definitive answer. Chiang Kai-shek had spent the four years after World War II fighting Mao Zedong's communist forces in a civil war. He lost mainland China to Mao in 1949 but the next year established a government-in-exile on the island of Taiwan, formerly Formosa, where he remained president until his death in 1975. Chiang kept Taiwan free from communism and advanced economic prosperity there but was also accused of dictatorial practices.[66]

Chiang always remained somewhat suspicious of American actions after 1942, probably because of the situation with the Doolittle Raid and its aftermath. He clearly understood the potential for brutal Japanese retaliation against his people at the time. It is estimated that as many as a quarter million Chinese civilians may have been murdered in the three months following the attack on Japan. Some historians theorize that President Roosevelt also recognized the risk to China but proceeded anyway. The Chinese suffering left an ever-present cloud hanging over all the Doolittle Raider celebrations.[67]

The printed program for the 1978 reunion featured cover art Smith would have appreciated: six B-25s flying in formation over Mount Rushmore. That Friday, 28 April, Hank Potter and Hoadley Dean arranged a bus trip to the mountain carving. The raiders also received a briefing at Ellsworth Air Force Base about its mission before enjoying a private dinner. On Saturday, the men drank their toast at noon and gathered for a public banquet at the Rushmore Plaza Civic Center that night, where 540 people paid fifteen dollars each to see and honor the raiders. At the head table sat three Medal of Honor recipients—Doolittle, Foss, and South Dakotan and Vietnam War veteran Leo Thorsness.

Doolittle also made certain that another South Dakotan attended: his friend, Smith's early mentor, and aviation pioneer Clyde Ice. Governors Richard Kneip of South Dakota and Stan Hathaway of Wyoming both spoke before Doolittle addressed the crowd.[68] Doolittle told the well-wishers that he appreciated coming to places like the Black Hills rather than major cities because, "out here people are thinking not only of themselves, but also of others, and that's what makes America what it is."[69]

The Rapid City reunion caused a revival of interest in Smith throughout South Dakota, but he returned to virtual anonymity with the next generation, even those from the Black Hills. Renewed attention came during the sixtieth anniversary of the Doolittle Raid, 18 April 2002. The year prior, South Dakota governor William J. Janklow proclaimed the date a day to honor Captain Smith. Belle Fourche staged a moving tribute that spring afternoon near the banks of the Belle Fourche River. The band from Don's high school played, and the United States Air Force, American Legion, and South Dakota National Guard took part in the ceremony, which included the dedication of a memorial plaque. Both Marie and Donna were too ill to accept their invitations to the tribute. Sadly, both mother and daughter passed away soon afterward.[70]

With each passing reunion, the surviving raiders turned more of their goblets upside down. Doolittle did not live to make the last toast as he had predicted, but he came closer than might have been expected. He lived until the age of ninety-six, dying in California in September 1993. His body made one last transcontinental flight for burial at Arlington National Cemetery in Virginia.[71]

In 1942, Ted Lawson had returned to the United States still suffering from the effects of the infection in his amputated left leg. He spent much of the year convalescing in Walter Reed General Hospital in Washington, D.C., during which he wrote *Thirty Seconds over Tokyo*. Growing tired of the public eye from his book and movie, Lawson requested an overseas assignment after his release from Walter Reed in 1943 and spent the rest of the war working as a liaison officer in Chile. He left the Army Air Corps in February 1945 and held several jobs until his retirement in 1965. Lawson died on 19 January 1992, just short of the fiftieth anniversary of the raid.[72]

Hank Potter, always remembered as "Doolittle's navigator" despite his many other professional accomplishments, served stateside through the rest of World War II, then made the Air Force his career. Potter rose to the rank of colonel and retired as commander of Bergstrom Air Force Base outside Austin, Texas, in 1970. He and his wife, Adell, raised six daughters and a son and made Austin their post-retirement home. In retirement, he became involved in a nonprofit organization that restored World War II-era aircraft and joined a few of the other raiders who traveled back to China. During one of their trips in 1992, Potter was re-introduced to Zho Xuesan, the English-speaking teacher who interceded after Chinese guerrillas seized Potter and Fred Braemer the morning following the raid.[73] "To be able to meet the man who helped me so much when I was wandering and tired and cold," Potter said, "it's just amazing." He died in May 2002, shortly after the raid's sixtieth anniversary.[74]

Tom Griffin, the navigator for Plane Nine who drove Smith to his B-26 on 12 November 1942, outlived his friend by seventy years. Later in the war, Griffin was shot down over Sicily and endured two years in a German prisoner-of-war camp. When he returned to the states, he ran an accounting business in Cincinnati until retiring in 1982. He died in February 2013 at the age of ninety-six.[75] Griffin gleefully chatted with anyone interested about the raid after the war, sometimes providing humorously self-effacing accounts.

All of Smith's *TNT* crewmates lived to see the raid's fiftieth anniversary. Doc White served in North Africa and the Mediterranean later in the war, then entered private medical practice in Hawaii and California. He succumbed to pneumonia and heart disease in November 1992. Smith's copilot Griffith Williams was shot down over Europe in July 1943 and held as a prisoner of war until 29 April 1945. He left the army as a major in 1952 and called southern California his home until his death in 1998. Navigator and bombardier Howard Sessler flew combat missions over the Mediterranean and Europe until 1945, left the army as a major, and enrolled at the University of Southern California. He earned a civil engineering degree and made heavy construction his career. He passed away in February 2001, just over a year before the raid's sixtieth anniversary. Ed Saylor, who repaired the *TNT*'s engine aboard the *Hornet*, gained high marks as an airplane maintenance expert and served both stateside and overseas. He stayed in the army after the war as an aircraft maintenance officer, making the rank of lieutenant colonel. Later, he was active in real estate and construction in Washington

State, always making time to share Doolittle Raider history with students, audiences, and researchers.[76] "I never knew a better pilot," Saylor said of Smith, "or a more generous man."[77] Saylor outlived the rest of the *TNT* crew, dying at ninety-four years old in January 2015.[78]

David Thatcher, the Plane Seven gunner who joined Smith's crew on the cross-country journey out of China, flew twenty-five more World War II missions over the Mediterranean and Europe. Doolittle made certain Thatcher received the Silver Star for gallantry for keeping his crewmates alive after their crash landing. He later lived in Missoula, Montana, and worked as a postman. Always loyal to his fellow raiders, Thatcher and his wife Dawn drove to Belle Fourche in 2001 for the ceremony honoring Don Smith.[79]

Thatcher was also one of the last four surviving raiders who made the final toast in November 2013. He, Saylor, and Richard Cole came together at the National Air Force Museum in Dayton, Ohio, to open the special bottle of cognac. The fourth surviving raider, Robert Hite, was too ill to attend but joined the three via webcam. Their advanced ages made any future reunions impossible, and they made this final toast a public ceremony for others to enjoy. Hite passed away at the age of ninety-five in March 2015, and Thatcher died at the age of ninety-four in Missoula in June 2016. Cole, Doolittle's copilot and the last living raider, died on 9 April 2019 at 103 years old.[80]

Although the raiders themselves have passed on, their story shows no sign of fading. What Griffin referred to as a "pin-prick of a raid" holds a secure spot in American military lore.[81] Many men and women who grew up in the postwar years drew inspiration from the daring mission. In July 2015, for example, famed astronaut Edwin E. ("Buzz") Aldrin came to the Black Hills. The man who, with Neil Armstrong, first landed a manned craft on the moon, visited Ellsworth Air Force Base as well as many of the places Don Smith fondly remembered. During the trip, South Dakotans told Aldrin how he had inspired them forty-six years earlier. Aldrin made sure to speak of the men who inspired him, the eighty fliers who volunteered for a challenging and dangerous mission in the first year of World War II. "The Doolittle Raiders," Aldrin said. "They were my heroes."[82]

Appendix I The Crews of the Doolittle Raid

Plane No. One, AC 40-2344
Pilot: Lt. Col. James H. Doolittle
Copilot: Lt. Richard E. Cole
Navigator: Lt. Henry A. Potter
Bombardier: S. Sgt. Fred A.
    Braemer
Flight Engineer/Gunner:
    S. Sgt. Paul J. Leonard

Plane No. Two, AC 40-2292
Pilot: Lt. Travis Hoover
Copilot: Lt. William N. Fitzhugh
Navigator: Lt. Carl R. Wildner
Bombardier: Lt. Richard E. Miller
Flight Engineer/Gunner:
    S. Sgt. Douglas V. Radney

Plane No. Three, AC 40-2270
    (*Whisky Pete*)
Pilot: Lt. Robert M. Gray
Copilot: Lt. Jacob E. Manch
Navigator: Lt. Charles J. Ozuk Jr.
Bombardier: Sgt. Aden E. Jones
Flight Engineer/Gunner:
    Cpl. Leland D. Faktor

Plane No. Four, AC 40-2282
Pilot: Lt. Everett W. Holstrom
Copilot: Lt. Lucien N.
    Youngblood
Navigator: Lt. Harry C. McCool
Bombardier: Sgt. Robert J.
    Stephens
Flight Engineer/Gunner:
    Cpl. Bert M. Jordan

Plane No. Five, AC 40-2283
Pilot: Capt. David M. Jones
Copilot: Lt. Rodney R. Wilder
Navigator: Lt. Eugene F. McGurl
Bombardier: Lt. Denver V.
    Truelove
Flight Engineer/Gunner:
    Sgt. Joseph W. Manske

Plane No. Six, AC 40-2298
    (*Green Hornet*)
Pilot: Lt. Dean E. Hallmark
Copilot: Lt. Robert J. Meder
Navigator: Lt. Chase J. Nielsen
Bombardier: Sgt. William J.
    Dieter
Flight Engineer/Gunner:
    Sgt. Donald E. Fitzmaurice

Plane No. Seven, AC 40-2261
    (*Ruptured Duck*)
Pilot: Lt. Ted W. Lawson
Copilot: Lt. Dean Davenport
Navigator: Lt. Charles L. McClure
Bombardier: Lt. Robert S. Clever
Flight Engineer/Gunner:
    Cpl. David J. Thatcher

Plane No. Eight, AC 40-2242
Pilot: Capt. Edward J. York
Copilot: Lt. Robert G. Emmens
Navigator/Bombardier:
　Lt. Nolan A. Herndon
Flight Engineer:
　S. Sgt. Theodore H. Laban
Gunner: Sgt. David W. Pohl

Plane No. Nine, AC 40-2303
　(*Whirling Dervish*)
Pilot: Lt. Harold F. Watson
Copilot: Lt. James M. Parker Jr.
Navigator: Lt. Thomas C. Griffin
Bombardier: Sgt. Wayne M.
　Bissell
Flight Engineer/Gunner:
　T. Sgt. Eldred V. Scott

Plane No. Ten, AC 40-2250
Pilot: Lt. Richard O. Joyce
Copilot: Lt. J. Royden Stork
Navigator/Bombardier:
　Lt. Horace E. Crouch
Flight Engineer: S. Sgt. George E.
　Larkin Jr.
Gunner: S. Sgt. Edwin W.
　Horton Jr.

Plane No. Eleven, AC 40-2249
　(*Hari Kari-er*)
Pilot: Capt. C. Ross Greening
Copilot: Lt. Kenneth E. Reddy
Navigator: Lt. Frank A. Kappeler
Bombardier: S. Sgt. William L.
　Birch
Flight Engineer/Gunner:
　Sgt. Melvin J. Gardner

Plane No. Twelve, AC 40-2278
　(*Fickle Finger of Fate*)
Pilot: Lt. William M. Bower
Copilot: Lt. Thadd H. Blanton
Navigator: Lt. William R.
　Pound Jr.
Bombardier: T. Sgt. Waldo J.
　Bither
Flight Engineer/Gunner:
　S. Sgt. Omer A. Duquette

Plane No. Thirteen, AC 40-2247
　(*Avenger*)
Pilot: Lt. Edgar E. McElroy
Copilot: Lt. Richard A. Knobloch
Navigator: Lt. Clayton J.
　Campbell
Bombardier: Sgt. Robert C.
　Bourgeois
Flight Engineer/Gunner:
　Sgt. Adam R. Williams

Plane No. Fourteen, AC 40-2297
Pilot: Maj. John A. Hilger
Copilot: Lt. Jack A. Sims
Navigator/Bombardier:
    Lt. James H. Macia Jr.
Engineer: S. Sgt. Jacob Eierman
Gunner: S. Sgt. Edwin V. Bain

Plane No. Fifteen, AC 40-2267
    (*TNT*)
Pilot: Lt. Donald G. Smith
Copilot: Lt. Griffith P. Williams
Navigator/Bombardier:
    Lt. Howard A. Sessler
Engineer: Sgt. Edward J. Saylor
Physician/Gunner: Lt. Thomas R.
    White

Plane No. Sixteen, AC 40-2268
    (*Bat Out of Hell*)
Pilot: Lt. William G. Farrow
Copilot: Lt. Robert L. Hite
Navigator: Lt. George Barr
Bombardier: Cpl. Jacob D.
    DeShazer
Engineer/Gunner: Sgt. Harold A.
    Spatz

Appendix II Timeline

WORLD WAR II AND DON SMITH'S LIFE

Events in Don Smith's life and related to the Doolittle Raid are italicized.

15 January 1918

Donald Gregory is born to Chuck and Eva Gregory in Oldham, South Dakota.

4 July 1918

Belle Fourche, South Dakota, holds the first Black Hills Roundup to raise funds for Red Cross efforts in World War I.

July 1919

The Treaty of Versailles officially ends World War I. The "War Guilt clause" requires Germany to pay reparations to the victorious nations, creating instability in its economy and society throughout the 1920s. Japan gains former German territories in China.

Early 1920s

Cousins of Donald Gregory find him in a Sioux Falls orphanage. He becomes Donald Smith when Dr. A. W. and Laura Smith adopt him.

November 1920

The League of Nations meets for the first time but is missing a key nation: the United States.

February 1922

Britain, France, Italy, Japan, and the United States sign the Washington Naval Treaty, setting limits on the size of their navies to prevent another arms race.

9 October 1922

Benito Mussolini is appointed Prime Minister of Italy.

1927

The Smith family moves to Belle Fourche, South Dakota.

12 April 1927

Chiang Kai-shek, leader of the nationalist Kuomintang, attacks members of the Chinese Communist Party in Shanghai, initiating civil war.

29 October 1929

The Wall Street Stock Market Crash instigates the Great Depression.

Early 1930s

Smith meets aviator Clyde Ice, who probably gives Smith his first flying lesson.

18–19 September 1931

The Imperial Japanese Army occupies the province of Manchuria, creating a puppet state named Manchukuo the next spring.

Fall 1932

Smith enters Belle Fourche High School.

30 January–March 1933

Adolf Hitler is appointed chancellor of Germany. The following month, a fire breaks out in the German Reichstag, the nation's parliament building, and German officials suspend most civil liberties. The Nazi Party opens the first concentration camp, Dachau, initially used for political prisoners.

4 March 1933

Franklin Delano Roosevelt begins his first term as president of the United States.

27 March 1933

Japan leaves the League of Nations after the organization refuses to recognize Manchukuo. Hitler becomes dictator of Germany.

19 October 1933

Germany withdraws from the League of Nations citing lack of support for military parity among the members.

1933–1934

South Dakota experiences drought-caused "black blizzards," which, along with economic depression, impact A. W. Smith's veterinary practice.

29 December 1934

Japan renounces the Washington Naval Treaty.

31 August 1935

Congress passes the Neutrality Act, the first in a series of laws preventing the United States from trading materials with warring nations.

15 September–2 October 1935

The Nuremberg Laws strip German Jews of their basic rights. Italy invades Ethiopia, starting the Second Italo-Abyssinian War.

1 November–23 December 1935

Albert Stevens and Orville Anderson pilot the *Explorer II* balloon out of the Stratobowl near Rapid City. Smith launches a balloon that lands three hundred miles northeast of Belle Fourche.

7 March 1936

German forces reoccupy the Rhineland in violation of the Treaty of Versailles.

May 1936

Smith graduates from Belle Fourche High School.

Fall 1936

Smith enters South Dakota State College, where he joins the Reserve Officer Training Corps and plays junior varsity football for two years.

24 December 1936

The Kuomintang and Chinese Communists suspend civil war, uniting to form the Second United Front against the Japanese.

20 January 1937

Roosevelt begins his second term as president.

7 July 1937

Imperial Japanese Army units exchange fire with Kuomintang soldiers near Peking (Beijing). Japan invades China, starting the Second Sino-Japanese War.

August 1937–January 1938

Japanese forces defeat China at the battles of Shanghai and Nanking (Nanjing), committing atrocities during the Rape of Nanking. Italy leaves the League of Nations due to economic sanctions placed on them after invading Ethiopia.

13 March 1938–15 March 1939

Germany annexes Austria, the Sudetenland, and Czechoslovakia.

September–December 1938

Smith starts as center for South Dakota State's varsity football team.

9–10 November 1938

The Nazi Party destroys the property of Jews throughout Germany during Kristallnacht.

14 April 1939

Roosevelt sends letters to Hitler and Mussolini seeking peace.

1 September–6 October 1939

Germany conquers Poland. Britain and France declare war on

Germany. The war between Japan and China becomes part of the Pacific Theater of World War II.

September–December 1939

Smith plays his final year of college football and earns a Little All-American honorable mention.

April 1940

Nazi Germany establishes Auschwitz concentration camp in Poland, the first and largest in the system of death camps used in the Holocaust.

May 1940

Smith graduates from South Dakota State College and enters the United States Army Air Corps as a second lieutenant.

10 May–25 June 1940

Germany invades and conquers France.

26 May–4 June 1940

British, French, and Belgian troops are evacuated from Dunkirk, France.

Summer 1940

Smith begins flight training at Oxnard Airport in California.

10 June 1940–8 November 1942

German and Italian forces invade North Africa.

10 July–31 October 1940

The German and British air forces engage in the Battle of Britain.

19 August 1940

The first B-25 Mitchell takes flight.

20–27 September 1940

Japanese forces conquer French Indochina. Japan, Germany, and Italy sign the Tripartite Pact, creating the Axis Powers.

Fall–Winter 1940

Smith transfers to bomber school at Randolph Air Force Base in San Antonio, Texas.

January–26 November 1941

Imperial Japanese Navy leadership plan for a possible assault against the United States fleet at Pearl Harbor.

20 January 1941

Roosevelt begins his third term as president.

Mid-February 1941

Smith meets Marie Crouch, his future wife.

March 1941

Smith graduates from flight school at Randolph Air Force Base.

11 March 1941

Congress passes the Lend-Lease Act, authorizing the transfer of war material to American allies.

April–mid-May 1941

Smith joins the Eighty-ninth Reconnaissance Squadron at McChord Field, Camp Lewis Army Base in Tacoma, Washington. They eventually transfer to Felts Field near Spokane, Washington, for training in the B-25 Mitchell.

20 June 1941

The Army Air Corps becomes part of the newly organized Army Air Forces.

21 June 1941

Don Smith and Marie Crouch are married in Seattle.

22 June 1941–January 1944

German forces invade the Soviet Union. They eventually threaten Moscow and lay siege to Leningrad (St. Petersburg) for nine hundred days.

26 July–1 August 1941

Roosevelt orders the seizure of all Japanese assets in the United States and places an oil embargo on the Axis, eliminating 80 percent of Japan's oil supply.

Late August 1941

Smith is promoted to first lieutenant.

September–December 1941

Smith and his squadron train in the American South.

18 October 1941

General Hideki Tojo, who supports a more aggressive stance against the United States, becomes prime minister of Japan.

26 November–7 December 1941

The Japanese navy attack fleet sails toward Pearl Harbor. Japanese ground forces prepare to launch assaults against the Philippines, Hong Kong, and Guam, among other territories.

7 December 1941

Japanese airplanes attack Pearl Harbor Naval Station, destroying most of the United States Pacific Fleet. Japan's ground troops attack

American, British, and Dutch territories in southeast Asia and the Pacific.

8 December 1941

The United States declares war on Japan.

8 December 1941–21 February 1942

Japanese forces capture Guam, Wake Island, Hong Kong, and Malaysia.

11 December 1941

Germany and Italy declare war on the United States.

January 1942

Under instructions from General Hap Arnold, Lieutenant Colonel Jimmy Doolittle plans a strike on Japan, identified as the "B-25 Special Project."

3 February 1942

Two B-25s take off successfully from the deck of the USS *Hornet*. Smith and 119 other Air Corps volunteers are chosen for the B-25 Special Project.

19 February 1942

Roosevelt signs Executive Order 9066, resulting in the establishment of Japanese internment camps.

27 February–22 March 1942

Fliers in the B-25 Special Project train at Eglin Air Base in Florida.

23 March–1 April 1942

The B-25 Special Project transfers to Alameda Naval Air Station where sixteen bombers are loaded onto the *Hornet*.

2–18 April 1942

Task Force 16.2, led by the *Hornet*, departs San Francisco Bay for Japan. The group meets up with Task Force 16.1 ten days into the journey.

9–11 April 1942

Approximately 70,000 American and Filipino troops surrender to Japanese forces on the Bataan Peninsula. The subsequent Bataan Death March kills between 500 and 650 American and between 5,000 and 18,000 Filipino troops.

18 April 1942

Doolittle and his raiders conduct the first strike of the war on the Japanese homeland. After Smith and his crew bomb targets in Kobe, the *TNT* crash lands near Tantou Island.

18 April–June 1942

Japanese occupation troops retaliate against Chinese civilians in response to the raid.

19–24 April 1942

The *TNT* crew arrives on the Chinese mainland via Nantien Island. The injured crew of Plane Seven are taken to a hospital in Linhai, China, where Smith and his squad meet them. The crews of Planes Six and Sixteen are captured and imprisoned by the Japanese. Plane Eight lands in Siberia and the crew is imprisoned by the Soviet Air Force. Doolittle gains the help of Chinese nationalists to search for the other raiders.

24 April–16 May 1942

Smith and his crew cross the Chinese countryside and arrive in Chungking. They are then transferred to Calcutta, India.

3–8 May 1942

The United States and Australian navies defeat the Imperial Japanese Navy at the Battle of the Coral Sea.

16 May–7 June 1942

Smith helps prepare Army Air Force bombers for continued action in the Pacific Theater while in India.

4–7 June 1942

The Imperial Japanese Navy suffers a crushing defeat at the hands of the United States Navy in the Battle of Midway.

7–26 June 1942

Smith and several other raiders return to the United States.

18 June 1942–16 July 1945

Scientific teams in the United States, Canada, and Great Britain work on the Manhattan Project to construct the first atomic weapon.

27 June 1942

Smith and twenty-four other raiders receive the Distinguished Flying Cross from General Arnold at Bolling Field in Washington, D.C.

2–5 July 1942

Smith visits Belle Fourche for the final time.

6 July 1942

Donna Marie Smith is born in San Antonio, Texas.

7 August 1942–9 February 1943

American forces take part in the Guadalcanal Campaign, initiating the Allies' strategy of "island hopping" against the Japanese.

23 August 1942–2 February 1943

The Soviets turn back the German offensive at the Battle of Stalingrad.

27 September 1942

Smith arrives in England with the 439th Bomb Squadron.

15 October 1942

Japanese troops execute Dean Hallmark, Bill Farrow, and Harold Spatz, three of the captured Doolittle Raiders, in China.

8 November 1942–13 May 1943

American and British troops defeat German and Italian forces in North Africa.

12 November 1942

Smith and his new crew perish in a B-26 crash outside of London.

28 November 1942–May 1943

Bombers from Smith's last squadron attack Axis forces in North Africa.

24 December 1942

A. W. Smith dies after having suffered a stroke weeks earlier.

18 April 1943

Doolittle arranges the first reunion of the Doolittle Raiders in North Africa.

20 April 1943

The War Department releases the full details of the Doolittle Raid to the public.

May 1943

The Plane Eight crew escapes the Soviet Union to a British consulate in Iran.

9 July 1943

Allied forces land in Sicily, initiating the Italian Campaign.

20-23 November 1943

United States Marines defeat Japanese forces at the Battle of Tarawa.

22-26 November 1943

Roosevelt meets with British Prime Minister Winston Churchill and Chiang Kai-shek in Cairo, Egypt, to discuss future strategy and postwar plans for Asia.

28 November–1 December 1943

Roosevelt, Churchill, and Soviet Premier Josef Stalin meet in Tehran, Iran, where the three agree to fight the war until the Axis Powers submit to an unconditional surrender.

11 December 1943

Robert Meder of Plane Six dies in Japanese custody due to malnutrition.

4 June 1944

Allied troops capture Rome.

6 June 1944

Allied troops establish a beachhead in Normandy, France, during the D-Day landings.

15 June–9 July 1944

United States forces capture the island of Saipan.

19–20 June 1944

The United States Navy wins a decisive victory over the Imperial Japanese Navy at the Battle of the Philippine Sea.

10 July 1944

Americans bomb Tokyo for the first time since the Doolittle Raid. Bombing runs continue for the next year.

21 July–10 August 1944

United States Marines recapture Guam.

25 August 1944

Allied troops liberate Paris.

15 September–27 November 1944

United States Marines fight in the Battle of Peleliu, the first in a string of increasingly bloody battles on the approach to the Japanese main islands.

17 October–26 December 1944

The battles of Leyte and Leyte Gulf give American forces a foothold in the Philippines.

15 November 1944

The film *Thirty Seconds over Tokyo* premiers in New York City and Chungking.

16 December 1944–25 January 1945

American forces hold off German counterattacks in the Battle of the Bulge.

13 January–25 April 1945

The Soviets begin their final push on Germany in the East Prussian Offensive.

20 January 1945

Roosevelt begins his fourth term as president.

3 February–3 March 1945

United States and Filipino troops reconquer the Philippines.

13–15 February 1945

American and British bombers firebomb Dresden, Germany.

19 February–26 March 1945

United States Marines defeat the Japanese at the Battle of Iwo Jima.

9–10 March 1945

Over 270 American B-29s firebomb Tokyo.

23 March 1945

United States and British forces cross the Rhine River into Germany.

1 April–22 June 1945

Americans achieve victory at the Battle of Okinawa, the final stepping stone to Japan.

12 April 1945

Roosevelt dies in Warm Springs, Georgia. Harry S Truman takes office as president.

16–27 April 1945

Soviet troops encircle Berlin.

30 April–7 May 1945

Hitler commits suicide. Germany surrenders to the Allied forces.

16 July 1945

Scientists from the Manhattan Project perform first detonation of an atomic weapon at the Trinity Testing Site in New Mexico.

6–9 August 1945

Atomic bombs destroy Hiroshima and Nagasaki. The Soviet Union declares war on Japan.

15 August 1945

Emperor Hirohito announces Japan's unconditional surrender.

20 August 1945

The surviving captured raiders, Jacob DeShazer, Robert Hite, George Barr, and Chase Nielsen are liberated from a Japanese prison.

2 September 1945

Japanese officials sign the surrender terms aboard the USS *Missouri*.

20 November 1945–1 October 1946

Twenty-one Nazi leaders are charged with crimes against humanity for their roles in the Holocaust and prosecuted in the Nuremburg Trials. All but three are found guilty. Eleven receive death sentences.

15 December 1945

The first official Doolittle Raiders reunion takes place in Miami, Florida.

29 April 1946–12 November 1948

An International Military Tribunal, during which raider Chase Nielsen testifies, finds Prime Minister Tojo and twenty-four other defendants guilty of war crimes. Tojo is executed on 23 December 1948.

August 1948

Don Smith's remains are reinterred at Pine Slope Cemetery in Belle Fourche.

3 September 1964

Don's mother, Laura Smith, dies.

27–30 April 1978

The thirty-sixth Doolittle Raider Reunion is held in Rapid City, South Dakota.

27 September 1993

Doolittle dies at the age of ninety-six.

18 April 2001

Governor William J. Janklow declares "Captain Donald Smith Day."

17 October 2001

Smith's daughter Donna dies.

1 May 2005

Smith's widow Marie dies.

17–20 April 2013

The last Doolittle Raiders Reunion is held in Fort Walton Beach, Florida.

9 November 2013

Edward Saylor, David Thatcher, Richard Cole, and Robert Hite give the final toast to the raiders at the National Air Force Museum in Dayton, Ohio.

9 April 2019

Richard Cole, the last surviving Doolittle Raider, dies at the age of 103.

Notes

Chapter 1: Black Hills Boyhood

1. [Richard Young], "World War II," in *Above and Beyond: A History of the Medal of Honor from the Civil War to Vietnam* (Boston: Boston Publishing Co., 1985), pp. 202–3.

2. Ibid.

3. Richard Sassaman, "The Impossible Raid," *America in WWII Magazine*, (June 2007), americainwwii.com/articles/the-impossible-raid/; Craig Nelson, *The First Heroes: The Extraordinary Story of the Doolittle Raid—America's First World War II Victory* (New York: Penguin Books, 2003), p. 129.

4. Carroll V. Glines, *The Doolittle Raid: America's Daring First Strike against Japan* (Altgen, Pa.: Schiffer Publishing, 1991), pp. 16–19.

5. David M. Kennedy, *Freedom from Fear: The American People in Depression and War, 1929–1945* (New York: Oxford University Press, 1999), pp. 526–31.

6. James H. Doolittle, *I Could Never Be So Lucky Again: An Autobiography*, with Carroll V. Glines (New York: Bantam Books, 1991), p. 2.

7. Kennedy, *Freedom from Fear*, pp. 526–31.

8. Glines, *Doolittle Raid*, pp. 79–82, 132–33.

9. Telephone interview with Edward Saylor, Graham, Wash., by Paul Higbee and Tim Velder, 17 Apr. 2001.

10. Glines, *Doolittle Raid*, pp. 24–27, 43–44, 70.

11. Interview with Saylor.

12. United States Army Air Force, *Pilot's Handbook of Flight Operating Instructions for Models B-25C and B-25D*, foreword by Leo J. Kohn (1942; reprint ed., Appleton, Wisc.: Aviation Publications, 1978), pp. ii–v, 5; James Bradley, *Flyboys: A True Story of Courage* (New York: Little, Brown & Co., 2003), pp. 99–100.

13. Don Smith to Dear Folks, 8 Aug. 1941, Don Smith Letters, Tri-State Museum, Belle Fourche, S.Dak. Unless otherwise noted, all correspondence to and from Smith family members comes from this collection.

14. James M. Scott, *Target Tokyo: Jimmy Doolittle and the Raid That Avenged Pearl Harbor* (New York: W. W. Norton, 2015), p. 229.

15. "Remember Pearl Harbor," *Time*, 27 Apr. 1942, p. 18.

16. Bradley, *Flyboys*, pp. 110–11; Alan D. Coox, "Air War against Japan," in *Case Studies in Achievement of Air Superiority*, ed. Benjamin Cooling (Washington, D.C.: Center for Air Force History, 1994), pp. 393, 395.

17. Coox, "Air War against Japan," pp. 394–96; Scott, *Target Tokyo*, pp. 194–96; Bradley, *Flyboys*, pp. 106–7.

18. Smith to Dear Folks, 13 Oct. 1941.

19. Smith to Dear Folks, 5 June 1941.

20. Kennedy, *Freedom from Fear*, pp. 389–92, 424.

21. Ibid., pp. 392–94.

22. Ibid., p. 394.

23. Ibid., p. 386.

24. Ibid., p. 433.

25. Ibid., pp. 387–88.

26. Ibid., p. 420.

27. Ibid., pp. 415–20.

28. Ibid., p. 420.

29. Ibid., p. 423.

30. Ibid., pp. 423–24.

31. Barbara W. Tuchman, *Stilwell and the American Experience in China, 1911–1945* (London: Macmillan, 1970), pp. 164–70.

32. Ibid., pp. 177–78; Kennedy, *Freedom from Fear*, p. 401.

33. Tuchman, *Stilwell and the American Experience in China*, pp. 179–80; Kennedy, *Freedom from Fear*, pp. 428–30; Lowell Thomas and Edward Jablonski, *Doolittle: A Biography* (Garden City, N.Y.: Doubleday, 1976), p. 61.

34. Herbert S. Schell, *History of South Dakota* (Lincoln: University of Nebraska Press, 1961), pp. 298–99.

35. Interview of Ruth Streeter Woodall, Belle Fourche, S.Dak., by Julia Monczunski, South Dakota Public Radio, 21 Apr. 2007.

36. Ibid.

37. Ibid.

38. Ibid.

39. Interview with Faye Kennedy, Belle Fourche, S.Dak., 25 June 1996; *Pioneer Footprints* (Belle Fourche, S.Dak.: Black Hills Half Century Club, 1964), p. 125.

40. Interview with Kennedy; *Pioneer Footprints*, pp. 125–26.

41. Interview with Kennedy; *Pioneer Footprints*, pp. 292–93.

42. *Fencing the West: Buffalo to Barbed Wire*, museum exhibit, 2008, Journey Museum & Learning Center, Rapid City, S.Dak.

43. Smith to Dear Folks, 13 Oct. 1941.

44. *Pioneer Footprints*, pp. 284–88; interview of Woodall.

45. Schell, *History of South Dakota*, pp. 357–60; *Pioneer Footprints*, pp. 284–85.

46. [Lynwood Oyos and Bob Lee], "Farming: Dependency and Depopulation," in *A New History of South Dakota*, ed. Harry F. Thompson (Sioux Falls, S.Dak.: Center for Western Studies, Augustana College, 2005), pp. 231–32; Schell, *History of South Dakota*, p. 283.

47. Interview with Jack Wells, Belle Fourche, S.Dak., 25 Oct. 2011.

48. Ibid.

49. Interview of Woodall.

50. "Spearfish Canyon," visitspearfish.com/things-to-do/spearfish-canyon.

51. "Various Nicknames Found in Belle H.," *Hi Times* (Belle Fourche High School student newspaper), 12 Nov. 1934.

52. "Dr. No-Yong Park Assembly Speaker," ibid., 14 Oct. 1932.

53. *Hi Times*, 6 May 1935.

54. Ibid., 23 Sept. 1935.

55. Ibid., 12 Nov. 1934.

56. Interview with Harold Brost, Belle Fourche, S.Dak., 25 Oct. 2011.

57. Ibid.

58. Ibid.

59. *Hi Times*, 11 Nov. 1932.

60. Ibid., 1 Oct. 1934; "Purple and White Win Final Contest," *Hi Times*, 12 Nov. 1934.

61. "3 New Instructors Teach in Belle H.," ibid., 23 Sept. 1935.

62. *Hi Times*, 14 Oct. 1935.

63. Interview of Woodall.

64. David Eagleman, "Secret Life of the Mind," *Discover Magazine* 32 (Sept. 2011): 50–53.

65. Rhonda Coy Sedgwick, *Sky Trails: The Life of Clyde W. Ice* (Newcastle, Wyo.: Quarter Circle A Enterprises, 1988), pp. 137–39.

66. Clayton F. Smith, "Clyde W. Ice: A Name Writ Large in South Dakota Aviation History," in *Fifth Annual West River History Conference September 18, 19, & 20, 1997 Papers*, comp. Herbert W. Blakely and Beverly M. Pechan (Keystone, S.Dak.: West River History Conference/Keystone Area Historical Society, 1998), pp. 63–65.

67. Interview of Woodall.

68. Sedgwick, *Sky Trails*, p. 24. Emphasis in original.

69. Joe Foss, foreword to *Sky Trails*, by Sedgwick, p. v.

70. Sedgwick, *Sky Trails*, pp. 70–72; Smith, "Clyde W. Ice," pp. 65–66.

71. Gene Bauer, "On the Edge of Space: The *Explorer* Expeditions of 1934–1935," *South Dakota History* 12 (Spring 1982): 9–15.

72. Albert W. Stevens, "Man's Farthest Aloft," *National Geographic* 69 (Jan. 1936): 95.

73. Ibid., p. 69.

74. Ibid., pp. 79–80.

75. Ibid., p. 80.

76. Ibid., pp. 59, 84–86.

77. Interview with Murial Jeffry, Belle Fourche, S.Dak., 6 Oct. 2012.

78. Smith, handwritten note, 23 Dec. 1935, copy in author's collection.

79. J. J. Guthmiller to Smith, 24 Dec. 1935, Janice Evans Collection, Rapid City, S.Dak.

80. Interview with David Junek, Belle Fourche, S.Dak., 16 Aug. 2011; [Oyos and Lee], "Farming," p. 236.

81. *Jack Rabbit* (1939), 2 vols., 2:234–35.

Chapter 2: Smith Earns His Wings

1. George Nolta, *The Doolittle Raiders: What Heroes Do after the War* (Altgen, Pa.: Schiffer Publishing, 2018), pp. 128–33.

2. Telephone interview with Edward Saylor, Graham, Wash., by Paul Higbee and Tim Velder, 17 Apr. 2001.

3. Lieutenant Donald G. Smith, Mission Report, 14 May 1942, in Summary of Targets in Japanese Raid and Memoranda of Personal Interviews with Major J. F. Pinkney,

Entry NM-53 293-C, Box 188, Central Decimal Files, Oct. 1942–1944, Security Classified General Correspondence, 1941–1944, Records of the Army Air Forces, 1902–1964, Record Group 18, National Archives and Records Administration, College Park, Md.

4. James Bradley, *Flyboys: A True Story of Courage* (New York: Little, Brown & Co., 2003), pp. 108–10.

5. Ibid., pp. 106–7; James H. Doolittle, *I Could Never Be So Lucky Again: An Autobiography*, with Carroll V. Glines (New York: Bantam Books, 1991), p. 270.

6. Washington State University Extension, "What is a Land-Grant College?," ext.wsu .edu/documents/landgrant.pdf; Interview of Ruth Streeter Woodall, Belle Fourche, S.Dak., by Julia Monczunski, South Dakota Public Radio, 21 Apr. 2007.

7. Course Bulletin, 1936, College of Agriculture and Mechanical Arts, South Dakota State College, copy in author's collection.

8. *Jack Rabbit* (1940), p. 251.

9. Ibid., p. 216.

10. Chuck Cecil, *Becoming Someplace Special: Gleanings from the Past: The Brookings Story* (Brookings, S.Dak.: By the Author, 2001), p. 78; *Jack Rabbit* (1940), p. 10.

11. Cecil, *Becoming Someplace Special*, p. 78, 80; R. Alton Lee, *A New Deal for South Dakota: Drought, Depression, and Relief, 1920–1941* (Pierre: South Dakota Historical Society Press, 2016), p. 205; Steven J. Bucklin, "Fly Over Country?: A Glimpse of South Dakota through Its Aviation History," *South Dakota History* 45 (Summer 2015): 114–16.

12. *Jack Rabbit* (1940), pp. 69, 179–86.

13. Ibid., pp. 180, 194; *Jack Rabbit* (1939), 2 vols., 2:251.

14. Ibid. (1940), p. 129.

15. Ibid. (1939), 2:228–35.

16. Ibid., 2:233.

17. Ibid. (1940), pp. 20, 51–52.

18. Ibid., pp. 31, 54–56.

19. Ibid., p. 119.

20. Ibid., pp. 57–58.

21. Ibid., pp. 51–52, 59–61.

22. Ibid., pp. 52–53.

23. *Daily Belle Fourche Post*, 8 Dec. 1939.

24. *Jack Rabbit* (1940), pp. 66–68.

25. Ibid., p. 122.

26. Ibid., p. 344.

27. Ibid., pp. 178–85, 251.

28. Bruce Ashcroft, *We Wanted Wings: A History of the Aviation Cadet Program* (Randolph Air Force Base, Tex.: HQ, AETC, Office of History and Research, 2005), p. 23.

29. Ibid., pp. 23–25.

30. Ibid., pp. 25–26.

31. Ibid., p. 30.

32. John Caughy, *California: A Remarkable State's Life History* (Englewood Cliffs, N.J.: Prentice-Hall, 1970), pp. 493–94.

33. Ibid.

34. Ashcroft, *We Wanted Wings*, pp. 25–27.

35. Ibid.

36. Ibid., p. 27.

37. Don Smith to Dear Folks, 25 May 1941, Don Smith Letters, Tri-State Museum, Belle Fourche, S.Dak. Unless otherwise noted, all correspondence to and from Smith family members comes from this collection.

38. Lloyd L. Kelly, *The Pilot Maker* (New York: Grosset & Dunlap, 1970), pp. 30–31.

39. Alan B. Shepard Jr., foreword to *Pilot Maker*, by Kelly, p. v. Emphasis in original.

40. Kelly, *Pilot Maker*, pp. 31–55.

41. Ibid., pp. 50–58.

42. Ibid., pp. 33, 37–38.

43. DeWitt S. Copp, *A Few Great Captains: The Men and Events That Shaped the Development of U.S. Air Power* (McLean, Va.: Air Force Historical Foundation, 1980), pp. 155–85.

44. Seth Tupper, *Calvin Coolidge in the Black Hills* (Charleston, S.C.: The History Press, 2017), pp. 70–73.

45. Copp, *A Few Great Captains*, pp. 155–85; Kelly, *Pilot Maker*, pp. 52–53.

46. Leonard Baker and Benjamin F. Cooling, "Developments and Lessons before World War II," in *Case Studies in the Achievement of Air Superiority*, ed. Cooling (Washington, D.C.: Center for Air Force History, 1994), pp. 49–53.

47. Smith to Dear Folks, 5 June 1941.

48. "The President Speaks," *Time*, 6 Jan. 1941, pp. 9–10.

49. Smith to Dear Folks, 23 Jan. 1941.

50. Smith to Dear Folks, 16 Feb. 1941.

51. Ibid.

52. Smith to Dear Folks, 24 Feb. 1941.

53. Ibid.

54. Smith to Dear Folks, undated.

55. Ibid; Smith to Dear Folks, 23 Jan. 1941; Ashcroft, *We Wanted Wings*, pp. 36–37.

56. Smith to Dear Folks, 17 Mar. 1941.

57. Ibid.

58. Smith to Dear Folks, undated; "17th Bomb Group WWII," bombgroup17.com /17th_bg_wwii.

Chapter 3: Training for War

1. Don Smith to Dear Folks, 3 Oct. 1941, Don Smith Letters, Tri-State Museum, Belle Fourche, S.Dak. Unless otherwise noted, all correspondence to and from Smith family members comes from this collection.

2. Telephone interview with Edward Saylor, Graham, Wash., by Paul Higbee and Tim Velder, 17 Apr. 2001; J. H. Doolittle, Report on the Aerial Bombing of Japan, 5 June 1942, Entry NM-53 294-C, Box 516, Central Decimal Files, Oct. 1942–1944, Security Classified General Correspondence, 1941–1944, Records of the Army Air Forces, 1902–1964, Record Group 18, National Archives and Records Administration, College Park, Md. (These records are hereafter cited Security Classified Correspondence).

3. Doolittle, Report on the Aerial Bombing of Japan.

4. Carroll V. Glines, *The Doolittle Raid: America's Daring First Strike against Japan* (Atglen, Pa.: Schiffer Publishing, 1991), pp. 132–34.

5. Lt. Donald G. Smith, Mission Report, 14 May 1942, in Summary of Targets in Japanese Raid and Memoranda of Personal Interviews with Major J. F. Pinkney, Entry NM-53 293-C, Box 188, Security Classified Correspondence.

6. Smith to Dear Folks, undated.

7. Ibid.

8. Smith to Dear Folks, 14 Apr. 1941.

9. Smith to Dear Folks, 22 Apr. 1941.

10. Smith to Dear Folks, 14 Apr. 1941.

11. Ibid.

12. Smith to Dear Folks, 22 Apr. 1941.

13. U.S. Army Air Force, *Pilot's Handbook of Flight Operating Instructions for Models* B-25C *and* B-25D, foreword by Leo J. Kohn (1942; reprint ed., Appleton, Wisc.: Aviation Publications, 1978), p. 1.

14. Geoffrey Perrett, *Winged Victory: The Army Air Forces in World War II* (New York: Random House, 1993), pp. 92–94.

15. Army Air Force, *Pilot's Handbook*, p. 1.

16. Smith to Dear Folks, 25 May 1941.

17. Smith to Dear Folks, 28 May 1941.

18. Army Air Force, *Pilot's Handbook*, p. 5.

19. Ibid., p. 75.

20. Ibid., p. 82.

21. Ibid., p. iii.

22. "Gen. Doolittle, at 81, Still Endeavors to Be Useful," *Rapid City Journal*, 28 Apr. 1978.

23. Smith to Dear Folks, 3 July 1941.

24. Smith to Dear Folks, 7 May 1941.

25. Ibid.

26. In the summer of 1941, the United States Army reorganized the command structure of the Army Air Corps, giving the group more autonomy and renaming it the Army Air Forces. Both units were officially dissolved when the United States Air Force became a separate branch in 1947. The two names were used interchangeably during World War II. "Army Aviation: Army Air Forces," army.mil/aviation/airforces/index .html; "Army Aviation: Army Air Corps," army.mil/aviation/aircorps/.

27. Smith to Dear Folks, 29 Apr. 1941.

28. Smith to Dear Folks, 14 May 1941.

29. Ibid.

30. Smith to Dear Folks, 18 May 1941.

31. Ibid.

32. Smith to Dear Folks, 25 May 1941.

33. Franklin D. Roosevelt, "Fireside Chat 17: On an Unlimited National Emergency," 27 May 1941, transcript, Miller Center, University of Virginia, Charlottesville, millercenter

.org/the-presidency/presidential-speeches/may-27-1941-fireside-chat-17-unlimited
-national-emergency.

34. Ibid.

35. Smith to Dear Folks, 28 May 1941.

36. "Acts and Intentions," *Time*, 9 June 1941, pp. 17–18. The American Institute of Public Opinion sponsors the popular Gallup and *Fortune* polls. In the poll from 1941, 76 percent of Americans responded that they supported the government "forbidding strikes in industries manufacturing materials for our national defense program" ("Gallup and Fortune Polls," *Public Opinion Quarterly* 5 [Autumn 1941]: 489).

37. "Acts and Intentions," p. 18.

38. Smith to Dear Folks, 28 May 1941.

39. Smith to Dear Folks, 25 May 1941.

40. Smith to Dear Folks, 5 June 1941.

41. Smith to Dear Folks, 8 Aug. 1941.

42. Smith to Dear Folks, 21 Aug. 1941.

43. *San Antonio Express*, 13 July 1941; Donald G. Smith and Marie R. Crouch, Marriage Certificate, King County Marriage Records, 1855–Present, Digital Archives, Washington State Archives, digitalarchives.wa.gov, accessed 18 Apr. 2019.

44. Smith to Dear Folks, 25 June 1941.

45. Smith to Dear Folks, 3 July 1941.

46. Smith to Dear Folks, 25 July 1941.

47. Ibid.

48. Lowell Thomas and Edward Jablonski, *Doolittle: A Biography* (Garden City, N.Y.: Doubleday, 1976), p. 163.

49. Smith to Dear Folks, 31 July 1941.

50. Ibid.

51. Smith to Dear Folks, 29 Sept. 1941.

52. Marie Smith to Dear Folks, undated.

53. Smith to Dear Folks, 15 Aug. 1941.

54. Smith to Dear Folks, 2 Sept. 1941.

55. Ibid.

56. Smith to Dear Folks, 11 Sept. 1941.

57. Smith to Dear Folks, 17 Sept. 1941.

58. Smith to Dear Folks, 25 Sept. 1941.

59. Smith to Dear Folks, 8 Nov. 1941.

60. Smith to Dear Folks, 25 Sept. 1941.

61. Smith to Dear Folks, 29 Sept. 1941; "Discipline Wanted," *Time*, 13 Oct. 1941, p. 34.

62. Marie Smith to Dearest Folks, undated.

63. Ibid.; Smith to Dear Folks, 29 Sept. 1941; "Test for the Fourth," *Time*, 3 Nov. 1941, p. 34.

64. "Discipline Wanted," p. 34.

65. Marie Smith to Dearest Folks, undated.

66. Smith to Dear Folks, 6 Nov. 1941.

67. Marie Smith to Dearest Folks, undated.

68. Smith to Dear Folks, 20 Nov. 1941. Although Smith used the figure for an enlisted man's pay, he would have made about double that amount as an officer.

69. Smith to Dear Folks, 31 Oct. 1941.

70. Smith to Dear Folks, 21 Oct. 1941. Another South Dakotan, Frank Leahy, coached Notre Dame at the time ("Frank Leahy, Notre Dame Coach, Dead," *New York Times*, 22 June 1973).

71. Smith to Dear Folks, 20 Nov. 1941.

72. Marie Smith to Dearest Folks, undated.

73. Smith to Dear Folks, 20 Nov. 1941.

74. Smith to Dear Folks, 3 Dec. 1941.

75. Smith to Dear Folks, 9 Dec. 1941.

76. "Tragedy at Honolulu," *Time*, 15 Dec. 1941, pp. 19–23; David M. Kennedy, *Freedom from Fear: The American People in Depression and War, 1929–1945* (New York: Oxford University Press, 1999), p. 522.

77. "Tragedy at Honolulu," p. 19.

78. Smith to Dear Folks, 9 Dec. 1941.

79. The Japanese assaults on Guam and the Philippines, among other British and American possessions, took place on the same day as the Pearl Harbor attacks. Because the offensive occurred across the international date line, however, the date is given as 8 December 1941. "Guam Bombed: Army Ship Is Sunk," *New York Times*, 8 Dec. 1941.

80. "Turn Back to Sea," ibid., 9 Dec. 1941.

81. Larry Pressler, *U.S. Senators from the Prairie* (Vermillion, S.Dak.: Dakota Press, 1982), p. 102.

82. Ibid.

83. Ibid., p. 99.

84. Ibid., p. 106.

85. Joseph Gies, *Franklin D. Roosevelt: Portrait of a President* (Garden City, N.Y.: Doubleday, 1971), p. 163.

86. "War Opened on US: Congress Acts Quickly as President Meets Hitler Challenge," *New York Times*, 12 Dec. 1941.

87. "Congress Decided: Roosevelt Will Address It Today and Find It Ready to Vote War," ibid., 8 Dec. 1941.

88. "Unity in Congress: Only One Negative Vote as President Calls to War and Victory," ibid., 9 Dec. 1941; "War Opened on US."

89. "War Opened on US."

90. Pressler, *Senators from the Prairie*, p. 100.

Chapter 4: The Special Project

1. James M. Scott, *Target Tokyo: Jimmy Doolittle and the Raid That Avenged Pearl Harbor* (New York: W. W. Norton, 2015), p. 291.

2. Ibid.

3. Carroll V. Glines, *The Doolittle Raid: America's Daring First Strike against Japan* (Atglen, Pa.: Schiffer Publishing, 1991), pp. 133–34.

4. Ibid., p. 134; Scott, *Target Tokyo*, p. 292.

5. Scott, *Target Tokyo*, p. 292.

6. Ibid., pp. 293–94.

7. Ibid.; Ted W. Lawson, *Thirty Seconds over Tokyo*, ed. Robert Considine (1943; new ed., New York: Simon & Schuster, 2004), pp. 142–44.

8. Scott, *Target Tokyo*, pp. 294–95.

9. Don Smith to Dear Folks, 17 Dec. 1941, Don Smith Letters, Tri-State Museum, Belle Fourche, S.Dak. Unless otherwise noted, all correspondence to and from Smith family members comes from this collection.

10. Scott, *Target Tokyo*, p. 18.

11. "Remember Pearl Harbor," *Life*, 22 Dec. 1941, p. 15.

12. Scott, *Target Tokyo*, pp. 24–28.

13. Ibid., pp. 28, 32–33.

14. "Bomber Pilot Tells of Air Raid on Japan," *Brookings Register*, 2 July 1942.

15. Glines, *Doolittle Raid*, pp. 18–20.

16. Lowell Thomas and Edward Jablonski, *Doolittle: A Biography* (Garden City, N.Y.: Doubleday, 1976), pp. 30–33.

17. Ibid., pp. 1–7.

18. Ibid., pp. 7–20.

19. Ibid., pp. 14–17; James H. Doolittle, *I Could Never Be So Lucky Again: An Autobiography*, with Carroll V. Glines (New York: Bantam Books, 1991), pp. 26–27.

20. Doolittle, *I Could Never Be So Lucky Again*, p. 27.

21. Ibid., pp. 33–43; Thomas and Jablonski, *Doolittle*, pp. 24–34, 40–41; DeWitt S. Copp, *A Few Great Captains: The Men and Events That Shaped the Development of U.S. Air Power* (McLean, Va.: Air Force Historical Foundation, 1980), p. 283.

22. Doolittle, *I Could Never Be So Lucky Again*, pp. 43–47, 50–51; Thomas and Jablonski, *Doolittle*, pp. 34–39, 51–52, 55–56.

23. Thomas and Jablonski, *Doolittle*, pp. 30, 136–37.

24. Ibid., p. 61.

25. Doolittle, *I Could Never Be So Lucky Again*, pp. 67–69; Thomas and Jablonski, *Doolittle*, pp. 60–62.

26. Thomas and Jablonski, *Doolittle*, pp. 74–75, 79–80; Glines, *Doolittle Raid*, p. 17.

27. Thomas and Jablonski, *Doolittle*, pp. 63–64.

28. Ibid., pp. 63–66.

29. Ibid., pp. 101–3; Glines, *Doolittle Raid*, p. 17.

30. "'Blind' Plane Flies 15 Miles and Lands; Fog Peril Overcome," *New York Times*, 25 Sept. 1929.

31. Thomas and Jablonski, *Doolittle*, pp. 112–27; Rhonda Coy Sedgwick, *Sky Trails: The Life of Clyde W. Ice* (Newcastle, Wyo.: Quarter Circle A Enterprises, 1988), p. 143.

32. Thomas and Jablonski, *Doolittle*, pp. 129–33, 144–48; David M. Kennedy, *Freedom from Fear: The American People in Depression and War, 1929–1945* (New York: Oxford University Press, 1999), pp. 72–74.

33. Thomas and Jablonski, *Doolittle*, pp. 132–33, 139–42.

34. Ibid., pp. 148–54, 203; Doolittle, *I Could Never Be So Lucky Again*, pp. 224–25, 227.

35. Lawson, *Thirty Seconds over Tokyo*, pp. 18–19.

36. Interview with Thomas Griffin, Rapid City, S.Dak., 23 Nov. 2002.

37. Smith to Dear Folks, undated.

38. Ibid.

39. Thomas and Jablonski, *Doolittle*, pp. 160–61.

40. Glines, *Doolittle Raid*, pp. 22, 28.

41. Smith to Dear Folks, 19 Feb. 1942.

42. Smith to Dear Folks, undated.

43. Glines, *Doolittle Raid*, pp. 28–29.

44. Ibid., p. 34; Doolittle, *I Could Never Be So Lucky Again*, p. 248.

45. Smith to Dear Folks, 18 Mar. 1942.

46. Glines, *Doolittle Raid*, p. 34.

47. William E. Aisenbrey, "Thirty Seconds over Tokyo—The South Dakota Connection," in *Papers of the Twentieth Annual Dakota History Conference*, comp. Herbert W. Blakely (Madison, S.Dak.: Dakota State College, 1988), p. 567; George Nolta, *The Doolittle Raiders: What Heroes Do after the War* (Atglen, Pa.: Schiffler Publishing, 2018), p. 25.

48. Smith to Dear Folks, 13 Jan. 1942.

49. Willibald C. ("Bill") Bianchi memorial marker, South Dakota State University, Brookings, S.Dak.; "Captain Willibald C. Bianchi," minnesotamedalofhonormemorial .org/wp-content/uploads/2017/12/Bianchi-Willibald-C.-Bio-July-16.pdf.

50. Glines, *Doolittle Raid*, pp. 29–30.

51. Smith to Dear Folks, 5 Mar. 1942; Doolittle, *I Could Never Be So Lucky Again*, p. 245; Glines, *Doolittle Raid*, p. 31.

52. Glines, *Doolittle Raid*, p. 31.

53. Interview with Griffin.

54. Glines, *Doolittle Raid*, pp. 29–30.

55. Thomas and Jablonski, *Doolittle*, p. 162.

56. Smith to Dear Folks, 5 Mar. 1942.

57. Glines, *Doolittle Raid*, p. 40.

58. "Third Report," *Time*, 2 Mar. 1942, p. 9.

59. Hanson W. Baldwin, "America at War: Three Bad Months," *Foreign Affairs* 20 (Apr. 1942): 395.

60. Ibid., p. 399.

61. "New Jap Planes," *Newsweek*, 16 Mar. 1942, p. 16.

62. "The New Tax Proposals," *The Nation*, 14 Mar. 1942, p. 302.

63. "The 40-Hour Week," *Time*, 30 Mar. 1942, p. 9. Emphasis in original.

64. Ibid., pp. 9–10; "Why the U.S. Can't Fight," *Time*, 2 Mar. 1942, p. 10.

65. "The 40-Hour Week," pp. 9–10.

66. Smith to Dear Folks, 18 Mar. 1942.

67. Thomas and Jablonski, *Doolittle*, p. 163.

68. Ibid.; Glines, *Doolittle Raid*, p. 33.

69. Glines, *Doolittle Raid*, pp. 42–43; Scott, *Target Tokyo*, pp. 93–94; Smith to Dear Folks, 18 Mar. 1942.

70. Doolittle, *I Could Never Be So Lucky Again*, p. 249; Thomas and Jablonski, *Doolittle*, pp. 164–65.

71. Doolittle, *I Could Never Be So Lucky Again*, p. 249; Thomas and Jablonski, *Doolittle*, p. 161.

72. Telephone interview with Edward Saylor, Graham, Wash., by Paul Higbee and Tim Velder, 17 Apr. 2001.

73. Glines, *Doolittle Raid*, p. 33; Scott, *Target Tokyo*, pp. 27–28.

74. Doolittle to Commanding General Army Air Forces, undated memorandum, in Doolittle, *I Could Never Be So Lucky Again*, p. 544.

75. Glines, *Doolittle Raid*, pp. 33, 111; Scott, *Target Tokyo*, pp. 27–28.

76. Don Sherman, "The Secret Weapon," *Air & Space Magazine* (Feb./Mar. 1995), archive.is/20060517184503/http://www.airspacemag.com/ASM/Mag/Index/1995/FM /swpn.html.

77. J. H. Doolittle, Report on the Aerial Bombing of Japan, 5 June 1942, Entry NM-53 294-C, Box 516, Central Decimal Files, Oct. 1942–1944, Security Classified Correspondence, 1941–1944, Records of the Army Air Forces, 1902–1964, Record Group 18, National Archives and Records Administration, College Park, Md.; Glines, *Doolittle Raid*, pp. 33–34.

78. Glines, *Doolittle Raid*, pp. 33–34.

79. Doolittle, Report on the Aerial Bombing of Japan; Glines, *Doolittle Raid*, pp. 33–34; Scott, *Target Tokyo*, p. 93.

80. Doolittle, *I Could Never Be So Lucky Again*, pp. 267–68.

81. Ibid., pp. 248–49.

82. Thomas and Jablonski, *Doolittle*, p. 166; Scott, *Target Tokyo*, pp. 166–67.

83. Lawson, *Thirty Seconds over Tokyo*, p. 36.

84. Doolittle, *I Could Never Be So Lucky Again*, p. 249.

85. Ibid., pp. 249–50; Smith to Dear Folks, 15 Apr. 1942.

86. Glines, *Doolittle Raid*, p. 42.

87. Doolittle, *I Could Never Be So Lucky Again*, pp. 251–54; Scott, *Target Tokyo*, p. 117.

88. Doolittle, *I Could Never Be So Lucky Again*, p. 254.

89. Ibid., p. 255.

90. Scott, *Target Tokyo*, pp. 119–28; Glines, *Doolittle Raid*, p. 50.

91. Interview with Griffin.

Chapter 5: Bombing Kobe

1. Ted W. Lawson, *Thirty Seconds over Tokyo*, ed. Robert Considine (1943; new ed., New York: Simon & Schuster, 2004), p. 141.

2. James Scott, *Target Tokyo: Jimmy Doolittle and the Raid That Avenged Pearl Harbor* (New York: W. W. Norton, 2015), p. 209.

3. Ibid., pp. 209–10, 250–54.

4. Ibid., pp. 154–55, 252–54.

5. Ibid., pp. 253–56.

6. Ibid., pp. 255, 280–82.

7. Ibid, pp. 282–83.

8. Ibid., pp. 283–86.

9. Lawson, *Thirty Seconds over Tokyo*, pp. 104–5.

10. Scott, *Target Tokyo*, pp. 285–86.

11. Thomas White, "Memoirs of 'Doc' White," p. 26, quoted in Scott, *Target Tokyo*, p. 297.

12. Ibid., pp. 296–97.

13. Lawson, *Thirty Seconds over Tokyo*, pp. 146–54; Scott, *Target Tokyo*, pp. 336–39. According to Lawson's account, Smith provided the blood for the first of his transfusions, but historian James M. Scott writes that Smith's crewmate Griffith P. Williams, having the same blood type as Lawson, was the donor.

14. Interview with David Thatcher, Belle Fourche, S.Dak., 18 Apr. 2001.

15. Ibid.; Lawson, *Thirty Seconds over Tokyo*, pp. 146, 173; Scott, *Target Tokyo*, p. 337.

16. Carroll V. Glines, *The Doolittle Raid: America's Daring First Strike against Japan* (Atglen, Pa.: Schiffer Publishing, 1991), photograph insert between pp. 82–83.

17. Ibid, p. 50; "Attack on the U.S.," *Time*, 2 Mar. 1942, p. 9; David M. Kennedy, *Freedom from Fear: The American People in Depression and War, 1929–1945* (New York: Oxford University Press, 1999), pp. 529, 750n5; Willibald C. ("Bill") Bianchi memorial marker, South Dakota State University, Brookings, S.Dak.; "Captain Willibald C. Bianchi," minnesotamedalofhonormemorial.org/wp-content/uploads/2017/12/Bianchi-Willibald-C.-Bio-July-16.pdf; James H. Doolittle, *I Could Never Be So Lucky Again: An Autobiography*, with Carroll V. Glines (New York: Bantam Books, 1991), pp. 250–51; Scott, *Target Tokyo*, pp. 151–53.

18. J. Royden Stork, response to questionnaire, Air Force Office of Information, 27 Mar. 1957, Folder 5, Box 66, Doolittle Raiders Questionnaires, The Doolittle Tokyo Raiders Association Records, Special Collections and Archives Division, History of Aviation Archives, Eugene McDermott Library, University of Texas, Dallas.

19. Doolittle, *I Could Never Be So Lucky Again*, pp. 262–63; Glines, *Doolittle Raid*, p. 50.

20. Scott, *Target Tokyo*, pp. 153–54, 162.

21. Ibid., pp. 153–54; Doolittle, *I Could Never Be So Lucky Again*, p. 272; Lawson, *Thirty Seconds over Tokyo*, p. 58; Glines, *Doolittle Raid*, p. 64.

22. Scott, *Target Tokyo*, p. 154.

23. Ibid.; Doolittle, *I Could Never Be So Lucky Again*, p. 272; Lawson, *Thirty Seconds over Tokyo*, p. 58; Glines, *Doolittle Raid*, p. 64.

24. Doolittle, *I Could Never Be So Lucky Again*, p. 269; Lawson, *Thirty Seconds over Tokyo*, p. 43; Glines, *Doolittle Raid*, p. 54.

25. Barbara W. Tuchman, *Stilwell and the American Experience in China, 1911–1945* (London: Macmillan, 1970), p. 151; Kennedy, *Freedom from Fear*, p. 502; Scott, *Target Tokyo*, pp. 102–5.

26. Scott, *Target Tokyo*, pp. 292–93.

27. Glines, *Doolittle Raid*, p. 54.

28. Doolittle, *I Could Never Be So Lucky Again*, pp. 265–67; Lawson, *Thirty Seconds over Tokyo*, p. 40.

29. Don Smith to Dear Folks, 15 Apr. 1942, Don Smith Letters, Tri-State Museum,

Belle Fourche, S.Dak. Unless otherwise noted, all correspondence to and from Smith family members comes from this collection.

30. Doolittle, *I Could Never Be So Lucky Again*, pp. 271–72; Lawson, *Thirty Seconds over Tokyo*, pp. 53–54.

31. Glines, *Doolittle Raid*, p. 63.

32. Doolittle, *I Could Never Be So Lucky Again*, p. 272.

33. Ibid.; Scott, *Target Tokyo*, pp. 169–70.

34. Doolittle, *I Could Never Be So Lucky Again*, p. 272; Lawson, *Thirty Seconds over Tokyo*, pp. 56–57.

35. Interview with Thatcher; Doolittle, *I Could Never Be So Lucky Again*, p. 274; Lawson, *Thirty Seconds over Tokyo*, pp. 60–63; James Bradley, *Flyboys: A True Story of Courage* (New York: Little, Brown & Co., 2003), p. 103.

36. Doolittle, *I Could Never Be So Lucky Again*, p. 274.

37. Lawson, *Thirty Seconds over Tokyo*, p. 63; Bradley, *Flyboys*, p. 103.

38. Telephone interview of Henry A. Potter, Austin, Tex., by William E. Aisenbrey, 6 Apr. 1988, transcript, copy in author's collection.

39. Ibid.; Glines, *Doolittle Raid*, p. 69.

40. Glines, *Doolittle Raid*, p. 69.

41. Telephone interview with Philip Hall, Spearfish, S.Dak., 30 Sept. 2018.

42. Robert J. Casey, *Torpedo Junction: With the Pacific Fleet from Pearl Harbor to Midway* (Indianapolis: Bobbs-Merrill Co., 1942), p. 305.

43. Lowell Thomas and Edward Jablonski, *Doolittle: A Biography* (Garden City, N.Y.: Doubleday, 1976), p. 183.

44. Lt. Donald G. Smith, Mission Report, 14 May 1942, in Summary of Targets in Japanese Raid and Memoranda of Personal Interviews with Major J. F. Pinkney, Entry NM-53 293-C, Box 188, Central Decimal Files, Oct. 1942–1944, Security Classified General Correspondence, 1941–1944, Records of the Army Air Forces, 1902–1964, Record Group (RG) 18, National Archives and Records Administration, College Park, Md. (These records are hereafter cited Summary of Targets in Japanese Raid).

45. Ibid.

46. Glines, *Doolittle Raid*, pp. 69–70.

47. Ibid., p. 90; Robert G. Emmens, *Guests of the Kremlin* (New York: Macmillan, 1949), p. 5; Scott, *Target Tokyo*, pp. 229–30.

48. "Don Smith Relates Story of Raid on Japan for Home Folk," *Daily Belle Fourche Post*, 3 July 1942.

49. Scott, *Target Tokyo*, pp. 229–30.

50. Ibid, p. 230; "Kobe," wikipedia.org/wiki/kobe.

51. Scott, *Target Tokyo*, p. 230.

52. Smith, Mission Report.

53. Ibid.; Scott, *Target Tokyo*, pp. 230–32.

54. Casey, *Torpedo Junction*, p. 306.

55. Scott, *Target Tokyo*, p. 261.

56. Ibid, pp. 261–63.

57. Smith, Mission Report.

58. James H. Doolittle, Personal Report, 4 May 1942, Entry NM-53 294-C, Box 516, Central Decimal Files, Oct. 1942–1944, Security Classified General Correspondence, 1941–1944, Records of the Army Air Forces, 1902–1964, RG 18, National Archives and Records Administration, College Park, Md.

59. Doolittle, *I Could Never Be So Lucky Again*, p. 9.

60. Ibid., pp. 9–10; Doolittle, Personal Report; Interview of Henry A. Potter, San Angelo, Tex., by John Garrett and Mike Strickler, undated, transcript, copy in author's collection.

61. Potter, Report of Navigator, 5 May 1942, in Summary of Targets in Japanese Raid.

62. Doolittle, Personal Report; Thomas and Jablonski, *Doolittle*, p. 186.

63. Thomas and Jablonski, *Doolittle*, pp. 187–88.

64. Potter, Report of Navigator.

65. Doolittle, *I Could Never Be So Lucky Again*, p. 276; "Col. Henry Potter, Navigator in Doolittle Raid, Dies At 83," *New York Times*, 4 June 2002.

66. Glines, *Doolittle Raid*, pp. 81–86.

67. Interview with Thomas Griffin, Rapid City, S.Dak., 23 Nov. 2002.

68. Doolittle, *I Could Never Be So Lucky Again*, pp. 547–54.

69. Emmens, *Guests of the Kremlin*, pp. 19–32.

70. Ibid., pp. 39–40; Scott, *Target Tokyo*, pp. 322, 352–54.

71. Scott, *Target Tokyo*, pp. 290, 369.

72. Glines, *Doolittle Raid*, pp. 93–94.

Chapter 6: The Final Trip

1. Quoted in James M. Scott, *Target Tokyo: Jimmy Doolittle and the Raid That Avenged Pearl Harbor* (New York: W. W. Norton, 2015), p. 320.

2. "No Help for Perplexity," *Time*, 18 May 1942, p. 22.

3. Interview of Henry A. Potter, San Angelo, Tex., by John Garret and Mike Strickler, undated, transcript, copy in author's collection.

4. Scott, *Target Tokyo*, pp. 292–93.

5. James H. Doolittle, *I Could Never Be So Lucky Again: An Autobiography*, with Carroll V. Glines (New York: Bantam Books, 1991), pp. 282–83; Scott, *Target Tokyo*, pp. xiv, 380–90.

6. Ted W. Lawson, *Thirty Seconds over Tokyo*, ed. Robert Considine (1943; new ed., New York: Simon & Schuster, 2004), pp. 187–88.

7. Barbara W. Tuchman, *Stilwell and the American Experience in China, 1911–1945* (London: Macmillan, 1970), p. 197.

8. Lowell Thomas and Edward Jablonski, *Doolittle: A Biography* (Garden City, N.Y.: Doubleday, 1976), pp. 201–5.

9. Lt. Col. James H. Doolittle to A. W. Smith, 21 May 1942, Don Smith Letters, Tri-State Museum, Belle Fourche, S.Dak. Unless otherwise noted, all correspondence to and from Smith family members comes from this collection.

10. Lawson, *Thirty Seconds over Tokyo*, p. 215.

11. Gerhard L. Weinberg, *A World at Arms: A Global History of World War II* (Cambridge, U.K.: Cambridge University Press, 1994), pp. 324–27.

12. Gordon W. Prange, with Donald M. Goldstein and Katherine V. Dillon, *Miracle at Midway* (New York: McGraw-Hill, 1982), pp. 13–16, 114–16; Jonathan Parshall and Anthony Tully, *Shattered Sword: The Untold Story of the Battle of Midway* (Dulles, Va.: Potomac Books, 2005), pp. 63–95.

13. Prange, with Goldstein and Dillon, *Miracle at Midway*, pp. 14–15, 147–48, 213–14.

14. Robert Casey, *Torpedo Junction: With the Pacific Fleet from Pearl Harbor to Midway* (Indianapolis: Bobbs-Merrill Co., 1942), p. 375.

15. Prange, with Goldstein and Dillon, *Miracle at Midway*, pp. 183–99, 240; Weinberg, *World at Arms*, pp. 336–39; "John Waldron, Fort Pierre Hero of WWII," *Pierre Capital Journal*, 11 Nov. 2015.

16. "John Waldon, Fort Pierre Hero of WWII"; Prange, Goldstein, and Dillon, *Miracle at Midway*, pp. 240–41; Parshall and Tully, *Shattered Sword*, p. 65.

17. "John Waldon, Fort Pierre Hero of WWII"; Prange, with Goldstein and Dillon, *Miracle at Midway*, pp. 240–48. According to Prange, Goldstein, and Dillon, only George Gay survived from Waldron's Squadron Eight, and four Devastators from Torpedo Squadron Six made it back to the *Enterprise*. One of those four, however, was damaged beyond repair, and the navy pushed it overboard (*Miracle at Midway*, pp. 247–48, 252).

18. Prange, with Goldstein and Dillon, *Miracle at Midway*, pp. 325, 331, 337, 373–74, 396; Parshall and Tully, *Shattered Sword*, pp. 65, 378, 380.

19. Doolittle, *I Could Never Be So Lucky Again*, p. 293; David M. Kennedy, *Freedom from Fear: The American People in Depression and War, 1929–1945* (New York: Oxford University Press, 1999), p. 543.

20. Casey, *Torpedo Junction*, p. 387; Doolittle, *I Could Never Be So Lucky Again*, p. 293; Scott, *Target Tokyo*, pp. xiii–xiv.

21. Lawson, *Thirty Seconds over Tokyo*, pp. 215–17; Scott, *Target Tokyo*, pp. 336–44.

22. Lawson, *Thirty Seconds over Tokyo*, pp. 215–17; "U.S. Awards Medals to 80 Heroes of the Army's Bombing Raid on Japan," *Life*, 1 June 1942, pp. 28–29.

23. "U.S. Awards Medals to 80 Heroes," p. 28.

24. Ibid.

25. Ibid.

26. Telephone interview with George S. McGovern, Mitchell, S.Dak., 23 Nov. 2009.

27. Lawson, *Thirty Seconds over Tokyo*, pp. 218–30.

28. "Bomber Pilot Tells of Air Raid on Japan," *Brookings Register*, 2 July 1942.

29. Ibid.

30. "Local Army Flier Was Honored Guest at Club Luncheon," *Belle Fourche Bee*, 9 July 1942.

31. "Don Smith Relates Story of Raid on Japan for Home Folk," *Daily Belle Fourche Post*, 3 July 1942.

32. "Local Army Flier Was Honored Guest."

33. "Unexpected Crowd Flocks to Belle for Celebration," *Daily Belle Fourche Post*, 6 July 1942.

34. Ibid.

35. Don Smith to Dear Folks, 9 July 1942.

36. Ibid.; Thomas and Jablonski, *Doolittle*, pp. 155–56.

37. Smith to Dear Folks, 9 July 1942.

38. Smith to Dear Folks, 28 July 1942.

39. Ibid.

40. Marie Smith to Dearest Folks, undated.

41. Smith to Dear Folks, 28 July 1942.

42. Ibid.

43. Smith to Dear Folks, 15 Aug. 1942.

44. Smith to Dear Folks, 22 Aug. 1942.

45. Marie Smith to Dearest Folks, undated.

46. Smith to Dear Folks, 2 Sept. 1942.

47. Smith to Dear Folks, 7 Sept. 1942.

48. Ibid.

49. "Mr. Gurney's Convictions," *Time*, 14 Sept. 1942, p. 18.

50. Smith to Dear Folks, 25 Sept. 1942.

51. Geoffrey Perret, *Winged Victory: The Army Air Forces in World War II* (New York: Random House, 1993), pp. 94–95.

52. J. H. Doolittle, Report on the Aerial Bombing of Japan, 5 June 1942, Entry NM-53 294-C, Box 516, Central Decimal Files, Oct. 1942–1944, Security Classified Correspondence, 1941–1944, Records of the Army Air Forces, 1902–1964, Record Group 18, National Archives and Records Administration, College Park, Md.; Perret, *Winged Victory*, pp. 94–95.

53. Perret, *Winged Victory*, pp. 94–95.

54. Interview of Jimmy Doolittle, Henry "Hank" Potter, and Dick Cole, Rapid City, S.Dak., by Steve Nelson, 27 Apr. 1978, ACC H93-101, Box 9290B, Rapid City Reunion Cassette Tapes, Doolittle Raiders Collection, State Archives, South Dakota State Historical Society, Pierre.

55. Perret, *Winged Victory*, p. 95.

56. Ibid., p. 96.

57. Interview of Doolittle, Potter, and Cole.

58. Perret, *Winged Victory*, pp. 95–96.

59. Thomas and Jablonski, *Doolittle*, p. 257.

60. Interview with Ansel Wooden Knife, Interior, S.Dak., Jan. 2015; Interview with Clifford Whiting, Kyle, S.Dak., Jan. 2015.

61. Telephone interview with Philip Hall, Spearfish, S.Dak., 10 Jan. 2016.

62. Ibid.; interviews with Wooden Knife and Whiting.

63. Smith to Dear Folks, 25 Sept. 1942.

64. Smith to Dear Folks, 20 Oct. 1942.

65. Carroll V. Glines, *The Doolittle Raid: America's Daring First Strike against Japan* (Atglen, Pa.: Schiffer Publishing, 1991), pp. 177–82; Scott, *Target Tokyo*, pp. 400–407.

66. Glines, *Doolittle Raid*, pp. 179–80.

67. Ibid., pp. 180–82; Scott, *Target Tokyo*, 407–9.

68. Lisle A. Rose, *The Ship That Held the Line: U.S.S.* Hornet *and the First Year of the Pacific War* (Annapolis, Md.: Naval Institute Press, 1995), pp. 219–78. The final location of the *Hornet* was unknown until February 2019, when the R/V Petrel expeditionary team relocated the sunken carrier. *See* Megan Eckstein, "WWII Aircraft Carrier USS *Hornet* Discovered in Solomon Islands," *USNI News*, 12 Feb. 2019, news.usni .org/2019/02/12/uss-hornet-found.

69. Smith to Dear Folks, 23 Oct. 1942.

70. "Capt. Donald Smith of Belle is War Victim," *Daily Belle Fourche Post*, undated, copy in author's collection.

71. Interview with Thomas Griffin, Rapid City, S.Dak., 23 Nov. 2002.

72. Ibid.; George Nolta, *The Doolittle Raiders: What Heroes Do after the War* (Atglen, Pa.: Schiffer Publishing, 2018), p. 129; "Belle Fourche's WWII Doolittle Raid Pilot to be Honored Saturday," *Butte County (S.Dak.) Post*, 6 Sept. 2012, rapidcityjournal .com/news/local/communities/belle_fourche/belle-fourche-s-wwii-doolittle-raid -pilot-to-be-honored/article_20efbd80-8ad4-52b9-b4c6-0261da7fc8df.html.

73. Interview with Griffin.

74. "Captain Don Smith Meets His Death in a Plane Accident," *Belle Fourche Bee*, 19 Nov. 1942.

75. "Memorial Services Held for Captain Don Smith," *Hi Times* (Belle Fourche High School student newspaper), 14 Dec. 1942.

76. Francis Case to A. W. and Laura Smith, 20 Nov. 1942.

77. "Funeral Rites Held for Dr. A. W. Smith Monday Afternoon," *Belle Fourche Bee*, 31 Dec. 1942.

Chapter 7: Remembering the Raiders

1. Jerry Scutts, *B-26 Marauder Units of the Eighth and Ninth Air Forces* (Oxford, U.K.: Osprey Publishing, 1997), pp. 7–21.

2. James H. Doolittle, *I Could Never Be So Lucky Again: An Autobiography*, with Carroll V. Glines (New York: Bantam Books, 1991), pp. 327–28.

3. Lowell Thomas and Edward Jablonski, *Doolittle: A Biography* (Garden City, N.Y.: Doubleday, 1976), pp. 218–20.

4. Doolittle, *I Could Never Be So Lucky Again*, p. 344.

5. Carrol V. Glines, *The Doolittle Raid: America's First Daring Strike against Japan* (Atglen, Pa.: Schiffer Publishing, 1991), pp. 227–33.

6. Ibid., pp. 221, 227–33.

7. Ted W. Lawson, *Thirty Seconds over Tokyo*, ed. Robert Considine (1943; new ed., New York: Simon & Schuster, 2004), p. 237.

8. "Notes, *Thirty Seconds over Tokyo*," tcm.com/tcmdb/title/451/Thirty-Seconds -Over-Tokyo/notes.html.

9. Ibid.

10. Ibid.

11. "William 'Bill' Phillips, Biography," imdb.com/name/nm0680883/bio; Lawson, *Thirty Seconds over Tokyo*, pp. 14, 224–27.

12. Keith Huxen, "America Responds: Hollywood, War and Propaganda," *V-Mail: The Newsletter of the National World War II Museum* (Spring 2018): 6–7.

13. Ibid.

14. "'Thirty Seconds over Tokyo,' a Faithful Mirror of Capt. Ted Lawson's Book, with Van Johnson, Tracy, at Capitol," *New York Times*, 16 Nov. 1943.

15. Steven J. Zolga, *Defense of Japan 1945* (Oxford, U.K.: Osprey Publishing, 2010), pp. 25–27; Barrett Tillman, *Whirlwind: The Air War against Japan, 1942–1945* (New York: Simon & Schuster, 2010), pp. 142–46; "Japan," *Oxford Companion to World War II*, ed. Ian C. B. Dear and M. R. D. Foote (Oxford, U.K.: Oxford University Press, 2001), p. 484.

16. Thomas R. H. Havens, *Valley of Darkness: The Japanese People and World War II* (New York: W. W. Norton, 1978), pp. 158–59; "Japan," *Oxford Companion to World War II*, p. 484.

17. Geoffrey Perret, *Winged Victory: The Army Air Forces in World War II* (New York: Random House, 1993), p. 451.

18. Perret, *Winged Victory*, pp. 447–49; David Willis, "Boeing B-29 and B-50 Superfortress," *International Air Power Review* 22 (2007): 136–37.

19. Tillman, *Whirlwind*, pp. 262–64; James Lea Cate and James C. Olson, "Urban Area Attacks," in *The Army Air Forces in World War II*, vol. 5, *The Pacific: Matterhorn to Nagasaki, June 1944 to August 1945*, ed. Wesley Frank Craven and Cate (Chicago: University of Chicago Press, 1953), pp. 622–27.

20. Lincoln LaPaz and Albert Rosenfeld, "Japan's Balloon Invasion of America," *Collier's* 131 (17 Jan. 1953): 10.

21. Waring Family, statement, Balloon Bombs, Japanese, Vertical Files, State Archives, South Dakota State Historical Society (SDSHS), Pierre. The balloon became a permanent piece in the collection of the Museum of the South Dakota State Historical Society.

22. Cornelius W. Conley, "The Great Japanese Balloon Offensive," *Air University Review* 19 (Jan.-Feb. 1968): 75–76.

23. Joint Memorandum to Franklin D. Roosevelt, 11 Dec. 1944, in *Guarding the United States and Its Outposts*, by Stetson Conn, Rose C. Engelman, and Byron Fairchild, vol. 2 of *The United States Army in World War II: The Western Hemisphere*, ed. Fairchild (Washington, D.C.: Office of the Chief of Military History, Department of the Army, 2000), p. 112.

24. Lee Juillerat, "Balloon Bombs," *The Oregon Encyclopedia*, oregonencyclopedia .org/articles/balloon_bombs/#.XJ4uBKBKiM9; Conley, "Great Japanese Balloon Offensive," p. 76; LaPaz and Rosenfeld, "Japan's Balloon Invasion of America," p. 10.

25. Gordon Thomas and Max Morgan-Witts, *Ruin from the Air: The Atomic Mission to Hiroshima* (London: Hamish Hamilton, 1977), pp. 12–13, 83.

26. Ibid., pp. 83–85; Perret, *Winged Victory*, p. 454.

27. Perret, *Winged Victory*, p. 455.

28. Ibid., p. 454; E. Bartlett Kerr, *Flames Over Tokyo: The U.S. Army Air Force's Incendiary Campaign against Japan, 1944–1945* (New York: Donald I. Fine Inc., 1991), p. 207; Niall Ferguson, *The War of the World: History's Age of Hatred* (London: Pen-

guin Books, 2007), p. 573; Richard B. Frank, *Downfall: The End of the Imperial Japanese Empire* (New York: Penguin Books, 1999), pp. 68–69; Max Hastings, *Nemesis: The Battle for Japan, 1944–45* (London: HarperPress, 2007), p. 330; Craven and Cate, "Victory," in *The Army Air Forces in World War II*, vol. 5, *The Pacific*, p. 754; Tillman, *Whirlwind*, p. 256.

29. James M. Scott, *Target Tokyo: Jimmy Doolittle and the Raid That Avenged Pearl Harbor* (New York: W. W. Norton, 2015), p. 449.

30. Thomas and Morgan-Witts, *Ruin from the Air*, pp. 50–52.

31. "First Atomic Bomb Dropped on Japan, Missile Is Equal to 20,000 Tons of TNT," *New York Times*, 7 Aug. 1945.

32. Ferenc Morton Szasz, *The Day the Sun Rose Twice: The Story of the Trinity Site Nuclear Explosion, July 16, 1945* (Albuquerque: University of New Mexico Press, 1984), pp. 3–92; Frank, *Downfall*, p. 262.

33. "U.S. Strategic Bombing Survey: The Effects of the Atomic Bombings of Hiroshima and Nagasaki," p. 37, 19 June 1946, Atomic Bomb-Hiroshima, President's Secretary's File, Truman Papers, Harry S. Truman Presidential Library & Museum, Independence, Mo.; Thomas and Morgan-Witts, *Ruin from the Air*, pp. 323–32.

34. Interview with Thomas Griffin, Rapid City, S.Dak., 23 Nov. 2002.

35. "First Atomic Bomb Dropped on Japan."

36. "U.S. Strategic Bombing Survey," p. 37; Perret, *Winged Victory*, p. 460; "Terms Will Reduce Japan to Kingdom Perry Visited," *New York Times*, 15 Aug. 1945.

37. "Terms Will Reduce Japan to Kingdom Perry Visited."

38. Interview with Doris Shipley, Spearfish, S.Dak., 5 Sept. 2006; Phil White, "The Black 14: Race, Politics, Religion, and Wyoming Football," *WyoHistory Online Encyclopedia*, wyohistory.org/encyclopedia/black-14-race-politics-religion-and-wyoming-football.

39. "Captain Willibald C. Bianchi," minnesotamedalofhonormemorial.org/wp-content/uploads/2017/12/Bianchi-Willibald-C.-Bio-July-16.pdf; Amy Dunkle with V. J. Smith, *The College on The Hill: A Sense of South Dakota State University History* (Brookings: South Dakota State University Alumni Association, 2003), pp. 347–56; Linda Goetz Holmes, *Unjust Enrichment: How Japan's Companies Built Postwar Fortunes Using American POWs* (Mechanicsburg, Pa.: Stackpole, 2001), pp. 32, 38–39; Robert C. Daniels, "Hell Ships—From the Philippines to Japan," *Military History Online*, militaryhistoryonline.com/wwii/articles/hellship.aspx#; [Peggy Davis and Billie Jane Hamlin], *The War Years: A Fiftieth Anniversary Album of World War II Center of The Nation Area* (Sturgis, S.Dak.: 54 Printing, 1995), pp. 13–21.

40. [Davis and Hamlin], *The War Years*, pp. 13–21.

41. Interview with Jack Wells, Belle Fourche, S.Dak., 25 Oct. 2011; "Body of Belle War Hero Enroute Home," *Rapid City Journal*, 17 Aug. 1948.

42. William O'Dyer to Laura Smith, n.d. Aug. 1948, copy in Janice Evans Collection, Rapid City, S.Dak.

43. Telephone interview with Edward Saylor, Graham, Wash., by Paul Higbee and Tim Velder, 17 Apr. 2001.

44. Robert G. Emmens, *Guests of the Kremlin* (New York: Macmillan, 1949), p. 290.

45. Ibid., pp. 76, 133–241.

46. Ibid., pp. 260–89; Doolittle, *I Could Never Be So Lucky Again*, pp. 550–51.

47. The United States Air Force was officially established as a separate branch in October 1947. Doolittle, *I Could Never Be So Lucky Again*, p. 482.

48. George Nolta, *The Doolittle Raiders: What Heroes Do after the War* (Altgen, Pa.: Schiffer Publishing, 2018), pp. 58–61, 135–41; Scott, *Target Tokyo*, p. 299.

49. Scott, *Target Tokyo*, p. 299.

50. Ibid., pp. 459–60.

51. Doolittle, *I Could Never Be So Lucky Again*, p. 462.

52. Scott, *Target Tokyo*, pp. 460–61.

53. Ibid., p. 478.

54. Doolittle, *I Could Never Be So Lucky Again*, pp. 519–22.

55. Ibid., p. 519.

56. Ibid., p. 531.

57. Ibid., pp. 555–59.

58. "Celebrity Pheasant Hunt," *The American Sportsman*, ABC Television, 1962, Historical Footprints Archive, Lead, S.Dak.

59. "Doolittle Raiders Reunion Begins Thursday In City," *Rapid City Journal*, 26 Apr. 1978; "Doolittle Raider's Widow Attending First Reunion," ibid., 28 Apr. 1978; "Memorial Page for Laura B. Smith (1886–1964)," *Find a Grave*, findagrave.com/memorial/41765110/laura-b-smith, accessed 21 May 2019.

60. "Doolittle Raider's Widow Attending First Reunion."

61. "Simple Toast Marks Ritual of Doolittle Raiders," *Rapid City Journal*, 27 Apr. 1978.

62. "Doolittle's Daring Raiders Have Another Common Interest—Grandchildren," ibid.

63. Interview of Father William J. Glynn and Richard Knobloch, Rapid City, S.Dak., by Steve Nelson, 27 Apr. 1978, ACC H93-101, Box 9290B, Rapid City Reunion Cassette Tapes, Doolittle Raiders Collection, SDSHS.

64. "Gen. Doolittle, at 81, Still Endeavors to Be Useful," *Rapid City Journal*, 28 Apr. 1978.

65. Interview of Jimmy Doolittle, Henry "Hank" Potter, and Dick Cole, Rapid City, S.Dak., by Steve Nelson, 27 Apr. 1978, Doolittle Raiders Collection.

66. Jonathan Fenby, *Chiang Kai-Shek: China's Generalissimo and the Nation He Lost* (New York: Carroll and Graf, 2003), pp. 500–501.

67. Ibid.; Scott, *Target Tokyo*, p. 389.

68. "More than 500 Attend Banquet to Express Gratitude to Doolittle Raiders," *Rapid City Journal*, 1 May 1978; Rhonda Coy Sedgwick, *Sky Trails: The Life of Clyde W. Ice* (Newcastle, Wyo.: Quarter Circle A Enterprises, 1988), p. 143.

69. "More than 500 Attend Banquet to Express Gratitude to Doolittle Raiders."

70. "Belle Fourche to Honor WWII Veteran," *Black Hills Pioneer* (Spearfish, S.Dak.), 16 Apr. 2001; Belle Fourche Tribute to Don Smith, 18 Apr. 2001; Telephone discussions with Teresa Schanzenbach, tribute coordinator, Belle Fourche, S.Dak., Feb.–Apr. 2001.

71. Interview with Griffin; "James Doolittle, 96, Pioneer Who Led the First Raid on Japan Dies," *New York Times*, 28 Sept. 1993.

72. Lawson, *Thirty Seconds over Tokyo*, pp. 213–36; Nolta, *Doolittle Raiders*, pp. 66–67.

73. "Col. Henry Potter, Navigator in Doolittle Raid, Dies At 83," *New York Times*, 4 June 2002; Nolta, *Doolittle Raiders*, pp. 25–26.

74. "Col. Henry Potter, Navigator in Doolittle Raid, Dies At 83."

75. "Maj. Thomas C. Griffin, 96, B-25 Navigator," *New York Times*, 5 Mar. 2013; Nolta, *Doolittle Raiders*, pp. 85–86.

76. Nolta, *Doolittle Raiders*, pp. 130–31; "Howard A. Sessler; Engineer, WWII Bomber Pilot," *Los Angeles Times*, 10 Mar. 2001; "'Doolittle Raider' Saylor Dies," *Air Force Times*, 29 Jan. 2015, airforcetimes.com/news/your-air-force/2015/01/29/doolittle -raider-saylor-dies-at-94/; Interview with Saylor.

77. Interview with Saylor.

78. "'Doolittle Raider' Saylor Dies"; Nolta, *Doolittle Raiders*, p. 133.

79. "David Thatcher, Part of Famed 1942 Raid on Japan, Dies at 94," *New York Times*, 23 June 2016.

80. "David Thatcher, Part of Famed 1942 Raid on Japan, Dies at 94"; "Missoula's Doolittle Raider Thatcher, Just Part of the War Effort," *The Missoulian* (Mont.), 12 Nov. 2013; Nolta, *Doolittle Raiders*, pp. 23–24; "Richard Cole, Last Survivor of Doolittle Raid on Japan, Dies at 103," *New York Times*, 10 Apr. 2019.

81. Interview with David Thatcher, Belle Fourche, S.Dak., 18 Apr. 2001.

82. Edwin E. ("Buzz") Aldrin, book signing question and answer session, 11 July 2015, Rushmore Mall, Rapid City, S.Dak.

Bibliography

Unpublished Materials

Harry S. Truman Presidential Library & Museum, Independence, Mo.
  Truman Papers. President's Secretary's File. Atomic Bomb-Hiroshima.
    "U.S. Strategic Bombing Survey: The Effects of the Atomic Bombings of Hiroshima and Nagasaki," 19 June 1946.
Historical Footprints Archive, Lead, S.Dak.
  "Celebrity Pheasant Hunt." *The American Sportsman*. ABC Television. 1962.
History of Aviation Archives, Eugene McDermott Library, University of Texas at Dallas.
  The Doolittle Tokyo Raiders Association Records.
South Dakota State Historical Society, Pierre.
  Doolittle Raiders Collection.
  Vertical Files.
South Dakota State University, Archives and Special Collections, H. M. Briggs Library, Brookings, S.Dak.
  Jack Rabbit. Yearbooks. 1939–1940.
Tri-State Museum, Belle Fourche, S.Dak.
  Don Smith Letters.
U.S. National Archives and Records Administration, College Park, Md.
  Record Group 18, Records of the Army Air Forces, 1902–1964.
Washington State Archives, Digital Archives, Cheney, Wash.
  King County Marriage Records, 1855–present.

Interviews

Brost, Harold. Interview by author. Belle Fourche, S.Dak., 25 Oct. 2011.
Griffin, Thomas. Interview by author. Rapid City, S.Dak., 23 Nov. 2002.
Hall, Philip. Interview by author. Spearfish, S.Dak., 10 Jan. 2016.
———. Interview by author. Spearfish, S.Dak., 30 Sept. 2018.
Jeffry, Murial. Interview by author. Belle Fourche, S.Dak., 6 Oct. 2011.
Junek, David. Interview by author. Belle Fourche, S.Dak., 16 Aug. 2011.
Kennedy, Faye. Interview by author. Belle Fourche, S.Dak., 25 June 1996.
McGovern, George S. Interview by author. Mitchell, S.Dak., 23 Nov. 2009.
Potter, Henry A. Interview by John Garrett and Mike Strickler. San Angelo, Tex., undated. Transcript. Author's Collection.
———. Interview by William E. Aisenbrey. Austin, Tex., 6 Apr. 1988. Transcript. Author's Collection.
Saylor, Edward. Interview by Paul Higbee and Tim Velder. Graham, Wash., 17 Apr. 2001.

Schanzenbach, Theresa. Telephone discussions with author. Belle Fourche, S.Dak., Feb.–Apr. 2001.

Shipley, Doris. Interview by author. Spearfish, S.Dak., 5 Sept. 2006.

Thatcher, David. Interview by author. Belle Fourche, S.Dak., 18 Apr. 2001.

Wells, Jack. Interview by author. Belle Fourche, S.Dak., 25 Oct. 2011.

Whiting, Clifford. Interview by author. Kyle, S.Dak., Jan. 2015.

Woodall, Ruth Streeter. Interview by Julia Monczunski. South Dakota Public Radio. Belle Fourche, S.Dak., 21 Apr. 2007.

Wooden Knife, Ansel. Interview by author. Interior, S.Dak., Jan. 2015.

Newspapers and Magazines

Air Force Times, 2015.

Daily Belle Fourche Post, 1939–1942.

Belle Fourche Bee, 1942.

Black Hills Pioneer, 2001.

Brookings Register, 1942.

Butte County Post, 2012.

Hi Times, 1932–1936, 1942.

Life, 1941–1942.

Los Angeles Times, 2001.

The Missoulian (Mont.), 2013.

The Nation, 1942.

New York Times, 1941, 1943, 1945, 1993, 2002, 2013, 2015–2016, 2019.

Newsweek, 1942.

Rapid City Journal, 1978.

San Antonio Express, 1941.

Time, 1941–1945.

USNI News, 2019.

Books

Ashcroft, Bruce. *We Wanted Wings: A History of the Aviation Cadet Program.* Randolph Air Force Base, Tex.: HQ, AETC, Office of History and Research, 2005.

Bradley, James. *Flyboys: A True Story of Courage.* New York: Little, Brown & Co., 2003.

Casey, Robert J. *Torpedo Junction: With the Pacific Fleet from Pearl Harbor to Midway.* Indianapolis: Bobbs-Merrill Co., 1942.

Caughy, John. *California: A Remarkable State's Life History.* Englewood Cliffs, N.J.: Prentice Hall, 1970.

Cecil, Chuck. *Becoming Someplace Special: Gleanings from the Past: The Brookings Story.* Brookings, S.Dak.: By the Author, 2001.

Conn, Stetson, Rose C. Engelman, and Byron Fairchild. *Guarding the United States and Its Outposts.* Vol. 2 of *The United States Army in World War II: The Western Hemisphere.* ed. Byron Fairchild. Washington, D.C.: Office of the Chief of Military History, Department of the Army, 2000.

Cooling, Benjamin, ed. *Case Studies in the Achievement of Air Superiority.* Washington, D.C.: Center for Air Force History, 1994.

Copp, Dewitt S. *A Few Great Captains: The Men and Events That Shaped the Development of U.S. Air Power.* McLean, Va.: Air Force Historical Foundation, 1980.

Craven, Wesley Frank, and James Lea Cate, eds. *The Army Air Forces in World War II.* 7 vols. Chicago: University of Chicago Press, 1948–1958.

[Davis, Peggy, and Billie Jane Hamlin]. *The War Years: A Fiftieth Anniversary Album of World War II Center of the Nation Area.* Sturgis, S.Dak.: 54 Printing, 1995.

Dear, Ian C. B., and M. R. D. Foote, eds. *Oxford Companion to World War II.* Oxford, U.K.: Oxford University Press, 2001.

Doolittle, James H., with Carroll V. Glines. *I Could Never Be So Lucky Again: An Autobiography.* New York: Bantam Books, 1991.

Dunkle, Amy, with V. J. Smith. *The College on the Hill: A Sense of South Dakota State University History.* Brookings: South Dakota State University Alumni Association, 2003.

Emmens, Robert G. *Guests of the Kremlin.* New York: Macmillan, 1949.

Fenby, Jonathan. *Chiang Kai-Shek: China's Generalissimo and the Nation He Lost.* New York: Carroll & Graf, 2004.

Ferguson, Niall. *The War of the World: History's Age of Hatred.* London: Penguin Books, 2007.

Frank, Richard B. *Downfall: The End of the Imperial Japanese Empire.* New York: Penguin Books, 1999.

Hastings, Max. *Nemesis: The Battle for Japan, 1944–45.* London: HarperPress, 2007.

Holmes, Linda Goetz. *Unjust Enrichment: How Japan's Companies Built Postwar Fortunes Using American POWs.* Mechanicsburg, Pa.: Stackpole, 2001.

Gies, Joseph. *Franklin D. Roosevelt: Portrait of a President.* Garden City, N.Y.: Doubleday, 1971.

Glines, Carroll V. *The Doolittle Raid: America's Daring First Strike against Japan.* Atglen, Pa.: Schiffer Publishing, 1991.

Havens, Thomas R. H. *Valley of Darkness: The Japanese People and World War II.* New York: W. W. Norton, 1978.

Kelly, Lloyd L. *The Pilot Maker.* New York: Grosset & Dunlap, 1970.

Kennedy, David M. *Freedom from Fear: The American People in Depression and War, 1929–1945.* New York: Oxford University Press, 1999.

Kerr, E. Bartlett. *Flames Over Tokyo: The U.S. Army Air Force's Incendiary Campaign against Japan, 1944–1945.* New York: Donald I. Fine Inc., 1991.

Lawson, Ted W. *Thirty Seconds over Tokyo.* ed. Robert Considine. 1943; new ed., New York: Simon & Schuster, 2004.

Lee, R. Alton. *A New Deal for South Dakota: Drought, Depression, and Relief, 1920–1941.* Pierre: South Dakota Historical Society Press, 2016.

Manning, Robert, et al., eds. *Above and Beyond: A History of the Medal of Honor from the Civil War to Vietnam.* Boston: Boston Publishing Co., 1985.

Nelson, Craig. *The First Heroes: The Extraordinary Story of the Doolittle Raid—America's First World War II Victory*. New York: Penguin Books, 2003.

Nolta, George. *The Doolittle Raiders: What Heroes Do after the War*. Altgen, Pa.: Schiffer Publishers, 2018.

Parrish, Thomas. *Roosevelt and Marshall: Partners in Politics and War*. New York: William Morrow & Co., 1989.

Parshall, Jonathan, and Anthony Tully. *Shattered Sword: The Untold Story of the Battle of Midway*. Dulles, Va.: Potomac Books, 2005.

Perret, Geoffrey. *Winged Victory: The Army Air Forces in World War II*. New York: Random House, 1993.

Pioneer Footprints. Belle Fourche, S.Dak.: Black Hills Half Century Club, 1964.

Prange, Gordon W., with Donald M. Goldstein and Katherine V. Dillon. *Miracle at Midway*. New York: McGraw-Hill, 1982.

Pressler, Larry. *U.S. Senators from the Prairie*. Vermillion: Dakota Press, 1982.

Rose, Lisle A. *The Ship That Held the Line: U.S.S.* Hornet *and the First Year of the Pacific War*. Annapolis, Md.: Naval Institute Press, 1995.

Schell, Herbert S. *History of South Dakota*. Lincoln: University of Nebraska Press, 1961.

Scott, James M. *Target Tokyo: Jimmy Doolittle and the Raid That Avenged Pearl Harbor*. New York: W. W. Norton, 2015.

Scutts, Jerry. *B-26 Marauder Units of the Eighth and Ninth Air Forces*. Oxford, U.K.: Osprey Publishing, 1997.

Sedgwick, Rhonda Coy. *Sky Trails: The Life of Clyde W. Ice*. Newcastle, Wyo.: Quarter Circle A Enterprises, 1986.

Szasz, Ferenc Morton. *The Day the Sun Rose Twice: The Story of the Trinity Site Nuclear Explosion, July 16, 1945*. Albuquerque: University of New Mexico Press, 1984.

Thomas, Gordon, and Max Morgan-Witts. *Ruin from the Air: The Atomic Mission to Hiroshima*. London: Hamish Hamilton, 1977.

Thomas, Lowell, and Edward Jablonski. *Doolittle: A Biography*. New York: Doubleday, 1976.

Thompson, Harry, ed. *A New History of South Dakota*. Sioux Falls, S.Dak.: Center for Western Studies, Augustana College, 2005.

Tillman, Barrett. *Whirlwind: The Air War against Japan, 1942–1945*. New York: Simon & Schuster, 2010.

Tuchman, Barbara W. *Stilwell and the American Experience in China, 1911–1945*. London: Macmillan, 1970.

Tupper, Seth. *Calvin Coolidge in the Black Hills*. Charleston, S.C.: The History Press, 2017.

Weinberg, Gerhard. *A World at Arms: A Global History of World War II*. Cambridge, U.K.: Cambridge University Press, 1994.

Zolga, Steven J. *Defense of Japan 1945*. Oxford, U.K.: Osprey Publishing, 2010.

Articles

Aisenbrey, William E. "Thirty Seconds over Tokyo—The South Dakota Connection." *Papers of the Twentieth Annual Dakota History Conference*. comp. Herbert W. Blakely. Madison, S.Dak.: Dakota State College, 1988.

Baldwin, Hanson W. "America at War: Three Bad Months." *Foreign Affairs* 20 (Apr. 1942): 393–401.

Bauer, Gene. "On the Edge of Space: The *Explorer* Expeditions of 1934–1935." *South Dakota History* 12 (Spring 1982): 1–16.

Bucklin, Steven J. "Fly Over Country?: A Glimpse of South Dakota through Its Aviation History." *South Dakota History* 45 (Summer 2015): 99–179.

Conley, Cornelius W. "The Great Japanese Balloon Offensive." *Air University Review* 19 (Jan.-Feb. 1968): 68–83.

Eagleman, David. "Secret Life of the Mind." *Discover Magazine* 32 (Sept. 2011): 50–53.

Huxen, Keith. "America Responds: Hollywood, War and Propaganda." *V-Mail: The Newsletter of the National World War II Museum* (Spring 2018): 6–7.

LaPaz, Lincoln, and Albert Rosenfeld. "Japan's Balloon Invasion of America." *Collier's Magazine* 131 (17 Jan. 1953): 9–11.

Stevens, Albert W. "Man's Farthest Aloft." *National Geographic* 69 (Jan. 1936): 59–94.

Willis, David. "Boeing B-29 and B-50 Superfortress." *International Air Power Review* 22 (2007): 136–69.

Government Document

U.S. Army Air Force. *Pilot's Handbook of Flight Operating Instructions for Models B-25C and B-25D*. Foreword by Leo J. Kohn. 1942; reprint ed., Appleton, Wisc.: Aviation Publications, 1978.

Websites

"17th Bomb Group WWII." bombgroup17.com/17th_bg_wwii.

"Captain Willibald C. Bianchi." minnesotamedalofhonormemorial.org/wp-content /uploads/2017/12/Bianchi-Willibald-C.-Bio-July-16.pdf.

Daniels, Robert C. "Hell Ships—From the Philippines to Japan." *Military History Online*. militaryhistoryonline.com/wwii/articles/hellship.aspx#.

Juillerat, Lee. "Balloon Bombs." *The Oregon Encyclopedia*. oregonencyclopedia.org /articles/balloon_bombs/#.XJ4uBKBKiM9.

Sassaman, Richard. "The Impossible Raid." *America in WWII Magazine*. June 2007. americainwwii.com/articles/the-impossible-raid/.

Sherman, Don. "The Secret Weapon," *Air & Space Magazine*. Feb./Mar. 1995. archive.is/20060517184503/http://www.airspacemag.com/ASM/Mag/Index /1995/FM/swpn.html.

"Spearfish Canyon." visitspearfish.com/things-to-do/spearfish-canyon.

Roosevelt, Franklin D. "Fireside Chat 17: On an Unlimited National Emergency." Miller Center, University of Virginia, Charlottesville, millercenter.org/the -presidency/presidential-speeches/may-27-1941-fireside-chat-17-unlimited -national-emergency.

Turner Classic Movies. "Notes: *Thirty Seconds over Tokyo*." tcm.com/tcmdb/title/451/Thirty-Seconds-Over-Tokyo/notes.html.

U.S. Army. "Army Aviation: Army Air Forces." army.mil/aviation/airforces/index.html.

U.S. Army. "Army Aviation: Army Air Corps." army.mil/aviation/aircorps/.

Washington State University Extension. "What is a Land-Grant College?" ext.wsu.edu/documents/landgrant.pdf.

White, Phil. "The Black 14: Race, Politics, Religion, and Wyoming Football." *WyoHistory Online Encyclopedia*. wyohistory.org/encyclopedia/black-14-race-politics-religion-and-wyoming-football.

"William 'Bill' Phillips, Biography." imdb.com/name/nm0680883/bio.

Wikipedia. wikipedia.org.

Index

Page numbers in italics indicate photographs

and B-26, 117, 136; childhood and education of, 59–60; death of, 139, 157; in Doolittle Raid, 65–69, 72–76, 90–94, 152; and Doolittle Raiders, 123, 135, 137–39, 154, 157; and Dwight D. Eisenhower, 122–23, 136; family of, 59–60, 64, 110, 135–36; and Shell Oil Co., 63–64; as test pilot, 61–64; and World War I, 59, 60–61. *See also* Plane No. One

Doolittle, James H., Jr., 64, 135–36

Doolittle, John, 64

Doolittle, Josephine, 110

Doolittle, Rosa, 59–60

Doolittle Raid, ix, 1–4, 20–21, 36, 75–94, *98–101*, 105–7, 110–12, 119, 143–45, 152–53. *See also* Smith, Donald G. ("Don"); Doolittle, James H. ("Jimmy"); USS *Hornet*; individual raider plane numbers

Doolittle Raider reunions, xi, 13, 123, 136–41, 154, 157

Douglas Aircraft Corp., 32, 39

Douglas Dauntless, 108–09

Douglas Devastator, 108–09, 173n17

DuFran, Madam Dora, 9

Duquette, Omer A., 144. *See also* Plane No. Twelve

Eaton, Lloyd, 14, 42, 131–32

Edwards, I. H., 29

Eglin Air Force Base (Fla.), xiv, 66–69, 71, 73–75, 124, 126, 152

Egypt, 110–11, 154

Eierman, Jacob, 145. *See also* Plane No. Fourteen

Eighth Air Force, 123

Eighty-ninth Reconnaissance Squadron, 35, 38–39, 65–66, 151

Eisenhower, Dwight D., 122–23, 136

Ellington Field (Tex.), 47–48

Ellsworth Air Force Base (S.Dak.), 118, 141

Emmens, Robert G., 133, 144. *See also* Plane No. Eight

Enola Gay, 130

Explorer II, 16–18, 149

Faktor, Leland D., 93, 143. *See also* Plane No. Three

Farrow, William G. ("Bill"), 119, 134, 145, 154. *See also* Plane No. Sixteen

Felts Air Field (Wash.), 38, 42, 44, 151

Fickle Finger of Fate. See Plane No. Twelve

Fifteenth Air Force, 123

Firebombing, 126–31, 156

Fitzgerald, John, 65

Fitzhugh, William N., 143. *See also* Plane No. Two

Fitzmaurice, Donald E., 93, 143. *See also* Plane No. Six

Flight operations, 1, 3–4, 20, 29–33, 44–45, 48, 61, 64, 69, 72, 75, 110–11, 122, 126, 129–31, 156

Florida, 62, 66–68, 70–74, 117, 124, 152, 157

Ford, Henry, 15

Ford, John, 125

Foreign Affairs (journal), 70

Formosa. *See* Taiwan

Foss, Joe, 16, 136, 138

439th Bomb Squadron, 114, 154

Frazier, Lynn, 4

Gardner, Melvin J., 144. *See also* Plane No. Eleven

Gay, George, 109

Gehrig, Lou, 89

Germany: and World War II, 5–6, 26, 28, 53, 63–64, 70, 126, 147–50, 152, 156

The Good Earth (Buck), 7

Gowdy, Curt, 136

Gray, Robert M., 143. *See also* Plane No. Three

Great Depression, 22

Green Bay Packers, 132

Green Hornet. See Plane No. Six

Greening, C. Ross, 73–74, 110, 144. *See also* Plane No. Eleven

Lawson, Ellen, 124. *See also Thirty Seconds over Tokyo* (movie)

Lawson, Ted W., 56, 77–80, 110, 124, 139, 143. *See also* Plane No. Seven; *Thirty Seconds over Tokyo*

League of Nations, 6, 147

LeMay, Curtis, 128–29

Leonard, Paul J., 73, 93, 143. *See also* Plane No. One

Levee, Douglas, 132

Life (Hutton), 22

Lindberg, Charles, 5, 15

Linhai, China, xv, 57, 77, 79–80, 110, 153

Link, Ed, 30

Link flight simulator, 29–32

Lockheed Corp., 32

Loewenstein, Hubertus zu, 26

The Lord of the Rings (Tolkien), x

Lost Horizon (Hilton), 105

Louisiana, 48–49, 77, 114–15

Lowry Air Force Base (Colo.), 34, 113

Ma Liagshui, 36–37, 55

McCarthy, James, 65

McChord Air Field (Wash.), 35, 37–40, 44, 64–65, 134, 151

Macia, James H., Jr., 145. *See also* Plane No. Fourteen

McClelland Field (Calif.), 75–76

McClure, Charles L., 78, 80, 143. *See also* Plane No. Seven

McCool, Harry C., 143. *See also* Plane No. Four

MacDill Air Field (Fla.), 117

McElroy, Edgar E., 64, 144. *See also* Plane No. Thirteen

McGee, Bob, 132

McGovern, George S., xii, 111

McGurl, Eugene F., 143. *See also* Plane No. Five

McNair, Lesley, 49

Manch, Jacob E., 143. *See also* Plane No. Three

Manchuria (Manchukuo), 148

Manske, Joseph W., 143. *See also* Plane No. Five

Mao Zedong, 138

Mariana Islands, 128–29

The Mark Twain (bombsight), 73–74

Martin, Frederick, 116

Martin, Joseph, 53

Maxwell Airfield (Ala.), 49, 51

Meder, Robert J., 134, 143, 155. *See also* Plane No. Six

Metro-Goldwyn-Mayer Studios (MGM), 124

Midway Island, 107–10, 125, 153

Military operations. *See* Flight operations; Pilot training

Military units. *See* individual units

Miller, Hank, 73, 74–75, 86–87

Miller, Richard E., 143. *See also* Plane No. Two

Miller, S.Dak., 136

Mitchel Field (New York), 63

Mitchell, William L. ("Billy"), 40, 61

Mitscher, Marc, 81–82, 109

Mugs (dog), 15, 34, 42, 50, 95, 112, 119, 120

Mussolini, Benito, 5–6, 147, 149

Nagasaki, Japan, 131

Nagoya, Japan, xv, 81, 88, 129, 134

Nanking, China, xv, 7, 149

Nantien Island, China, ix, xv, 55–57, 77–79, 153

Napalm, 126–27. *See also* Firebombing; Incendiary explosives

National Aeronautics and Space Administration (NASA), 16

National Air Force Museum, 141

National Football League, 131–32

National Geographic Magazine, 7, 17

National Geographic Society, 16–17

Neutrality Act of 1935, 5–6, 148. *See also* Isolationists

New York Yankees, 89, 119

Newell, Lon, 112

Newell, S.Dak., 11

USS *Panay*, 7
USS *Yorktown*, 107, 109

Vietnam War, 138
Vladivostok, Soviet Union, xv, 73, 93
Vultee Aircraft Corp., 32

Wadsworth, James, 116
Waldron, John C., 108–9
Wall, Robert, 88, 134
Walter Reed General Hospital, 139
Waring ranch, 128
Washington, George, 5
Watson, Harold F., 144. *See also* Plane
    No. Nine
Wells, Jack, xii, 11–12
West Point. *See* United States Military
    Academy
Whirling Dervish. See Plane No. Nine
Whisky Pete. See Plane No. Three
White, Thomas R. ("Doc"), 20, 36, 55–58,
    66–67, 73, 80, 83, 90, *101*, 110, 140, 145.
    See also Plane No. Fifteen
White Lake, S.Dak., 18
White Sands, N.Mex., 130
Why We Fight (film), 125
Wright, Orville, 58
Wright, Wilbur, 58
Wilder, Rodney R., 143. *See also* Plane
    No. Five
Wildner, Carl R., 143. *See also* Plane No.
    Two
Williams, Adam R., 144. *See also* Plane
    No. Thirteen
Williams, Frank, 132
Williams, Griffith P., 20, 73, 90, *101*, 105,
    111, 140, 145, 170n13. *See also* Plane No.
    Fifteen
Woman's Air Service Pilots (WASPs),
    117
Woodall, Ruth Streeter, x–xi, 8–9, 10, 12, 15
World Series (1942), 118–19
World War I, 5, 9–10, 40, 63, 147

Yamamoto, Isoroku, 107–8
Yankton College, 67
Yokohama, Japan, xv, 81
York, Edward J. ("Ski"), 93–94, 133, 144.
    See also Plane No. Eight
Youngblood, Lucien N., 143. *See also*
    Plane No. Four

Zho Xuesan, 92, 140
Zimmerman, Marie. *See* Smith, Marie
    Crouch